GrowerTalks®
on Structures
and Equipment

Edited by

Rick Blanchette

Ball Publishing
Batavia, Illinois, U.S.A.

Ball Publishing
335 North River Street
Batavia, IL 60510, USA
www.ballpublishing.com

Cover design by Anissa Paterson.
Interior design by Bay Graphics.

Reference in this publication to a trademark, proprietary product, or company name is intended for explicit description only and does not imply approval or recommendation to the exclusion of others that may be suitable.

Library of Congress Cataloging-in-Publication Data

GrowerTalks on structures and equipment / edited by Rick Blanchette.
    p. cm.
  ISBN 1-883052-29-7 (alk. paper)
  1. Greenhouses. 2. Greenhouse management. I. Blanchette, Rick, 1966- II. GrowerTalks.
  SB415 .G77 2001
  690'.8924—dc21

                                  2001002522

Printed in the United States of America
06 05 04 03 02 01 1 2 3 4 5 6

Contents

Contributing Authors

Kurt Becker, greenhouse technical sales, Dramm Corporation, Manitowoc, Wisconsin.

Chris Beytes is editor of *GrowerTalks* magazine, Batavia, Illinois.

A. J. Both is assistant extension specialist, Bioresource Engineering, Rutgers University, New Brunswick, New Jersey.

Troy Bouk is Director of Florida Operations, Fernlea Flowers, Quincy, Florida.

Sherri Bruhn is former editor of *Seed Trade News International* magazine, Batavia, Illinois.

Ted Deidrick is a research scientist with Green-Tek, Edgerton, Wisconsin.

Ratus Fischer is owner of GreenLink LLC, Asheville, North Carolina.

Jim Fowler is sales manager, Bouldin & Lawson, McMinnville, Tennessee.

Gene A. Giacomelli is professor in the Department of Agricultural and Biosystems Engineering and director of the Controlled Environment Agriculture Center, University of Arizona, Tuscon.

Don Grey is a freelance writer from Oregon City, Oregon.

P. Allen Hammer is professor, Department of Horticulture and Landscape Architecture, Purdue University, West Lafayette, Indiana.

Debbie Hamrick is editor of *FloraCulture International* magazine, Batavia, Illinois.

Bob Johnson is a freelance writer from Corralitos, California.

Fred Kaiser is chairman, Q-COM Corp., Irvine, California.

Lloyd D. Lemons Jr. is a freelance writer from Scottsdale, Arizona.

Peter P. Ling is associate professor, Department of Food, Agricultural, and Biological Engineering, Ohio Agricultural Research and Development Center, The Ohio State University, Columbus.

Robert W. McMahon is associate professor, Ohio State University, Wooster.

Chris Millar is information systems manager, Knox Nursery Inc., Orlando, Florida.

Lesa Morey is a freelance writer from Sebring, Florida.

Anna Peerbolt is a freelance writer and marketing consultant in Portland, Oregon.

Jim Rearden is president, TrueLeaf Technologies, Petaluma, California.

William J. Roberts is former director of the Center for Controlled Environment Agriculture (CCEA), Cook College, Rutgers University, New Brunswick, New Jersey.

Sara Rowekamp is responsible for inside sales and estimating, Rough Brothers Inc., Cincinnati, Ohio.

Bill Sheldon is a freelance writer from Gardner, Kansas.

Ted H. Short is professor and associate chair, Food, Agricultural, and Biological Engineering, The Ohio State University, Wooster, Ohio.

David Steiner is vice president, Blackmore Company, Belleville, Michigan.

Roger C. Styer is president, Styer's Horticultural Consulting Inc., Batavia, Illinois.

John Walters is former president of the North and South American division of Svensson, Charlotte, North Carolina.

Jennifer Duffield White is associate editor for *GrowerTalks* magazine, Batavia, Illinois.

Don C. Wilkerson is professor and extension horticulturist, Department of Horticultural Sciences, Texas A&M University, College Station, Texas.

Paula A. Yantorno is a freelance writer and a member of Garden Writers Association of America. She is Advertising/Promotions Coordinator for Center Greenhouse Inc., her family's business.

Introduction

We don't need to tell you that there have been dramatic changes in the greenhouse industry: retractable-roof structures, computerized controls, Dutch trays, bar code tracking systems. Houses can range from inexpensive hoop houses to multimillion-dollar expanses with the latest in automation and computerized technology.

What's best? That depends on where you're located, what you grow, how large your operation is, and, well, . . . how much you like cool toys.

One of the best things about being at Ball Publishing is that we get to see the latest and most innovative structures, equipment, and technology on the market—and even some stuff that's still in development. Our editors travel to the Netherlands and Denmark to see what's new and likely to cross the pond. They also make stops all across the U.S. and Canada to see what growers are doing to make their operations more productive and less costly. And we pass that information along to you in *GrowerTalks* magazine.

GrowerTalks on Structures and Equipment brings you the best articles from *GrowerTalks* relating to your greenhouse and the equipment you need to make it run at peak performance. You'll find articles on structures, new technology, transplanters, environmental control, irrigation, carts, and maintaining your facility. And given the dramatic rise in fuel costs we've seen so far in the new millennium, we've included a chapter featuring articles related to controlling your energy bills.

We hope you'll find the articles here informative and inspiring. Maybe you'll come away with a new tool to add to your house, or a new use for existing equipment. Or maybe you'll find a new toy to put on your Christmas list!

Chapter 1
Structures

Selecting the Right Greenhouse

Don Grey

Growers take their greenhouses seriously. With so many different greenhouses, designs, and manufacturers on the market, which one is best? It's a question growers often struggle and argue over. Whether you grow in a poly-covered freestanding house, the latest Venlo design, or a retractable roof, you can't afford to go wrong in selecting the right greenhouse. The best house for you, however, depends on answers to several key questions.

Crops

What do you grow, when do you grow it, and what do you want it to look like? It seems obvious, of course, but the crops you grow or plan to grow should be your main criterion in selecting a greenhouse, tradition and preference aside.

"Growers don't want a greenhouse; they want the crops that come out of it," says Jim Stuppy of Stuppy Inc., North Kansas City, Missouri.

If you grow only spring bedding plants, you can tailor your greenhouses just for those crops. But even if you add hanging baskets to this mix, you've changed the demands on your structures because they must now support the extra weight and there's reduction in available light. And still, if you add a fall program of poinsettias, your crop cultures have changed radically, and so must your equipment and structural requirements. If you grow for the mass market and turn your benches too many times to count, your houses have to sustain fast growth and a certain level of efficiency, a far cry from the needs of a niche grower who focuses on low-volume, high-margin products.

Before you select a structure, take a critical look at the demands of your market. Will you be able to meet the needs of a changing market with your products? Or could some new demand dictate you grow in another direction?

Location

Where do you grow? Crop selection is tied closely to the region in which you live and thus in what structures you grow.

First, consider local building codes and design loads. Growers in cold climates must have frames that tolerate snow loads, say at least 25 lbs. per sq. ft., and that's in addition to live loads from hanging baskets, trolleys, booms, and other equipment. In areas that receive particularly heavy snows, the threat of unbalanced loads, where snowdrifts can cause excessive pressure on one side of the house, must be considered. Snow load is not as critical for growers along the U.S. Gulf Coast, of course, but wind and hail are. Manufacturers say growers and insurance companies are demanding stronger structures capable of withstanding harsh weather.

Understanding your local building code is important. You don't want to purchase or install a house without first checking the codes and zoning regulations. You can't always expect the manufacturer to be versed on each local code.

In what kind of environment do you grow? Light levels, for example, influence selection of structures and their coverings. Light is your only free resource, so take advantage of it. Glasshouses, especially Venlo-style ranges, are popular in northern areas where light transmission levels are critical, even though energy costs may be higher. Growers typically add curtains to them for energy conservation. The big gutter-to-peak glass panes allow maximum light penetration, and the high gutters and roof trusses common in the newer houses aid in better crop ventilation. Meanwhile, growers in warm-weather areas—say Southern California, Texas, and Florida—often can get by with a single layer of poly film.

Budget

What can you afford? In the end, it usually comes down to money. "Cheapest isn't always the best out there," Jim advises. "But you don't need to overspend, either. You need a greenhouse that's going to do the job."

Buy the most greenhouse you can afford now to do that job. Go for volume first, then plan to add to it later, in stages. How many greenhouses have you ripped out lately because you didn't need the space? With an eye on your checkbook but dreams of the future, you can add equipment as it becomes necessary to do so. Many systems can be upgraded or older structures retrofitted.

That's where developing long-term plans for your business counts the most. You do have a long-term goal or business plan, don't you? Growers are good at working backwards, calculating sow date from desired finish date, for example, or planning next year's production based on last year's spreadsheets. But what about the future? Developing a long-term vision is just as important, especially in the fast-paced economic world we live in.

Of course, plans and business strategies do change, so flexibility is important, too. Are you growing the same crops now as when you first started? Do you have the same customer base? Being able to change with the industry, and your markets, will be essential for your business health.

Structures

Growers can find a wide variety of structural designs on the market, from unheated poly-covered hoop houses that can be installed for well under $1 per sq. ft., to Venlo styles that cost upwards of $9 or more per sq. ft. Here's a look at three general types of structures and how they can fit into your decision-making process.

Freestanding houses

These houses are the most basic of structures and often are the choice for the beginning or small grower. The tradeoff here is cost versus efficiency.

For starters, these structures are fairly inexpensive. You can install one house at a time and add more when necessary. If all you need is a structure to protect against weather extremes, say to overwinter or shade your plants, unheated cold frames or hoop houses are hard to beat.

These low-profile structures can be covered with single- or double-poly film to protect nursery stock or perennials from cool temperatures. They also make good houses in which you can finish or hold crops like spring bedding plants. In warm weather, they can be covered with shadecloth instead of poly to guard against searing heat. In areas with prolonged heat, some growers use permanent shade structures, often constructed with high flat roofs for maximum ventilation.

Hoop houses come in numerous shapes and sizes, so you have lots of options regarding width, height, length, and curvature designs. Different end wall configurations can be added. Look for galvanized steel bows with a load factor (snow and wind) suitable for your region. Most are skinned with poly film, though some models come with acrylic sheets. And, they are relatively easy to install, even for the novice grower.

Because these hoop houses are fairly small, unheated, and poorly venti-lated, they limit what you can grow and when you can grow it. Sooner or later you'll want a structure that can do more than protect against weather extremes: You'll want one in which you can modify the environment.

With a larger single-unit Quonset-style structure, you can easily expand your crop diversity and grow year-round. Add an inflated double-poly cover, a heater (two are better, in case one fails), and exhaust fans for powered ventilation. Sidewalls that roll up or roof vents that open provide additional natural ventilation. For longer houses, include fan-jet units and convection tubes for even air dissipation.

These single-unit double-poly houses can support a wide range of crops in most areas of the country, including bedding plants, potted crops such as poinsettias and chrysanthemums, perennials, and even cut flowers.

One thing you sacrifice with single freestanding structures, however, is efficiency. It's simply not as efficient to heat or cool single houses compared to multispan gutter-connect structures. Another drawback is labor efficiency. It's much more labor intensive to move from one house to another to manage your crops.

Gutter connect

Multispan houses, usually connected by a series of gutters, offer better flexi-bility and efficiency—and a bigger up-front price tag than single freestanding structures.

Gutter-connect houses save in heating, cooling, and ventilating costs. Growers like the typically wide bays and the greater air volume. Bigger inte-rior space can result in more efficient labor and materials costs.

Another advantage to a multispan house is high gutters, a noticeable trend today. Over the last few years, greenhouse heights have inched from what was once a standard 8 to 10 ft., up to 14 ft. or more, and for good reason: Growers like the extra height for improved ventilation, climate control, and space for automated equipment. Up in the trusses now sit auto-mated hanging basket systems, slick rail trolleys, energy and shade curtains, and watering booms. Growers find they can grow better plants, both in baskets and on the bench, with the extra room high gutters and trusses afford. With that equipment up higher, air circulation and light infiltration improves, especially for crops on the bench or floor.

Gutter-connect houses also expand the choice of coverings available to growers. Poly film is the No. 1 covering of choice for many growers and is common on multispan houses because it's comparatively inexpensive, easy to install, and offers good light transmission. And today's film is better than ever. It's no stretch that many growers can pull four years or more from their double-poly film, depending on the area of the country and winter severity. Polycarbonate sheets have also come a long way. Today's sheets drip far less from condensation, have improved protection against ultraviolet rays, and are durable in severe weather, particularly hail. And with sophisticated environmental control and plant-handling equipment making coverings a smaller percentage of the overall greenhouse cost, glass has again become a glazing option for growers who, a few years ago, considered it too expensive.

Retractable roofs

Retractable-roof greenhouses have been described as a brand-new style of growing structure because crops can be fully exposed to the outside environment or the houses can be buttoned up for maximum crop protection.

They are probably the most flexible of growing systems. For example, growers have better control over lighting. Roofs can be opened wide to allow for maximum light transmission, or they can be closed and shaded in minutes to help control plant height and stretch. Likewise, growers can force or slow flowering by altering light and temperature levels.

Furthermore, these houses are the best ventilated of any on the market. The idea of natural ventilation is driving innovation in greenhouse structures today, and retractables are clearly out front. Not only do the roofs open wide, but many of the houses that use curtains have roll-up end walls and sidewalls. This degree of outside exposure allows growers to acclimate plants to the natural environment. Also, increased ventilation helps reduce disease by keeping foliage drier. Growers can react in minutes to nighttime temperatures and daytime heat buildup, especially during winter, to produce hardier crops. Natural DIF control is easier because temperatures can be timed better.

Last, but not least, retractable-roof houses are efficient. Growers can lower their labor costs through improved traffic flow and materials handling, as well as by not needing to whitewash or cover and uncover houses by hand.

Retractables have been on the market for about six years now and have evolved into several designs. Flat- and peaked-roof systems covered by durable, woven polyethylene curtains are most prevalent. Flat-roof houses are most popular in the Pacific Northwest (which has the highest concentration in the country), Texas, and the Southeast. There they are used for basic cold protection and shading. The roofs are opened when it rains or snows. As a result, they're used most often for finishing bedding plants and perennials, and for overwintering nursery stock. Prices typically run about $0.86 to $1.00 per sq. ft., installed.

Peaked-roof curtain houses provide even more flexibility and are used for production of bedding plants and perennials in colder climates, poinsettias, mums, cut flowers, and plug production. That's because the A-frame roof when closed can stand up to inclement weather, including heavy snow loads, and can open wide for maximum light transmission and ventilation. The houses also can be equipped like conventional structures with heaters, energy curtains, hanging basket systems, watering booms, etc. Northern growers love the light intensity they get from retractables, but often must equip them with energy curtains because they feel the houses are not as efficient in the cold as Venlo-style ranges. Prices for an installed structure and covering run about $2.86 to $3.00 per sq. ft.

Now, new peaked-roof designs with rigid panels of glass or polycarbonate material that open like hinges are coming on the market. They can be closed tight but still provide excellent ventilation when the roof panels are opened. A new low-profile structure, covered by a curtain, sports a slightly pitched roof, which can be closed during light rain; the water channels away via grooves in the fabric.

Retractables are the hottest in greenhouse structures today and show no sign of cooling off. Look for their technology to keep improving and the installed costs to drop even more.

Whether you have designs on one of these new structures or opt for a traditional single poly-covered Quonset house, get the most out of your house by considering your crops, location, budget, and the many designs available.

Summer 1999

Three Growers, Three Greenhouse Styles

Chris Beytes

Despite the wide array of designs, configurations, and options available on today's modern greenhouses, you really only have one main decision to make: freestanding, gutter-connected, or retractable. Beyond that, your decision comes down to details pertaining to crops, land use, labor, and personal preference.

So why is it often so tough, even for experienced growers, to decide between the three types? Why do growers who for years have succeeded by growing exclusively in freestanding houses suddenly decide they need a gutter-connected range? Why would a grower with a large gutter-connected range suddenly decide to build a dozen freestanding houses? Why have retractables become the choice of many expanding growers?

We asked growers who use a large area of one style of house what they like about that particular design. It's not that they don't use other styles—each of our three growers has at least two of the three styles. Instead, it's that they think enough of that one style to have made a very large investment in a lot of square feet of it—hundreds of thousands, in all three cases. Also, they have plenty of experience with that particular greenhouse style, so they know the ins and outs of building, maintaining, and growing in it.

Freestanding: Low Cost

For low-cost entrance into the greenhouse business, nothing beats a free-standing greenhouse. That's what sold bedding plant grower Glen Hart, owner of Hart's Nursery, Jefferson, Oregon, on the design. The vast majority of his 900,000 sq. ft. of greenhouse space consists of freestanding houses—more than 130 of them, each 6,000 sq. ft. In Glen's mind, it's also the only way he can stay competitive in the very tough West Coast bedding plant market.

"[Bedding plants are] a pretty cheap item, and you've got to figure out a way to grow them [profitably]." says Glen. "I can grow it as good as anybody else can in a freestanding greenhouse."

Glen worked with a local company to design a 30-by-200-ft. house that—with ground cloth, one heater, one fan for airflow, and roll-up side vents—can be built for about $1 per sq. ft., including labor. Retractable-roof houses start at two to three times that; gutter-connected houses start at close to four times that price.

Thanks to natural ventilation via the roll-up sides, Glen says he can operate his freestanding houses cheaper than he could a large gutter-connected range that would require fans and pads for cooling. This doesn't apply to heating costs, however; in a cold winter, Glen says he's sure his heating bill is higher than that of a grower with one large house. But that's the exception, not the norm, in the Northwest.

Another advantage is in meeting Worker Protection Standards. "We don't have to shut down a large area to do our spraying," Glen says. "We can quarantine one house and move on to others and work in them."

Culturally, Glen has 130-plus separate zones, which makes growing impatiens and pansies at the same time a snap. Scheduling houses is done via computer. Early spring crops are put into houses farthest from his soil mixing area, and later crops are nearer the soil area. This way, as his labor force gets more crunched for time later in the spring, they're not moving materials as far.

Labor cost is one question Glen says he can't answer: "I don't have a range of gutter-connects to tell if I could do it cheaper." He uses sixteen John Deere Gators to pull low trailers that carry his shipping carts. Employees load the carts at each greenhouse, then trailer the carts to the shipping area. Two employees can pull about 1,000 flats a day. "I don't know if that's good or bad," Glen says," because I don't have anything to compare with, but we can pull 15,000 flats a day if we have to."

Another cost of freestanding houses is in land use. Glen has almost maxed out his forty acres; gutter-connected houses would require fewer access roads and aisles between houses. But it's a small price to pay for the overall low investment versus return he gets from his business.

While his freestanding houses are inexpensive, Glen will make a big investment in facilities where warranted: He recently built a state-of-the-art, 60,000-sq. ft. gutter-connected house for plugs. "For plugs, where we've got roof ventilation and end ventilation with fans in the house, we feel we're doing a great job," he says. "Costwise, well, it was an expensive 60,000 sq. ft.!"

As tough as the competition is today among the mass-market outlets that Glen serves, his individual houses do everything he needs, and at the right price: "How do you justify putting [$0.60 bedding plants] in a house that you spend $12 to $14 per sq. ft. on?" he asks. "You'll spend a long time trying to recoup that money."

Gutter-Connected: Efficiency

It's not hard to argue the functionality of gutter-connected greenhouses, as most growers in the country use them. It's also not hard to find growers to represent the gutter-connected point of view. We chose Young's Plant Farm, Auburn, Alabama, for one interesting reason: Their thirteen-acre range is built on land that other growers might have put individual houses on, or might not have built on at all. Rather than a nice, flat site, Young's land consists of three levels, each with blocks of gutter-connected houses ranging in size from a half acre to three acres. The houses on each level are connected by tunnels, breezeways, or ramps, and the three levels are connected by ramps and tunnels that let workers and plants move from house to house without going outside. An underground chain drive system like the one used at the Dutch auctions hauls carts around the range, making packing and shipping from the unique site fairly efficient.

Vice President Rob Young says they went down the "individual house road" years ago when getting started and experienced the labor problem of pulling product from a wide range of individual houses. "With a gutter-connected house, you've got aisles either around the perimeter or down the center of the house," he says. "We pull a lot of our orders by taking the carts themselves through the greenhouse."

One potential drawback to gutter-connected houses is the lack of flexibility, because the house may be all one climate. Young's setup automatically eliminates that problem because they have seven individual houses, each of which can be kept at a particular temperature. One of their houses is equipped with Hired Hand roll curtains around all four sides. This is where they start their cool crops, such as cool-weather vegetables, pansies, snaps, and dianthus. Later crops all require roughly the same conditions, so zones aren't as big of an issue, he says.

The Youngs have built a second location on a flatter piece of ground, which gave them the opportunity to build a more efficient range. They chose a six-acre glass structure, but rather than create one big zone, they divided it into two-acre zones, four acres on one side of their shipping barn and two on the other. This way they get the efficiency of having everything under one roof with the flexibility of being able to heat or cool each zone as needed.

When asked about cost of the new range compared to the old range or to other alternatives, Rob says, "You're talking about a lot of money per square foot." So why make the investment? Rob says it was in part because of one important lesson they learned from their No. 1 range: Build so you don't have to come back and redo it in five or ten years. "The way we're putting that place up, we shouldn't have to touch anything for years to come," he says.

For even more flexibility, the Youngs have also built three acres of Cravo retractable-roof house at their No. 2 location. And for their next expansion, Rob says, "We'll probably be considering a house like the one Tom Van Wingerden is putting up."

Retractables: The Best of Two Worlds

So, what's Tom putting up that has Rob Young interested? Six acres of Van Wingerden Greenhouse Company's MX greenhouse, which, for lack of a better name, is a "rigid retractable."

Tom, owner of Metrolina Greenhouses, Huntersville, North Carolina, learned the value of growing outdoors by using a ten-acre rollout area for his spring bedding plants. The drawback was the time and labor required to move a crop back inside when it got windy or cold or started to rain.

So, they began looking for a way to cover their rollout area without losing its benefits, says Art Van Wingerden, Tom's son and the company vice president. That led them to Cravo, which at that time had just built its first retractable-roof greenhouse. Metrolina put up an acre to test the concept, then quickly followed with more. Today, out of their forty-five acres, twelve are Cravo retractables. Obviously, they're happy with the results.

"It definitely makes the crop better and gets it ready for the stores," Art says of growing in a retractable-roof house. "Pansies do better out there, as do petunias." He says they'll start pansies off in the regular greenhouses, "to get them going," then put them into the retractable-roof house because they stretch more in a standard greenhouse. Perennials and fall mums are two other crops Metrolina likes to grow in the outdoor climate of the retractables, which they use for six to eight months of the year.

Their Cravo houses are equipped with enough heat to keep the plants growing, but not enough to make them a year-round house. Like many retractables, Metrolina's are equipped with a single layer of flexible, transparent, waterproof fabric. "We can't heat it very well because we've only got one roof layer, not a double layer of plastic," Art explains. You can more efficiently heat a retractable-roof house if you put an energy curtain in it, and they're looking at it. Some manufacturers use 6-mil. poly, and one company, Jaderloon, has designed a retractable that uses two layers of poly that inflate, creating a standard double-poly house when the roof is closed.

Over the years, Metrolina has learned some tricks about growing in retractables. At first, they'd move pansies and other crops into the house just for finishing, about two weeks before shipping. Now they put them out right away, saving the regular greenhouse space for impatiens and other crops that need more protection.

Ventilation needs were also a learning experience. At first, they thought they'd need rollup sidewalls to get adequate airflow through the houses, despite the open roof. They've discovered that sidewalls are important for keeping crops from being wind damaged. The open roof provides plenty of ventilation. Sidewalls are glazed with inexpensive rigid plastic.

Mechanically, their Cravo houses "are basically maintenance free," says Art. They replaced the pull wires on the original house (later designs use a heavier wire), but the roof material, now more than four years old, looks fine, Art says. (Roof life is still a question mark for retractables: Rob Young isn't as happy with how his fabric is holding up.)

To give them even more flexibility, Metrolina is now building six acres (part of a twenty-acre expansion plan) of the latest generation of retractable greenhouses, the MX. These look like standard, peaked, gutter-connected houses, but each roof section is hinged at the gutter and sealed with a gasket at the peak. A rack-and-pinion mechanism pushes each roof section to the vertical position, opening the roof and providing 100% ventilation. Linked to a computer to sense wind, rain, or temperature, the roofs can quickly be closed. (Private Garden, Hampden, Massachusetts, markets a similar European design called the Cabrio that's hinged at one gutter and the peak; the two roof sections fold together to open the roof.)

"We can grow everything with it and still get the benefits of the Cravo," Art says of the MX. "It gives us more in one house." Cost, of course, is also more than a standard retractable and slightly more than a typical gutter-connected house.

Each Has Its Purpose

So what can we learn from the experiences of these three growers? First, while all three depend heavily on one style of house, none of them uses one design exclusively. Art Van Wingerden sums it up best: "If I were building a forty-acre range, I wouldn't build forty acres of retractable, nor would I build forty acres of glass. Each one has its purpose. You do your best to match the greenhouse style to the crops you want to grow."

March 1998

The Rolls Royce Greenhouse

Don Grey

It seems everyone wants to be a millionaire. If you won a cool million on a TV game show, what would you do with it? Imagine the greenhouse you could build and equip with an unlimited budget! So we asked a few growers to dream big about the greenhouses they'd build if money didn't matter— the Rolls Royce greenhouse.

For Ken Van Der Ende, Burnaby Lake Greenhouses, Surrey, British Columbia, Canada, dreaming big isn't a problem. The potted plant grower is expanding and recently opened a new 260,000-sq. ft. facility.

Ken prefers glass because of its optimal light transmission and would build wide-span houses rather than Venlo-style houses. Inside would be a motorized roll-up shading system, one preferably inside the purlins, an inch or two from the glass. Ken wants to control shading as much as possible.

Burnaby Lake already has a Dutch tray internal support system, but Ken would build on that technology and install overhead cranes that could pick up trays and move them throughout the houses. Any movable container system would be completely automated. Ken would build an automated order picking and sorting system that could select and convey plants to the shipping facility, where a mechanized boxing system would prepare them for transport.

"An ebb-and-flood system is the way to go," Ken says of his benches. "But I'd like to see better control with fertilizer mixing." In addition, he wants environmental control computers designed for pot plant greenhouses, not for vegetable crops. Monitoring the physiology of a crop itself would be a big plus—sensors that could measure leaf and soil temperatures, transpiration, and nutrient uptake, for example.

Mike Gooder of The Plantpeddler in Cresco, Iowa, would install more robotics in his Rolls Royce greenhouse to improve efficiency and costs. "We're looking at the automation side of things in the greenhouse that doesn't require a lot of people," Mike says. Their crops are mums and poinsettias, but they typically ship twenty different flowering crops a week.

One of Mike's biggest desires would be to automate as completely as possible all irrigation. Today, for example, he estimates that 40 to 50% of his budget is spent on labor to irrigate.

Mike also wants Dutch trays to move plants around. Although several good systems are on the market, he'd like to see microtube heat perfected within the benching system. "It's at the top of my wish list," he says. Microclimatic heat would be everywhere, right at the plant level, making it easier to provide the necessary heat right on the bench.

Mike likes polycarbonate coverings but would like to see better fastening systems than exist today.

Any new greenhouse for Don Spence, head grower for bedding plant producer Smith Gardens, Aurora, Oregon, would be built to save on labor costs. He says irrigation—and the cost and labor it takes—is his biggest issue. He wants to automate his irrigation program as much as possible and wants a system of high-tech watering booms and a program that could automatically monitor, trigger, and adjust his irrigation regimens.

In fact, everything in the greenhouse would run through a sophisticated environmental control system that would be reliable and as bulletproof as possible.

Another priority for Don is a Dutch tray system or an automated container handling system to improve efficiency and cut down on labor. He'd like to have large, gutter-connected houses where he can "have enough space to move people, product, and carts though—a big time- and labor-savings issue," Don says. A house with good roof venting and roll-up sidewalls is a necessity.

Arch Vermeer, manager of Westbrook Greenhouse Systems Ltd., Grimsby, Ontario, Canada, believes greenhouse and equipment manufacturers aren't far behind what growers are dreaming about. "Look at what you can buy now," he says. "It's there."

Manufacturers say that more growers are now shopping not for greenhouses, but for plant-growing systems. Richard Van Wingerden, of Van Wingerden Greenhouse Company, Horseshoe, North Carolina, says the structure may account for less than half of the total job cost; internal automation is now the biggest percentage of the price tag.

Some structure builders, such as Colorado's Nexus Corporation, which has partnered with Hawe for internal transport and Visser for automation, have become one-stop shops that let growers deal with one vendor to design a complete, unified plant production facility.

"In the end, it doesn't come down to your dream house," says Arch Vermeer. "It's a matter of choice."

August 2000

What Growers Want in a Greenhouse

Chris Beytes

While construction of new greenhouses may be declining in some parts of the world (in the Netherlands, greenhouse construction declined from 904 acres in 1992 to 395 acres in 1995), many growers are still building new structures. *FloraCulture International, GrowerTalks'* sister publication, surveyed eighteen greenhouse manufacturers serving more than sixty countries to find out what specifications growers are requesting in their new structures. While our survey isn't an exact description of greenhouse structures worldwide, it still provides a good representation of what growers in various parts of the world want in their new greenhouses.

What Kinds of Structures Are They Building?

Gutter-connected houses are most common worldwide, with 50% of respondents listing them as the greenhouse style they most often build. Freestanding houses are most popular with 33% of respondents. However, freestanding houses are ranked No. 1 by 71% of U.S. manufacturers, with gutter-connected houses rated second. Dutch manufacturers rate Venlo-style houses No. 1. Retractable-roof greenhouses are gaining in popularity in both North America and Europe.

Average Greenhouse Dimensions

The average size of new greenhouses built by survey respondents varies widely—from just 3,228 sq. ft. all the way up to 129,156 sq. ft. (three acres). The average is 45,797 sq. ft. (just over an acre). There are some regional differences: Dutch-built houses average 43,000 sq. ft., compared to 39,940 sq. ft. for houses built by North American companies. United Kingdom companies reported a much smaller average size of 7,962 sq. ft.

Bay widths range from as little as 10.5 ft. up to 41 ft., with the average bay width being 26 ft. Typical bay widths built by respondents include 21, 22, and 30 ft. The survey revealed very few regional differences. Bay width is determined by roof material dimensions and interior equipment (bench and automation) dimensions, which are fairly standard.

Bay lengths, however, are much more variable. Manufacturers reported averages ranging from 95 ft. all the way up to 579 ft. The average among all respondents is 192 ft., with the most common lengths being 96, 131, and 142 ft. Interestingly, average bay length for European and Canadian builders (285 ft.) is more than twice that of U.S. and United Kingdom builders (121 ft.).

How High Should You Go?

Gutter heights range from 7.0 ft. to 14.5 ft., with the average being 11.2 ft. Standard in Europe is 11.5 to 13.0 ft.; Canadian builders build the tallest houses at 14.0 ft. average; U.S. builders average 10.0 to 12.0 ft.; and the customers of United Kingdom builders request the lowest gutters, averaging just 7.5 ft.

What Will It Cost You?

Per-square-foot prices reported by individual companies vary wildly, from a low of $1.00 all the way up to $11.60. Average price is about $3.64 per sq. ft., with most companies ranging between $3.50 and $4.00 per sq. ft. Contrary to the popular belief that Dutch or European houses are the most expensive, our survey didn't reveal any regional differences, only differences between individual companies.

Preferred Coverings

Double poly is the world's most popular covering, the favorite of 61% of respondents. It ranks No. 1 in North America, Australia, and France. Glass is No. 1 for 22% of respondents (Italian and Dutch manufacturers), followed by single poly at 17% (primarily United Kingdom builders). Various types of rigid sheeting follow these three. With the increase in construction of retractable-roof houses, reinforced poly and other new coverings are gaining in popularity.

Ventilation and Heat

Regional climatic differences have a major effect on ventilation choices. According to survey respondents, 61% of new houses are naturally ventilated. Fans are No. 1 for 17% of builders; fans and pads are the first choice for 11%. Australia, the Pacific Rim, Europe, and Canada favor natural ventilation. U.S. builders are split among all three types.

Heat requests are also very climate specific. Gas-fired unit heaters are the top choice for 61% of new houses worldwide, followed by hot water perimeter pipe, 28%. U.S. and United Kingdom builders choose unit heaters first; European and Canadian builders say hot water perimeter pipes are No. 1. In-floor heat is gaining in popularity: It's the No. 3 system installed by many U.S. and European builders. Less widely used but still popular are under-bench heat and infrared and oil-fired unit heaters.

Controlling the Environment

Environmental control computers are now going into 40% of new greenhouses built by our survey respondents. One Dutch company reports installing them in 100% of their new structures. Computers are most common in northern Europe and Canada and least common for United Kingdom builders, who install them in less than 5% of new greenhouses.

Automatic shade curtains are less common than environmental control computers, going into 27% of new greenhouses, according to respondents. Regional popularity is identical to that of computers.

New Construction Outlook

The eighteen manufacturers we surveyed build greenhouses in one to sixty different countries and have sold 35 to 600 greenhouses so far in 1996, totaling 130,824 sq. ft. to 8.6 million sq. ft. Combined, our eighteen companies built 2,484 new structures covering more than 35.1 million sq. ft.

For 1997, 65% say they expect to sell more greenhouses (20% more on average), with 30% expecting to do about the same amount of business. Only 5% expect to do less business.

March 1997

The Fundamental Structure Question

Chris Beytes

"Should I build a freestanding or a gutter-connected greenhouse?"

That's probably the most common question greenhouse builders get. Certainly, new growers planning their first greenhouses want to know the difference between the two. But even experienced growers often have a tough time deciding between freestanding and gutter-connected structures, especially when their new house will be for a crop they've never grown before. Both types have their places in our industry. Knowing their strengths and weaknesses will help you make the best decision for your particular needs.

Why Freestanding?

Low cost. This may be the reason most growers start out with freestanding houses. A simple freestanding structure with minimal heating and ventilation can quickly be erected for under a dollar per square foot, for about a third to a quarter of the cost of an average gutter-connected structure. Of course, better environmental controls cost more money.

Easy to add. It's easy to build more freestanding houses without disrupting production in existing houses. Tearing off walls and roofs and tying in to existing electrical services when adding on to a gutter-connected house can affect crops in the existing portion of the house. Lost sales during construction are expenses most growers forget to account for.

Individual environments. This is another key reason most growers use freestanding houses. Because each has its own heating and ventilation system, you can maintain unique environments for each crop. You can keep pansies cool while your vinca stay warm. Perennials can be vernalized in one house and forced into bloom in another.

Isolation. Freestanding houses let you isolate one crop from another, preventing the spread of insects and diseases and containing any potential problems to one house. This is especially useful when you're handling virus- or bacteria-susceptible crops such as geraniums and New Guinea impatiens. You can spray only where needed, cutting chemical and labor costs.

Redundancy. If a fan, heater, irrigation line, or some other piece of equipment breaks in one freestanding house, you may lose the crop in that house, but you won't lose everything because you have other freestanding houses. However, don't be complacent: If all of your freestanding houses are on the same electrical service or water supply, a power or water problem will affect all of your houses. And more equipment usually means more costs.

Why Gutter-Connected?

Heating efficiency. Gutter-connected houses use less energy for a given amount of space compared with freestanding houses. Why? Any gutter-connected house, regardless of size, has only two end walls and two sidewalls through which heat can leak, whereas each freestanding house you have has two end walls and two sidewalls to leak heat. While a ground-to-ground freestanding house (one without sidewalls) doesn't have this problem, it and other freestanding houses will leak more heat through the roof, as it's difficult and expensive to equip freestanding houses with energy curtains. Most gutter-connected houses today have energy curtains to cut heating costs.

Space efficiency. Gutter-connected houses make the most use of your land, whereas freestanding houses are usually built a few feet apart from one another, leaving a narrow alley that gathers weeds and debris. Though some growers use the space for outdoor crops that don't need protection. Also, it's more difficult to use all of the space in a freestanding house with short sidewalls, especially for hanging crops.

Labor efficiency. With all of your crops under one roof, a gutter-connected house makes better use of your growing and shipping labor. Also, if you have any future plans to automate, it's *much* easier to do in a gutter-connected house.

Environmental consistency. While freestanding houses give you environmental flexibility, gutter-connected houses make it easier to maintain a consistent environment for a crop. Many growers will tell you that some of their freestanding houses have unique environments that require special cultural considerations, such as for growth regulator applications. Some growers find it easier to grow a consistent, uniform poinsettia crop in one big house rather than in twenty small ones.

Lower cost, long term. While freestanding houses are an inexpensive way to get started, they can actually cost more for a given area than gutter-connected houses. One builder says if you're planning to build five freestanding houses, you can cover the same area with a gutter-connected house for roughly the same cost.

The bottom line is that there's no best greenhouse, only the greenhouse that's best for you. Many growers have both types, giving them the best of both worlds.

December 1997

Greenhouse for a Growing Retail

Chris Beytes

Platt Hill Nursery has been a suburban Chicago institution for years, with locations in West Dundee and Bloomingdale. When growth and development finally pushed the garden center out of its small Dundee location, owner Platt Hill, a grower as well as a retailer, had the chance to build a state-of-the-art facility that would meet the dual challenges of growing and retailing.

To satisfy his grower side, Platt went with glass on his new structure, a Nexus Big Sky. It's a wide-span house, with 42-ft. bays and 5-by-8-ft. tempered-glass roof panels for maximum light transmission. Gutters are 12 ft. high. The four-bay house measures 168 by 100 ft.

Ventilation is through a side vent on the south wall and roof vents on both sides of the ridge. Cooling is handled by four United Metal Products positive pressure units ("swamp coolers") mounted on the north wall high overhead, which puts them out of the way. A 7-ft. overhang protects them from the elements. Platt likes the positive pressure units because they aid in pest control: By keeping the pressure inside the greenhouse higher than the pressure outside, insects can't fly in through vents.

BioTherm Hydronic engineered the heating system. Hot water from two Hamilton V-Tube mini boilers flows through tubes in the floor and through finned tubes overhead, around the perimeter and at the gutters.

A knee wall adds architectural interest to the structure, while vents keep it cool. Automatic doors are the same as used in grocery stores.

A Wadsworth Power Pull heat/shade controller operates the rack-and-pinion energy curtain. Eight Schaefer HAF fans per bay keep the air moving. All climate systems are tied into a Wadsworth MicroStep SA environmental control computer.

Platt satisfied his retail needs by specifying more space between columns, giving the house an open, airy look and lending flexibility to the retail layout. The concrete floor has herringbone-pattern brick paths accented by hexagonal stepping stones. Portable Midwest GROmaster ebb-and-flood benches suit both growing plants and retailing them. Automatic sliding glass doors give customers access, and a large overhead door allows large material to be moved in and out.

Most striking is the structure's brick knee wall, highlighted by diamond-shaped accents at the corners. Platt says this was the most challenging part of the structure because it had to be built to a precise height to meet the tempered glass sidewalls. Some of the glass had to be reordered because the mason didn't keep the wall at the specified 39-in. height.

So far Platt is pleased with his impressive new greenhouse. Now his challenge is making the rest of the nursery look as impressive.

November 1999

Designing Ambiance, Maintaining a Niche

Chris Beytes

When the Heidgen family, owners of Shady Hill Gardens, a longtime Batavia, Illinois, production and retail operation, decided to open a second location nine miles west in rural Elburn, they knew it had to be special enough to keep Shady Hill a destination for gardeners.

With the help of the greenhouse specialists at V&V Noordland, Medford, New York, the Heidgens have created a spectacular new glass conservatory-look garden center with three "clock towers" on the front facade. They designed the building to catch the attention of motorists on busy Route 38 and draw customers from nearby big boxes.

"We know that our old greenhouses have a certain amount of charm," says Joe Heidgen, who, with his father, Chuck, and brothers, Karl and Matt, run Shady Hill. "So we decided we needed a unique front on our new location, not something straight without personality. We wanted people to think of us not just as 'that garden center,' but as 'that place with geraniums and the really neat greenhouse.'"

Shady Hill's newest location is set back from the road, providing the opportunity for impressive display gardens and outdoor bedding plant merchandising and offering ample parking space. Joe looks at that as free advertising: "You've got to pay for permits for signs, but you don't have to pay for permits for flower beds."

To keep customers from feeling that one location is better than the other, both garden centers have the same square footage, and both will stock the same items.

Inside the original location's mazelike greenhouses, shoppers

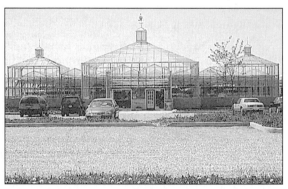

Shady Hill Gardens' new conservatory-style greenhouse offers a classy and comfortable retail environment.

can find something new at every twist and turn. To create the same sense of adventure and exploration in the new greenhouse, they'll use fencing, trellises, and large plants and vines, which will soften the interior and break it up into various rooms. Ebb-and-flood benches make plant maintenance a breeze, but they can easily be moved for merchandising flexibility. In-floor heating and modern environmental controls provide a perfect growing and retailing environment.

The new location opened April 1 to cloudy, cool weather. But by Mother's Day, they'd exceeded their sales goals at both stores, Matt says, showing they didn't lure customers away from the original location.

Summer 1998

Equipping Your Retractable-Roof Greenhouse

Don Grey

Growers have at least two demands from their greenhouses: flexibility to grow many different crops, and control over the environment.

To achieve this, growers worldwide are turning to retractable-roof greenhouses. They've become the darling of the industry the past few years, gaining in popularity as more manufacturers offer them and more growers install them.

But how much control over the environment do they really offer? And how do you need to equip them? Will conventional heaters, irrigation, and shading systems still work, or will you need to buy something much more sophisticated? The answers are as variable as the houses themselves.

What's Available

Retractable-roof greenhouses have been on the market for less than ten years, but the number of installations is rapidly increasing. Most growers who build such houses buy more in short order. That's why many top greenhouse manufacturing companies now offer various retractable-roof systems, including Conley's Manufacturing, Cravo Equipment, Harnois Industries, Nexus Corporation, United Greenhouse Systems, and Van Wingerden Greenhouse Company, among others.

It's worth noting that three retractable-roof greenhouse styles are on today's market: flat roof, peaked roof, and a new sawtooth design. Each can be used in many ways, but generally flat-roof houses are used more commonly as shade and frost protection structures, peaked-roofs are great for keeping out heavy snow or rain and often are heated, and the sawtooth design is a hybrid that allows open venting when other parts of the roof are closed. It's this ability to create the optimum growing environment that sets retractable-roof houses apart from fixed-roof, traditional houses. This flexibility is fueling the demand for retractable-roof houses. Growers now have the ability to create a greenhouse environment or an outdoor environment by a simple roof adjustment.

Control over Environment

This degree of exposure and "control" over the environment opens a grower's management options to produce healthier, hardier plants:

- Increased control over lighting. Just open or close the roof as needed to control plant growth. Control high- and low-light conditions that inhibit plant growth and that can lead to internode stretching.
- More exposure to the natural environment means better acclimation and plants that can survive better outdoors. Growers can force or slow flowering depending on timing of the season and how orders come in.
- Better ventilation means drier foliage, which means fewer disease problems. You can control daytime heat buildup, especially during winter, and control night temperatures for hardier crops.
- Easier, more effective DIF because proper and easier timing of temperature control.
- Lower labor costs. Fewer man-hours are needed to cover, uncover, or whitewash greenhouses. Improved traffic flow and materials handling; fewer pest and disease control applications also can cut labor.
- Lower irrigation needs by exposing crops to rainfall.

Greenhouse Selection

If you're thinking about a retractable-roof greenhouse, consider first what you want to grow in it, when you'll grow it, and where you live. For example, growing bedding plants in Texas, perennials in the Pacific Northwest, or poinsettias in Michigan all have different needs. That will lead to selecting a retractable style (flat, peaked, or sawtooth) and then adding equipment to meet your needs and conditions.

Flat roof

This style is becoming popular in parts of the country, such as Texas, the Pacific Northwest, and the Southeast, where snow load is not a critical factor yet weather is variable enough to cause concern and growers want basic protection against excess heat and cold. Houses commonly are used for finishing bedding plants and perennials or for overwintering nursery stock. They could be used for propagation in some locations if the conditions are right.

For example, Blooming Nursery Inc., Cornelius, Oregon, has three retractable-roof houses but uses them differently. Two are flat-roofed Cravo structures that are bare bones: no heat, no fans or other cooling, with standard sprinkler irrigation. The third house is a peaked roof Harnois. One Cravo is used to finish 4-in. bedding plants and hardy perennials, while the other contains 1-gal. stock. Both are used for overwintering and for shade in spring and summer. During cold months, owner Grace Dinsdale closes the roofs when temperatures dip below 36°F. The roofs are opened when it rains or snows. During warm months, they provide shade and are closed down to 80%.

To offer even more possibilities, Grace plans to retrofit the flat roofs by adding peaks (both were initially designed to be retrofitted). That modification will allow her to close the houses from rain, keep plants dry, and to add heat—she's considering an infrared Radiant-Aire heating system.

Peaked, sawtooth roof

Offering even more flexibility are peaked-roof retractable houses. Jerry Tuinier of Post Gardens in Rockwood, Michigan, is impressed with his new one-acre peaked-roof Cravo house. He's going into his second growing season, coming off a "really good looking 8-in. poinsettia crop and a great summer hardy mum crop." In addition, he's using it for seed geraniums and for forcing perennials.

Terry Smith of Smith Gardens in Bellingham, Washington, says growers are limited only by their creativity with how they can use retractable-roof greenhouses. Smith's 2 1/2-acre Cravo house is used for bedding plant production. He is better able to acclimatize the plants yet protect them from extensive cold. "The plants grow themselves," he says. "I'm very satisfied with the whole concept."

Meanwhile, Grace of Blooming Nursery uses her 30,000-sq. ft. Harnois house for propagating or dividing perennials and for growing on the 4-in.

transplants. She too is satisfied. "I want the best equipment to grow the best quality plants. I can't afford not to have the best structure."

Equipment Options

When you consider a retractable-roof greenhouse, your equipment options are just as varied as your structure options. "Basically, you can do anything in these houses you can do in any other greenhouse," says Graham McDonald, sales and technical service representative with Cravo. "A retractable-roof greenhouse when closed is just like any other greenhouse. They can be as simple or as complicated as you want to make them."

Depending on the house style you select, the list of what you won't need may be shorter than the options you can use. If you enjoy applying or removing whitewash or glazings to glass houses, you're out of luck. That's one thing you can dispense with. You won't need expensive rack-and-pinion, side, or ridge vents, or fan and pad cooling systems, for that matter. For the most part, you won't need outside exhaust fans.

Your equipment options then are as open as the houses you'll buy. Growers have installed everything from bare-bones systems, where they open and close the roof manually, to the most elaborate computer control systems. Both Graham and Gary Baze of Conley's say they've seen retractable-roof greenhouses where growers have installed environmental control computers, HAF fans, ECHO hanging basket systems, shade and heat-retention curtains, flood floors, overhead booms or sprinkler irrigation, Dutch trays, gas heaters, bottom heat, and more.

Here is a look at equipment options many growers use:

Air circulation

You would think that with all the ventilation that an open roof gives, horizontal airflow fans wouldn't be necessary in a retractable house. Not so. "HAF fans are almost a necessity," says Mike Van Wingerden of Van Wingerden Greenhouses, a bedding plant grower from Blaine, Washington. "It can get really moist in a cold greenhouse." Mike uses HAF fans with CO_2 burners to eliminate this humidity when the houses get moist in the cold, especially in the mornings, to keep the foliage as dry as possible. Grace at Blooming Nursery uses Schaefer HAF fans for optimum internal air circulation.

Benches

Growers have many options to consider. Some use benches (some equipped with ebb and flood) while others choose none. Terry at Smith Gardens has installed Dutch trays to move plants through the range for optimum conditioning. Mike uses a semiautomatic monorail system for some of his crops. Post Gardens uses a Carson rack system with double-wide pallet jacks that can move the racks two at a time up to 6 mph. Rolling benches are options some growers love, and they can work well in these houses.

Computers

Environmental control computers are common with both flat- and peaked-roof houses. Computers can be set to react to air temperature, CO_2, humidity, soil moisture, and many other factors. For example, Mike Van Wingerden uses an Argus computer system, and he sets his own thresholds according to the crop and season. Jerry Tuinier uses a Priva computer at Post Gardens to automate his houses. "You'd be a fool to buy a retractable-roof greenhouse and not operate it automatically," says Conley's Gary Baze. Flat- and peaked-roof systems can be automated by computer to open and close both the roof and sidewall vents. That can save a considerable amount in labor costs.

Heat

Heat is a fixed function in both fixed- and retractable-roof greenhouses: It takes the same output to heat a glass house to 70°F as it does a retractable-roof house. Post Gardens in Michigan and Smith Gardens in Washington use Modine unit heaters in their peaked-roof houses. Because you often don't want to expose the crops to much rainfall, you really don't have to worry about heaters getting wet. Fiberglass shields can help protect them if necessary.

Mike Van Wingerden uses bottom heat in one part of his house (with hot water heat under the gutters for snowmelt). Blooming Nursery also uses bottom heat (a Delta T system with two boilers). Gary Baze says hot water radiant heat systems work well in retractable-roof houses. Jerry at Post Gardens says he doesn't prefer heat in his floors because it takes too long to react to input changes. Nonetheless, he has been impressed at how well his house retains its heat.

Insect screening

Yes, retractable-roof greenhouses can be screened to exclude insects. Installing insect screens over the vents of a fixed-roof house can reduce airflow through the vents, causing an excessively hot house. Growers then often shade the house to cool it, but at the price of reduced light levels. On the other hand, when you install insect screen horizontally across the roof opening of a retractable-roof house as well as on side vents, about seven times more vent area exists for air to flow through. One California operation uses a motor to retract the insect screening when the roof is closed, to maximize light levels.

Irrigation

From simple overhead sprinklers to flood floors and traveling booms, growers again have many options to consider. Most flat-roof houses seem to employ common overhead sprinklers, while peaked houses are more variable. For example, Grace uses an ebb-and-flood floor in her Harnois house with good success, although she irrigates crops in the flat-roof houses with overhead sprinklers. And while Post Gardens is set up for flood floors, Jerry says he uses overhead sprinklers. The concrete floors let him collect and recycle the runoff. Mike Van Wingerden installed a heavy boom irrigation system from Cherry Creek Systems, Larksburg, Colorado. The booms are so sturdy, he says, workers can insert planks on them and sit out over the crops below to work.

Shading and energy curtains

Gary Baze says, "Shade screens are ideal for these houses. When you pull back the roofs, you wish you had shading." However, he says some growers don't install shading because of the expense. Mike Van Wingerden is one grower who doesn't use supplemental shading, but not necessarily because of cost. Rather, he finds his ECHO hanging basket machines provide just enough extra shade. Likewise, heat-retention curtains can help conserve heat in colder climates and may pay for themselves through lower overall energy bills.

Venting

"The most important thing is getting the heat out of the house," Jerry says. With the ability to retract the roofs as widely as possible and even roll up the sidewalls in many houses, venting is easy, especially if a computer controls the house. Jerry offers the high quality of his 1996 garden mum crop as proof. "We were able to get rid of the heat, especially at night," he says. "We also like to brush our plants with a little wind, which helps in hardiness."

It's this flexibility to grow many different crops and control the environment that's proving to be an open and shut case for retractable-roof greenhouses. An increasing legion of growers worldwide are seeing their options expand, rather than retract.

January 1997

Retractables: Ever-Expanding Flexibility

Don Grey

In the old days—four or five years ago—selecting a retractable-roof greenhouse was fairly simple: You could select among two or three manufacturers and a couple of basic styles. Today, no fewer than twenty manufacturers now have some style of retractable house either in production or on their drafting tables. Here's a look at current trends in today's hottest greenhouse structures.

Flat Roofs

From the beginning, flat-roofed retractable systems caught on quickly with nursery stock and hardy perennial growers for temporary crop protection. Now bedding plant, vegetable starter plant, and foliage growers are quickly adopting them. They can save in labor costs and reduce chemical applications—and grow a healthier crop. While they don't stop rain (the roof fabric is porous), they're popular because they can open nearly 100% to prevent heat buildup and give outdoor growing conditions, but quickly close tight to protect crops from occasional frost and cold weather.

As a result, new flat-roofed retractable systems are going up by the acre, replacing overwintering hoop houses and shade houses. They're especially popular in coastal areas with less harsh winters—the Pacific Northwest, Southwest, Southeast, and Middle Atlantic states, for example. Costs are coming down, too, so more growers can afford them.

With time comes better technology. For example, roof fabrics have been improved. Although today's roofs cut out a fair bit of light when closed, Cravo Equipment Ltd., Brantford, Ontario, a pioneer in retractable-roof houses, with more than three hundred acres constructed worldwide, plans to introduce a new fabric for their flat-roofed house which gives just 15 to 20% shading (compared with 45% for their original roof), while offering the same heat-retention capability—perfect for areas with less light or for crops that need more light. When closed, more light penetration also means more warmth inside. Marketing Manager Graham McDonald says the new fabric makes flat-roofed retractables work "more like greenhouses."

Many growers use their flat-roofed retractable houses mainly to protect against weather extremes, so they equip them sparsely. Many growers, though, will use environmental control computers to set roof and sidewall opening and closing thresholds.

Northwest growers use them for year-round nursery stock and perennial production. For example, Woodburn Nursery & Azaleas Inc., Woodburn, Oregon, installed a six-acre flat-roof range for nursery stock production two years ago and likely will build more. Three other nearby nurseries use them for perennial production.

Low Profile

Brand new on the market is the "low-profile" house, a hybrid between the flat-roof and A-frame house. This style offers rain protection without the structural costs of a peaked-roof house. They're sometimes built in a sawtooth configuration.

Hired-Hand Green of Bremen, Alabama, recently introduced its Meg-A-Frame retractable roof. The house has just a 4-ft. pitch between gutter height and peak. Key to the design is the self-guttering roof material from LS Americas, Charlotte, North Carolina. The QLS Abri Ultra fabric has a tough monofilament weave and built-in folds to better channel rain and dew from the fabric.

The Meg-A-Frame's roof drive is a push-pull system rather than cables. "The push-pull system is more expensive," says Steven Crider, company president, "but is more precise and dependable than cables."

The low pitch and self-guttering fabric can lower construction costs, as there's less structure. For example, at Powell Plant Farm, Gallatin, Tennessee, a new Meg-A-Frame house is 360 ft. wide with just one central gutter.

Steven says the trend in the South is toward lower-cost houses for basic frost protection that can be closed against rain and shaded during the summer. The company is looking to the big bedding plant grower. "Hired Hand is going after the big grower, big production houses, and ranges," Steven says. "I see this as a growing market." Still, he says a smaller grower can afford the house. Prices start at about three dollars per square foot for the structure, drive system, and roof.

Peak Roofs

Peak-roofed retractables give benefits of both retractables and traditional greenhouses: outdoor growing conditions and full weather and climate control. These houses have been equipped with everything from Dutch trays to flood floors to HID lights—anything a grower would put into a regular greenhouse.

Graham says that Cravo has developed three new "hybrids" of its popular northern-style peaked-roof house: shade above, insect screen, and a southern house design. The shade-above system suspends a shade curtain 18 in. above the roof fabric, which allows growers to easily choose to grow in the field, in a shade house, or in a greenhouse. Graham says it's especially good for warmer climates where cooling is a major challenge. Also, Cravo has a new Retract-A-Roof greenhouse covering that's heavier and expected to last longer than their original fabric, which can last for five years or more under good conditions.

They've used the second hybrid, retractable insect screening, on a 175,000-sq. ft. Costa Rican range they're building for Fides Plants. They can maximize light levels by retracting the screen when the roof is closed for rain protection and get maximum light and ventilation when the roof is open and the screen is closed. Another feature of the Fides project is a house design featuring A-frame trusses on 16-ft. centers instead of the standard 12-ft. centers. It's designed for areas of lower snow loads and is 5 to 7% cheaper to purchase and construct.

Rollup Roofs

For growers who want a large measure of ventilation capacity but more year-round climate control, one company now offers a double-poly house with a roll-up roof. Jaderloon, Irmo, South Carolina, has come out with the roll-A-roof house. This system uses inflatable double-poly film that fits over a frame, which can be rolled and unrolled. The system can be retrofitted to existing structures. Major benefits include the energy efficiency of double poly, along with the low replacement cost. AgraTech Greenhouse Manufacturers, Pittsburg, California, distributes the roll-A-roof house on the West Coast.

Hinged-Roof Greenhouses

Perhaps the houses garnering the most attention today are the peaked-roof houses with hinged roof panels. Instead of flexible curtains forming the roof, rigid panels open and close via rack-and-pinion drives. One immediate plus of this system: It allows flexibility in choosing different coverings. For example, if you're used to rigid coverings, you can choose among glass, acrylic, or polycarbonate sheeting. If you like film, you can install double-poly panels.

Van Wingerden Greenhouse Company, Horse Shoe, North Carolina, has a new house called the MXII. The house's price starts around $6.50 sq. ft. for roof, structure, and drive system. It can be covered by inflated double poly, polycarbonate, or glass.

Westbrook Greenhouse Systems Ltd., Grimsby, Ontario, has introduced something similar. Its Open Roof Greenhouse essentially is a house that features double-poly-covered panels that open at the ridge vents. The panels open by rack-and-pinion drives and stand straight up above the gutter. When closed, the top panel nestles on the bottom, creating a tight seal, thanks to a rubber gasket. The house roof can open partially like a traditional ridge vent or fully for maximum ventilation.

Private Garden Greenhouse Systems, Hampden, Massachusetts, offers another twist on the retractable-panel house, the Cabrio, which was introduced two years ago to the North American market from Europe. "Everybody doesn't need our type of house," says the company's Joe Hickson. "But when you purchase a Cabrio greenhouse, you purchase it on a twenty-year return on investment." From the outside, the house resembles a standard Venlo-style house. But rather than open at the ridge like the MXII, the roof, which is hinged at the peak, slides on Teflon wheels from gutter to gutter, a scissors effect. The roof can open in four minutes and close in two, Joe says, with 85% retractability. The end that moves also has a moving gutter under it that collects any dew or rain on the roof and prevents it from falling on the exposed crop below. Hickson says the roof panels have a good wind resistance of about 30 to 35 mph before they should be closed.

As with other systems, the roof can be covered with polycarbonate, acrylic, poly film, or glass. Joe prices an acre at $9.50 per sq. ft. Houses are specially designed for each grower, built to local codes.

Dutch greenhouse manufacturer Verbakel/Bomkas has a similarly styled house they call the Cabriolet. But they offer several advantages over the Cabrio, says Edward Verbakel; namely construction costs of up to 25% less and glazing with lightweight, flexible, and shatterproof SPS DynaGlas corrugated polycarbonate. Verbakel/Bomkas just completed a range at Van De Wetering Greenhouses, Jamesport, New York.

But How Do They Grow?

Retractable peaked-roof houses are proving to be versatile for many different crops. Sure, you can grow perennials and bedding plants in them. What about potted crops such as poinsettias and mums? How about plugs?

Blue Ridge Growers Inc., Stevensburg, Virginia, is learning how to grow mums, Easter lilies, and plugs in its new Cabrio house. Growers were able to hold Easter lilies longer this year and grow a hardier mum crop. Blue Ridge installed one acre one year ago (it also has eight acres under glass) and is so sold on the system it is looking at adding two more acres in the future.

"I'm sold on it," says Charles Jaber, plug grower. "I've grown in several systems, from the cheapest Quonsets to this house, and this is on the top of my list. It's an excuse-free greenhouse."

This year Blue Ridge is finishing its first bedding plant crop in the house, growing mainly in 606s and 1204s, and results look promising, Charles reports. The stem caliper definitely is bigger and leaf thickness greater, he says. He says he's using a little more ammonia because of the light levels. The most remarkable difference between the Cabrio and fixed-roof houses has been the ambient air temperature at leaf level compared to the outside. During one early season heat spike, for example, Charles noted just a 1°F difference between inside and outside temperatures, thanks to the house's ability to vent at 85% percent and supplemental shadecloth.

"The quality of the greenhouse is fantastic," says the company's Jim Soedler. "It's a little more expensive, but in the long run we won't have to change a thing."

Retail Houses

Growers aren't the only ones with retractable-roof greenhouses to show for their dollars. Another trend is their emerging popularity among retailers for open-air markets.

Many of the same advantages apply to retailing plants in these houses as growing in them. Indeed, you can give your plants—and customers—the best of both worlds: exposure to nice weather and protection against rain or nippy conditions.

Some manufacturers are modifying existing product lines for this new market. United Greenhouse Systems, Inc., Edgerton, Wisconsin, now offers its Ambassador Crown system as a retractable-roof house. Dave Johnson, operations manager, says the house is a classic shape for retailers.

The Ambassador can be fitted with a hard-glazed roof or a retractable-curtain system. The curtain system is called Skytrac, an LS Americas' fabric curtain, which operates with a push-pull drive system. Growers also use the house. "Ours is not just an investment in one system," Dave says. "You can grow anything in there. Once growers see the quality of goods going out of it, it will be an instant hit."

Dave says that when he was in Sweden a few years ago, he first saw a retractable-roof greenhouse used for retailing. He sees an increasing part of the market going toward garden centers. "The need for a retractable-roof greenhouse is two-pronged: for retailers and for sophisticated growers who want to harden off their crop," he says. "It's a growing segment of the market, a specialty."

Private Garden also is positioning its Cabrio house for the garden center market. "We have a major interest in garden centers," Joe says. "With this house, the consumer can shop in comfort."

Molbak's Inc., Woodinville, Washington, an independent garden center, is installing a Cabrio house at its new store nearing completion in Seattle. Molbak's wanted to create an open-air environment for customers, to take advantage of nice summer weather yet protect them from notorious Northwest winter and spring rains.

With so many different styles of greenhouses on the market today, retractable-roof houses represent a small but growing percentage, thanks in great part to the tremendous flexibility they offer.

"The future of growing is in an open-roof system," Private Garden's Joe Hickson says. "That's because plants were meant to grow outdoors. Now we can bring that natural light and fresh air in to our plants."

Summer 1998

Growing in Open-Roof Greenhouses

Don Grey

Retractable- and open-roof greenhouses have really taken the floriculture world by storm. But they're essentially a new production system, one in which plants can be exposed to the outdoor environment or fully protected from it, so growers are learning every day how to get the most from these structures.

To learn more about them, some 160 greenhouse professionals from throughout North America attended what may have been the world's first seminar devoted exclusively to retractable-roof greenhouses on March 22, 2000, in Wilsonville, Oregon. Cravo Equipment Ltd. and Argus Controls sponsored the seminar.

"The purpose was to learn how to grown in open-roof houses," explains Richard Vollebregt, Cravo's president. "Not much knowledge is out there because these structures only came on the scene six or seven years ago, compared to thirty years of [growing experience with] traditional structures."

The daylong event featured seminar presentations, a grower panel, and a tour of four nearby operations that use both peaked- and flat-roof structures for everything from woody ornamentals and florist azaleas to bedding plants and retail sales.

"Oregon, Washington, and British Columbia growers have the most overall experience growing plants in retractable-roof systems, so it seemed logical to locate the seminar in an area that encouraged their participation," says Sven Svenson, Ph.D., assistant professor of horticulture and research horticulturist at Oregon State University's North Willamette Research and Extension Center in Aurora. The center also hosted a lunch and a tour of its new retractable-roof research greenhouses.

Learning New Ways
Both Richard and Sven spoke about the importance of managing the soil temperatures of the plants to protect the containerized root systems from high heat, even during cool growing seasons.

"When you start to hit 95°F soil temperatures, you're getting in the danger zone," Sven says. "With anything over 90 to 100°F, you'll get root damage. The ability of retractable film coverings to diffuse light allows the use of films with higher light transmission without risking higher soil temperatures."

Keeping container media cool, especially in summer months, means the plants will use less water and fertilizer, exhibit less root damage and therefore suffer fewer diseases, avoid summer dormancy, and exhibit more uniform growth, Sven says.

Alec Mackenzie of Argus Controls spoke about how environmental control computers can help growers manage crops in these new systems. "Once you pick a structure, you lock yourself into a way of doing things, especially with environmental control and what kind of equipment you can put into it," Alec says. "Retractable-roof houses are not standardized systems. People are handling these houses in many different ways."

As a result, manual operation can be difficult when growers and managers are busy. That's why many use computerized environmental control systems. "Computer systems need to be customized to match each grower's site and

This A-frame retractable is equipped with an energy curtain, ECHO hanging basket system, heaters, watering booms, and more. The house, at Fessler Nursery Company near Woodburn, Oregon, is double-cropped: They grow florist azaleas on the floor and fuchsias above in hanging baskets.
Photo by Don Grey.

management style," Sven says. "The computer system doesn't substitute for a grower, but it's just a tool to make management of the retractable roof easier." Alec says it may be up to two years yet before growers will have specific programs written that can be used with environmental computers in retractable-roof greenhouses.

Sharing Ideas

A panel discussion involved a wide range of growers who grow everything from cut flowers and bedding plants to tree seedlings and nursery stock.

Tom Fessler of Woodburn Nursery & Azaleas Inc. shared his experiences with both flat- and peaked-roof houses. The nursery initially installed six acres of flat-roof houses for growing nursery stock, including thread-branch cypress, evergreen azaleas, maples, and more. The nursery later installed a peaked-roof house to grow floral azaleas from July through January and then tissue culture rhododendrons.

For Tom, the biggest thing in installing retractables was going through a learning curve. For example, he learned that how the nursery manages shade in the summer is as important as using the structure for cold protection during the winter.

Jim Finch of Washington Bulb Co. is also learning how to grow bulb crops in retractable structures. He grows cut flowers and bulbs for forcing and as a seed source—mainly tulips, irises, and lilies. Jim likes the retractable-roof house, now going into its second year of production, because of its ability to vent. Other types of structures, he says, are too hot for his crops during spring and summer. The retractable house is set to open when temperatures reach 62°F and provides the best maximum venting available.

"Retractables are working tools, but they only improve your crops if you actually use them," Sven says. "For example, if you forget to position the roof for shading on a hot summer day, you fail to prevent heat stress or crop damage. Similarly, retractable roofs don't grow crops faster for you or schedule the finishing time for you, but they do ease the management of growing crops faster or on a specific schedule."

Tom agrees. "Both systems are tools to help grow plants, not a cure-all. It still takes people to manage crops. You need to be out there with your crops."

July 2000

Open-Roof House Opens Eyes

Lesa Morey

Most retail customers spend their time looking at the shrubs and bedding plants displayed in and around the greenhouse. But at Sanders' Nursery & Distribution Center in Broken Arrow, Oklahoma, it's the greenhouse itself that awes first-time visitors. When the 140,000-sq. ft. house opened last year, the local newspapers came by to shoot pictures. Even the delivery truck drivers stepped out of their rigs to look around.

That's because Sanders Nursery was the first in Oklahoma to build a retractable-roof greenhouse.

"People come out and just marvel at it," says owner Berl Berry, whose family also operates two wholesale nursery operations in Tahlequah, Oklahoma. "They just stand there and can't believe the whole house just opens up to the sky above." They're even more impressed when a weather front approaches and Berry hits the switch to close the roof: Ultraquiet electric motors pull the series of rooftop curtains shut. In just minutes, tough overhead fabric tents the entire greenhouse. Now, instead of running for the shelter of their cars, customers can continue shopping under the two central rain-tight gabled bays.

"It's just a beautiful facility," says Berl. "Because everything's under one big roof, when your first walk in, the house looks a lot bigger than it really is."

Berl and his father, Bob, spent two years studying the retractable-roofing systems on the market. After making the decision to buy one, they haven't looked back. They've since bought not just one retractable, they've bought four—all different designs. Their initial purchase was a flat top Retract-A-Roof from Cravo Equipment, Brantford, Ontario, Canada, that covers 200,000 sq. ft. of woody ornamentals and perennials at the family's Park Hill location. Two other houses now stand at their Tri-B wholesale nursery location. One, covering 130,000 sq. ft., is another Cravo flat top. The other is from Northglenn, Colorado-based Nexus, a rain-tight 60,000-sq. ft. convertible that combines a flat top with a peaked gable.

The highest profile house, of course, is the retail center. Covering nearly 140,000 sq. ft., it combines two expanses of flat top connected by two rain-tight A-frame bays. The central drive-in bays measure 16 ft. high at the gutters and 24 ft. at the peaks—high enough for not only customer's cars, but even for semis. Before the grand opening, Berl had five rigs parked inside at once, unloading plant material. (He had room for three more.)

With two years of retractable-roof experience now behind him, Berl remains pleased with the decision to try the novel designs. "I think they're the wave of the future," he says. As operations expand, he plans to build more of them.

The up-front and maintenance costs of his new houses are comparable to those of conventional houses, Berl calculates. What swayed his decision to use them is the added flexibility the open roofs can provide. In the Plains, growers continually wrestle with daily weather extremes. Sudden winds can carry in temperatures that are extremely variable.

The Berrys spent $1.30 per sq. ft. for the basic flat top space, which features water-permeable roof fabric and roll-up side curtains. On fair days, such as those in late spring when temperatures can soar, opening the roof provides optimal light and natural ventilation. If the weather turns nasty, the overhead fabric protects plants from strong gusts and pelting rain. The options help Berry grow better plants year-round. The movable covers, however, prove especially useful in the colder months, when he uses them to overwinter and shade his fall perennials. "You can't do that [vernalize] in a regular greenhouse," Berl says, adding that he considers retractables "economical for what you get." He can also heat the retail space, keeping customers shopping year round. The rain-tight Nexus house, operated similarly, costs a more substantial $5.00 per sq. ft., plus installation.

The curtain materials are all rated to withstand winds of up to 60 to 70 mph, and the nursery has already weathered one 60-mph windstorm. "The [curtains] held up fine," he says confidently. In two years, he's had no problems with the fabric, and he sees no differences in overall maintenance costs compared with his more conventional houses. The retractable roofs don't seem to need any special preventive maintenance, and Berl calculates payback time to be comparable to a standard house, too.

Berl can't say retractable roofs are for everyone, however. "It all depends on your needs, whether you're doing potted plants, or flats, and the time of year you're doing it." He encourages any growers contemplating a retractable roof to visit other growers who are using them. During his research, Berl visited houses in Oregon and Michigan and had phoned a Florida grower who had built one. "I think everyone needs to look at them before you buy. It's quite an investment."

In Oklahoma, Berl predicts his house will remain a novelty for a while longer. In his state, the innovative design "caught [competitors] off guard," and he doubts they'll catch up anytime soon.

Summer 2000

Aerodynamic Design Improves Ventilation

Ted H. Short

Most naturally ventilated greenhouses have been designed by experience with little engineering input. Grower testimonials abound, and real data have been almost nonexistent—that is until now!

The Ohio State University engineers are changing the "guess and try" practice of naturally ventilated greenhouse design by aerodynamically modeling some of the newest double-poly, multispan greenhouses. Further, these same engineers have tested designs in a commercial grower's greenhouse and have had some very positive results.

How Natural Ventilation Works

Naturally ventilated greenhouses rely primarily on wind pressure blowing in one side and out the other. Wind can also create a vacuum pressure along the roof to suck air out while letting air in the same vent or in the side vents. A secondary, much smaller effect is that of buoyancy, which predominates only on hot, low-wind days. In all cases, it's essential to have at least one very effective inlet with multiple outlets, and air must move through the plants from inlet to outlet for good ventilation. Thus, for gutter-connected multi-spans, a combination of windward side vents and continuous leeward roof vents tends to result in the most effective ventilation design. With retractable-roof designs, open windward side vents are as important as the open roof area to achieve midsummer cooling.

The Role of Buoyancy

Buoyancy has many examples, such as wood rising to the surface of water because it's less dense than water. Also, from experience, most people know that hot air rises because it's less dense than cool air. Most, however, are surprised to learn that moist air rises because it is less dense than dry air.

The reason for the confusion is that water as a liquid is very dense; water as a vapor, however, is less dense than the surrounding air and rises until it forms clouds in the atmosphere. Therefore, the combination of hot, moist air in a naturally ventilated greenhouse must be given a smooth path up and out. The slightest entrapment will stall the natural ventilation process on a low-wind day.

The Role of Wind

Wind with a little buoyancy is the primary ventilation system driver. The ultimate test of a natural ventilation system design is the response to a no-wind day. We can all think of moments on hot days when it feels as if there is no wind. Such moments have been recorded for nearly twenty years on precision weather stations in Ohio, taking hourly data 16 ft. above the ground. From this data, Ohio engineers found that most of the no-wind cases occurred when the outside temperature was less than 75°F. From 75 to 80°F, there was approximately one hour of no wind in five years. Above 80°F, there was always measurable wind above 1 mph with the average being approximately 5 mph. Therefore, no-wind ventilation tests were defined by the engineers to be 1 mph. In other words, if a greenhouse ventilates well at 1 mph, it's a very good design and will ventilate better at higher wind speeds.

(At 1 mph near plants, one will tend to see very slight movements of plant leaves.)

Solar Radiation and Shading

Solar radiation drives the whole natural ventilation process, including the outside wind. Solar radiation provides heat to the internal greenhouse air and forces plants to transpire water vapor. Excess solar radiation above 50% clear day noon levels, however, requires some form of shading for most climates. Often the shading is put on the outside as a paint or shade net. It can also be done with a porous horizontal shade screen or net inside the greenhouse. With internal shading, it's very important that the ventilation air enters the sidewall openings and travels up through the shade screen to carry the heat out of the roof vents.

Aerodynamic Models

The Ohio State University agricultural engineers have computer modeled both multispan sawtooth and curved-roof designs with top vents at different locations. They're leasing highly sophisticated computer software that you may have seen in aerodynamic car advertisements on TV. The technique essentially places a greenhouse cross-sectional profile into an electronic wind tunnel. With an emphasis on multispans, variables studied have been greenhouse widths, roof and side vent locations, vent opening widths, windward side profiles, internal and external shading systems, internal temperature profiles, and benching for various wind speeds and directions. With the fastest PC computers available, the calculation process is so complex that one single run takes anywhere from eight to forty-eight hours of continuous calculations!

An On-Farm Test

I helped a small Ohio grower (Quailcrest Farm, Wooster) consolidate Quonset houses and plan a 4½-span, gutter-connected, naturally ventilated production and retail facility. The greenhouse uses a combination of a windward (west) side vent and leeward roof vents to achieve the configuration shown on page 40. During the summer of 1997, temperature, humidity, wind, and solar radiation sensors were placed inside and outside the greenhouse to evaluate the design. The greenhouse was modeled aerodynamically and evaluated for both westerly and easterly wind flows.

For westerly winds, 90% of the air came in the west side vent and 10% came in the first roof vent. The outlet percentages were 3% for roof vent 1,

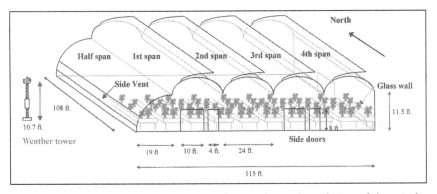

This sketch of the Quailcrest Farm greenhouse shows the relation of the wind-ward side vent to the roof vents as well as the wall, door, and plant locations. Most plants were on benches, and hanging baskets were over aisles.

13% for roof vent 2, 30% for roof vent 3, and 54% for roof vent 4. Amazingly, uniform temperatures were measured throughout the entire greenhouse at all times. The volumetric air exchange for this period was predicted to be 0.9 air changes per minute, with inside temperatures never exceeding outside temperatures by more than 5°F. In most cases, the inside temperature was within 2°F of outside.

For easterly winds (reverse flows), 95% of the air came in the east side in roof vent 4, 4% came in roof vent 3, and 1% came in roof vent 2. The outlet percentages were 2% for roof 3, 7% for roof 2, 41% for roof 1, and 50% for the west side vent. Again, uniform temperatures were measured throughout the entire greenhouse, with no temperature being more than 5°F above the outside. Average air exchange for an easterly wind was predicted to be half that of a westerly wind at the same velocity. East winds, however, tended to have higher velocities, making the actual air exchanges similar to west winds.

Retail buyer and grower responses to the Quailcrest Farm greenhouse have been extremely positive. All doors are typically open on warm and hot days, allowing easy access for browsing customers and plant-toting employ-ees. While the greenhouse was sometimes 5°F warmer than outside during the hottest part of the day, the greenhouse was still more comfortable than outside due to the 50% or more shading from direct solar radiation.

The Future Work
More work should be done to size and specify full-scale greenhouses, includ-ing retractable-roof designs. Side vent placement to prevent plant damage and short circuiting to the first roof vent is still being evaluated. Alternative

shading techniques such as internal nets are also being studied for use in naturally ventilated greenhouses in both humid and arid desert climates. While computer memory and speed have limited span width studies, this problem is changing with each new computer.

The engineers and horticulturists also want to improve the aerodynamic models to account for plant influences. The possibility exists that growers and manufacturers will eventually be able to give The Ohio State University engineers a sketch or layout of a proposed greenhouse design and get an "instant" aerodynamic evaluation of both fan and naturally ventilated systems.

Natural ventilation checklist

Advantages:
- Low energy requirements
- All side doors can be open in the summer
- Quiet internal working and shopping environment
- Unused greenhouse can be easily cooled in summer
- No ventilation restrictions on length of greenhouse
- Air temperature can be maintained very close to outside air
- Very high ventilation rates are possible
- Low temperature gradients across greenhouse

Disadvantages:
- Can easily be improperly designed
- Must be incorporated with some form of shade system
- Pad cooling can't be used
- May not allow for micro insect screening
- Plants near the side vent can be wind damaged
- Is dependent on wind speed and wind direction
- Vents are subject to wind damage
- Low light plants below open vents can be sun scorched

Design considerations:
- Roof vent opening should be 15 to 20% of floor area and open leeward to wind
- Minimum windward side vent should equal one roof vent
- For large multispans, windward side vent should be greater than 3% of floor area
- Windward side vent should be low enough to prevent air short circuiting to first top vent
- Higher gutter heights are generally better if windward side is aerodynamic
- A 50% shading system is necessary for summer growing
- Internal shapes should allow upward and outward convective flows (no traps)
- Computer control is essential for climate control and vent protection from high wind

Customization Key in Today's Greenhouses

Anna Peerbolt

In the early 1900s, Henry Ford declared that customers could have any color Model A they wanted as long as it was black. At the same time, greenhouse manufacturers were offering any greenhouse as long as it was glass. But in 1920, a German chemist, Hermann Staudinger, hypothesized that plastics were actually giant molecules, putting the development of plastics into high gear, affecting the greenhouse industry with change and infusing it with growth.

Greenhouses have continued to evolve. Today, the big news in greenhouse design is retractable roofs. But other than retractable roofs, what other trends are hot in greenhouse structures and coverings?

Customization

After speaking with a number of manufacturers and growers about what the industry wants, the overall answer is customization. Or, as Jim Stuppy, president of Stuppy Greenhouse Manufacturing, Kansas City, Missouri, says, "There is no trend, just a wide variety of new thoughts and innovations" keyed to each grower's particular need.

Just fifteen or twenty years ago, suggests Al Reilly, president, Rough Brothers, Cincinnati, Ohio, greenhouse options were still limited to choices A, B, or C (superior, mediocre, or inferior). Growers in Florida or Michigan with money to burn might choose greenhouse A not because it suited their individual crop, but because it was the top of the line. But today, Al says, growers are looking at what is the best combination of facilities and costs for a particular crop: "If you're a farmer, a Ferrari isn't going to do you a whole lot of good in your crops. And if you're a race-car driver, you're going to have a hell of a time winning with a John Deere."

Today's choices in greenhouses are staggering—the selection includes everything from a Quonset barely 6 ft. at the top of the bow to the new gutter-connected range planned by Cliff Powell at Powell's Plant Farm, Troup, Texas, which will eventually put 800,000 sq. ft. under one roof. "We're still making selections. We want to include all of the innovations on the market," says Cliff, adding that he's got two consultants working on the decision-making process. The focus of this new facility is the mass production of jumbo packs, and the goal is to streamline everything from production to shipping. He's concentrating on efficiencies in labor and energy and searching out exactly the materials and systems that will best suit his needs.

What growers choose depends on what crop is being grown, whether they're just starting out in the business, and if they have dozens of special tasks that need precise scheduling. Greenhouse decisions are made differently for those growing seasonally or growing year-round. There is a huge difference in growing one crop or a wide range of plant types. It makes a difference if you're doing baskets or starting from seeds or plugs. And for each difference, greenhouse manufacturers are offering individual solutions.

"There is absolutely more and more customization," says Jim. "Growers come with certain criteria: head room, maybe the ability to get a certain piece of mechanical equipment in or to hang it up from a structure or boom." Greenhouse manufacturers, as they always have, use their engineering know-how to accommodate their customers' needs. For the manufacturer, the trend is toward more sophisticated, usually computerized, design tools and a constant cutting-edge mentality.

Though crops and growing processes may be different, there are some similarities in what growers are look for in a greenhouse and in what manufacturers are designing.

Productivity and Efficiencies

"This country is at functional full employment," says Al. "We're no different from any other industry right now in our need to find labor." The trend is to find new ways to do the same or more with fewer people. This means that anything that will increase productivity or promote efficiencies is hot.

"In every CEO's speech or annual report, you get a line about driving the cost out of the business," says Jim. "Growers want to do the same thing, and they're thinking of the productivity return on a greenhouse investment. So they may add things that will cost more than the last time they built, but they can see that these things will drive costs out of labor, chemical uses, or ways to grow a better plant."

"You used to say that a grower could manage an acre," says Henry Mast Jr., president of Henry Mast Greenhouses, Byron Center, Michigan. However, today's greenhouse system allows a much larger space. A single grower can now monitor and control a three-acre block. Two years ago, Henry put in a block like that: nineteen gutter-connected bays, 228 ft. long by 30 ft. wide, with 14-ft.-high gutters, divided into one-acre zones with glass partitions for temperature control.

Efficiencies can be tied to monocropping. "We do 9 million seed geraniums in the spring," says Henry. "We focus on it, and we're efficient at it."

He also points out that retailers are getting more demanding: "We're being asked to participate in advertising and merchandising programs, supply people for training, do customer education. These all have to be paid for in some fashion, and the only way is through efficiencies."

So growers and greenhouse manufacturers are increasingly looking closely at ways to cut cooling and heating costs and to control or cut repetitious labor costs. They're looking for glazings with longer lives and greenhouse structural materials that span wider distances. All of these savings cost money and are leading to a trend that's forcing small, nonspecialized growers out of the market. "The cost of greenhouses hasn't escalated anywhere near the cost of other products," says Al. "No way does a greenhouse cost ten times as much as it did twenty years ago, as far as the basic structure goes. But the overall project might be considerably more expensive because it includes more items than it used to."

Natural Ventilation

Growers want to provide growing environments that are as close as possible to Mother Nature's ventilation system. In addition to roofs that come off completely, manufacturers are designing intriguing methods for getting a more natural flow of air through the greenhouse. "There's a tremendous move to natural ventilation," says John Pound, president, AgraTech, Pittsburg, California. Many of his customers are growing in the Temperate Zone and have been using a rack-and-pinion system to open their houses for many years. "But in the last ten years, we're also doing a lot of poly vents, drop-wall vents, roll-up vents, vents on poly roofs, rolling roofs," he says. "It's almost gotten so that it's a component in every structure that goes out." The natural ventilation trend is so popular that John is also retrofitting existing roofs in his older greenhouses for this option.

"An important aspect of natural ventilation is roof ventilation," says Steven Crider, president, Hired-Hand Green, Bremen, Alabama. His firm manufactures a sawtooth design that allows a roll-up or drop-down curtain inside that window. "When it gets hot in the house, you open up roof vents and roll up the side vents and literally create a chimney effect with the hot air going out the roof and cooler air being drawn in from the ground," he says. "It gives you a constant flow of air. You're ventilating the house naturally instead of paying the electrical company for fans to be running all day long."

The trend is toward houses that have few fans, smaller fans set to work together, or fans directed at a particular area. "We see this especially in garden centers," says Jim. He also mentions innovations in terms of condensation control and innovations in using equipment that hasn't been in greenhouses before, such as paddle ceiling fans that drive the air up or down, depending on the time of the year. "The trend is to move the air more gently," he says.

"There is definitely an effort to take advantage of nature wherever we can," Al says. What's driving this trend is a better understanding of how plants operate and how greenhouse structures work in terms of airflow. It isn't too far-fetched to say that there's a trend toward a much deeper understanding of science on the part of everyone involved in growing plants.

Glazings and Structural Materials

If you disregard the open roof and its impact on the industry, other elements that drive change in the greenhouse industry are new glazings or construction products. There's better and better technology for producing poly film, which is still the most popular glazing in the country. Some films have up to a four-year life, some offer anti-condensation, and some have UV inhibitors.

The same level of innovation is true of polycarbonate, and there is also a new flexible, tempered glass that's up to 1/4 in. thick and comes in 4-by-10-ft. sheets. But, according to Al, "There hasn't been a new glazing or structural product that would create major change in the industry for ten years—just refinements of existing products."

In structural materials, no one we spoke with suggested that there were any significant trends. "It's a battle to increase the quality without increasing the costs," says John. "Basically, we're still making greenhouses out of pipe; we're just trying to find a better pipe."

Taller, Wider, Bigger—More Sophisticated

"Growers want wider houses," John says. "The wider, the better. It gives them more flexibility. It's easier to arrange benches and move equipment around. Of course, wider also means taller. Taller houses, growers are finding, result in a better environment for growing plants because the glazing is farther away from the plants. You get a more stable temperature inside the house," he says. "The sun comes up, and it takes longer to get hot in the house; the sun goes down, and it stays warm longer. [Taller houses] offer a milder, gentler, easier-to-control mass of air."

"We're definitely going taller," says Steven. He regularly builds houses with gutters 14 ft. high; in fact, he says he's quoting one right now that's 18 ft. high. Everyone we talked with spoke of this height trend, many saying that 15, 16, and even 17 ft. aren't uncommon gutter heights. A future change in code may restrict the total height of garden center greenhouses and structures that allow public access, says Al. "We've had a patchwork of three or four different codes throughout the country." Codes are being consolidated into one International Building Code that will be the standard.

"We seem to be rediscovering that as you increase the volume of air in the greenhouse, you improve the growing environment," says Al. The more air in the house, the more buffer you have between the outside and inside environments. "The air itself actually serves to insulate the crop to a certain degree," he says. He uses a hot water system below the benches as an example, saying, "That heated air rises, and as it does, it cools. When it gets to the roof, there's a lower differential between the air temperature inside and the air temperature outside." This leads to less heat loss and more energy savings.

Another reason for taller houses is the need to accommodate additional equipment that's suspended from the roof of the house—shade systems, hanging baskets (sometimes three or four deep), automation systems, irrigation booms, and various material-handling systems. Indeed, manufacturers say the trend toward wider and taller greenhouses means bigger, more sophisticated growing environments. There is some talk of automation, but nothing so new, different, or economical as to truly excite growers. "There hasn't been a move in the United States to spend money on materials handling automation," says Al. He noted that automation and standardization go hand in hand, pointing to the European model, where greenhouse structures and container sizes are standardized, and monocropping is the norm. "[The U.S. has] a total lack of standardization from one operation to another," he says. "What I see is a move opposed to standards." And the reason has to do with big business.

Big Business and Industry Growth

The trend in all industries for mergers, consolidations, giant corporations, and mass merchandising has significantly affected the greenhouse manufacturing industry. "We used to advertise that we are a family business," says John. "Today, we advertise that we're a corporation."

As the massive baby boom generation has moved into the suburbs and discovered gardening, the entire composition of garden centers and nurseries has changed. The boomers, with the Generation X-ers following close on their heels, like shopping in the warehouse atmosphere offered by mass merchandisers. But no matter where they shop, they demand the full range of possible plant materials. Their expectation of value is many degrees higher than that of their parents. "If someone buys a bouquet of roses for fifty to a hundred dollars," says John, "the flowers can't die the day after Valentine's Day."

Growers are scrambling to have a high quality crop. Distributors, resellers, and wholesalers are also increasing their quality and service levels. The mass merchandisers at the top of the food chain, given the clout of boomer dollars, are in a position to insist that growers meet their demands.

To differentiate itself, a mass merchandiser will decide to change the size of flats or containers. This change, sometimes just inches, can have a major impact on how growers use their greenhouses. John notes that his company wants to be in on those discussions and the decisions that affect his business.

"There's definitely a shift toward growers growing what retailers want—and maybe not what they [the growers] want to grow," says Al.

"The retail marketplace doesn't want to buy just one plant from one grower," says Henry. "It wants to buy many products from one grower: hanging baskets, bedding plants, window boxes, and a whole host of other things." And because he can't do all of this efficiently, large, monocropping growers like Henry are subcontracting with smaller, specialized growers. Henry becomes the central point, or distributor, satisfying the large retail buyer. "Marketing is driving consolidation, which requires a distribution network, which, in turn, allows the grower to remain specialized and efficient," he says.

The umbrella trend for growers and greenhouse manufacturers is to get smarter about everything they're doing. "If you're a survivor, you're investing money very wisely," says John. Growers are planning farther out, taking more time to research their greenhouse decisions. They're making business plans and reviewing them more often.

"The business hasn't changed," says Jim. "It's just moving a lot faster."

August 1998

The High Points of Tall Greenhouses

Chris Beytes

If there's one modern trend that has done much to eliminate grower headaches, it's the move toward tall greenhouses. Average greenhouse height has increased by several feet in the past fifteen years. Why is that? What's the difference between a house with 10-ft.-high gutters and 14-ft.-high gutters? And the big question: Are tall houses really more expensive to heat?

How Low Can You Go?

Back in the early 1970s, during the height of the energy crisis, greenhouse builders tried to cut heating costs by reducing the overall volume of greenhouses. They did that by reducing gutter and sidewall heights down to the bare minimum, usually somewhere between 7 and 9 ft., though occasionally you found one that was built at 6 ft. or even lower.

By the early 1980s, some sanity had returned, thanks in part to the development of thermal screens, also called heat retention or energy curtains. Suspended below the gutters, they reduced interior heating space much more effectively than low gutters, as you aren't heating the airspace above the gutters. But installing energy curtains in an already short greenhouse is difficult. So, greenhouse builders began raising their gutters to make room for energy curtains and other new automated equipment such as boom irrigation systems. An added benefit was overhead space for hanging baskets.

Stable Air

In addition to the added headroom of a taller house, growers quickly found that the added air mass helped create a more stable growing environment. William Roberts, director, Center for Controlled Environmental Agriculture, Rutgers University, New Brunswick, New Jersey, calls this large volume of air a "larger sponge" that holds moisture in the greenhouse, helping to reduce the dramatic humidity swings often found in greenhouses as they cool at night.

This sponge effect also applies to temperature. Once the greenhouse is at a desired temperature, it maintains that temperature more consistently and with less fluctuation. Cool incoming air has more space to mix with the existing greenhouse air before reaching the crop, minimizing cold and hot spots and potential plant damage. While heating or cooling a tall greenhouse to a desired temperature may take longer than a short greenhouse, a tall greenhouse is more effective at maintaining that temperature.

What about Heating Costs?

With today's modern coverings and thermal screens, tall houses can be heated for just pennies more per square foot than short houses. William has run computer models that compare the heating costs for single- and double-glazed houses of various heights, with and without thermal screens.

The following chart shows the annual fuel consumption for a variety of different one-acre greenhouses. Regardless of height, single-glazed structures without curtains consume the most fuel. Just adding double glazing to a 10-ft. house can cut your fuel use by 33%! Double glazing *and* a thermal curtain will cut your fuel use by more than half! Yet a 14-ft. house consumes just 5½ to 7% more fuel than a similarly equipped 10-ft. house. At $1 per gallon, a 14-ft. house with double glazing and curtains will cost just $2,635 more to heat per year than a 10-ft. house.

Clearly, in an energy efficient greenhouse, height has little negative impact on heating costs but it has an extremely positive impact on the overall growing environment. There's no reason not to dream big—and tall—the next time you're shopping for a greenhouse.

The Effect of Height on Energy Use in a One-Acre Greenhouse

	Greenhouse style and equipment	Height	Gal./year	Gal./sq. ft./yr.	Increase gal./ sq. ft./yr.
A	Single-glazed structure with 10-ft. sidewall	10 ft.	71,536	1.66	
B	Single-glazed structure with thermal screen	10 ft.	50,983	1.18	
C	Double-glazed structure with 10-ft. sidewall	10 ft.	47,688	1.10	
D	Double-glazed structure with thermal screen	10 ft.	34,845	0.81	
E	Single-glazed structure with 12-ft. sidewall	12 ft.	73,509	1.70	0.04*
F	Single-glazed structure with thermal screen	12 ft.	52,960	1.23	0.05
G	Double-glazed structure with 12-ft. sidewall	12 ft.	49,006	1.13	0.03
H	Double-glazed structure with thermal screen	12 ft.	36,162	0.84	0.03
I	Single-glazed structure with 14-ft. sidewall	14 ft.	75,486	1.75	0.09**
J	Single-glazed structure with thermal screen	14 ft.	54,936	1.27	0.09
K	Double-glazed structure with 14-ft. sidewall	14 ft.	50,323	1.16	0.06
L	Double-glazed structure with thermal screen	14 ft.	37,480	0.87	0.06

* indicates the difference between A and E
** indicates the difference between A and I

Figures from a computer model developed by W. Roberts in 1980.

Greenhouses are ten bays each, 200 ft. by 216 ft. total. Degree days are 5,861. Costs can be determined by applying cost per gallon of oil to the table values. Inside set point temperature is 60°F. Design temperature difference is 60°F. Fifteen percent credit is given for solar energy contribution. Chart reprinted from the Rutgers Cooperative Extension Horticultural Engineering Newsletter.

Bay Watch

Chris Beytes

We previously discussed gutter height and its effect on the greenhouse. But another, more commonly discussed aspect of greenhouse dimensions is bay width.

Simply defined, a greenhouse bay is the space between two rows of posts. A freestanding house has only one bay. A gutter-connected house with ten rows of posts has nine bays.

How wide should those bays be? If your house is 150 ft. wide, should you have six 25-ft.-wide bays or five 30-ft. bays? Many options are available; most manufacturers offer bay widths from 20 up to 50 ft. or more. What's best for your application? While there's no definitive answer, here are some ways that bay width impacts your plants and your pocketbook.

Wider and Taller Equal Cooler

Last month we learned that a taller house maintains a more uniform climate, as the larger mass of air helps prevent drastic temperature swings. Plus, because hot air rises, the growing area stays cooler longer. Another benefit of a wide house is that, because there are fewer gutters, there's less energy loss from gutters and other uninsulated areas.

Bay width affects greenhouse height because as posts get farther apart, roof trusses have to span a greater distance. As trusses get wider, they also get taller. While a 21-ft.-wide house might be 14 ft. tall at the peak, a 36-ft.-wide house might be 18 ft. tall. That extra air mass in the roof offers some of the same climate balancing benefits of tall gutters.

More Costs Less

Interestingly, a house with wider bays actually requires less construction material. For example: a 150-ft.-wide house with six 25-ft. bays has seven rows of posts and five gutters. The same house built with five 30-ft. bays has six rows of posts and four gutters, so you've saved the material costs for a full row of posts and a gutter, along with all of the necessary hardware, poly lock, downspouts, and other materials. You've also saved on labor costs: Your builder had to dig fewer postholes and assemble fewer materials. One builder says he can erect a greenhouse frame (without covering) with 30-ft. bays for less money than it costs to build the same size house with 21-ft. bays because of the savings in materials and labor.

Another major cost savings comes when you equip your house. Our six-bay house requires six unit heaters and six irrigation booms. The five-bay house, while needing larger heaters and wider booms, needs only five of each, cutting the overall cost. You save more with the bigger job.

Flex Appeal

What are you going to do with your new greenhouse? Grow plugs or bedding flats? Poinsettias? Set up retail displays? Simply put, a greenhouse with wide bays is more flexible than one with narrow bays, especially if you're growing on the floor or moving retail displays from season to season.

If you're using rigid benches, rolling benches ("movable aisles") or Dutch trays, work with your greenhouse manufacturer and bench supplier to choose the bay width that best suits your bench system, such as the 42-ft., 8-in. bays designed to accommodate Dutch trays.

Spanning the Gap

How do you achieve a wide span? Some manufacturers use a single bow truss or peak truss to make the bay. Others use a beam truss to span the bay, then put short-span bows on top of it, i.e., three 16-ft. bows on a 48-ft. beam to create a 48-ft. house. While this method offers the benefits of an open floor plan and lower equipment costs, you don't gain the height benefits or the material cost benefits of a single truss house. However, a beam truss makes it easier to use double poly to cover a wide span. Also, if you want glass glazing, you may have to go with this construction method (a Venlo-style house), as glass comes in smaller sizes than rigid plastic sheets, which can be adapted to virtually any house configuration.

It seems that when it comes to greenhouse bays, wider is better. However, if you want to cover the largest area at the lowest possible cost, a gutter-connected house with 21-ft.-wide bays and no trusses may be the low price leader. But you're giving up the equipment savings, energy savings, and flexibility of wider models. Like much of this business, it all boils down to what you need, what you want, and what you can afford.

Bay Watch Update

Editor's note: This addendum to this article was printed in a later (January 1998) GrowerTalks *issue.*

A structure manufacturer let us know that, while we were right on with bay widths, one issue needs clarification: While a greenhouse with wider bays does require fewer posts and possibly less labor to construct, you may not save money. Why? To meet today's snow and wind load codes, a wider bay requires heavier posts and beefier trusses than a narrow bay, so the cost may actually be similar for the two.

November 1997

A Barn No More

Chris Beytes

Combine several decades' worth of peat moss, perlite, dust, cobwebs, old cardboard, used pots, and obsolete machines, and what have you got? The headhouse or production "barn" at your typical greenhouse business.

Yet it's in just these kinds of buildings that growers are now installing high-tech, high-dollar automation. And it's in just these kinds of buildings that employees are being asked to spend much of their day—employees who could easily choose to work for companies offering comfortable, well-lit work environments.

Admittedly, some of you insist upon operating room cleanliness throughout your business, but you're the exceptions. For the rest of you who haven't done much more than sweep the floor since the Nixon administration, is it time to bulldoze that dark, dingy old headhouse and start from scratch? Or is there a way to upgrade what you've got? And what considerations should you make if you're planning a new headhouse? We spoke to the experts—greenhouse and equipment manufacturers, along with two growers who've done recent upgrades—to get some ideas.

Clean It Up

Phil Ulery, owner of Ulery Greenhouses, Springfield, Ohio, planned to order some new soil handling and transplanting equipment. But the headhouse he was going to install it in, constructed in 1974, was long and narrow (40 by 260 ft.), dimly lit with dusty insulation on the sidewalls—your typical "pole barn," Phil says, and hardly the place to install hundreds of thousands of dollars' worth of new machinery. It was time for a change.

"We wanted to create a better working atmosphere for the employees and help morale that way," Phil says. "And it was just time to do something 'nice.'" Plus, the building was just too narrow to efficiently move product in and out during production and shipping.

The solution was to knock out one entire sidewall of the building and expand the width by 22 ft., to 62 ft. total. The new sidewalls and roof are glazed with Lexan, which lets in lots of light. The walls and ceiling of the old section were cleaned and lined with white metal panels to further brighten the space. New fluorescent fixtures top it all off. The electrical service was completely updated for the new equipment, which includes a new high-speed transplanter, bail shaver (equipped with mist nozzles to eliminate dust), new compressor, and new conveyors. Now there's plenty of space around the two transplant lines to efficiently move plants and materials.

Cost for the upgrade and equipment was "$300,000 to 400,000," Phil estimates, and was well worth the price. "We're getting our transplanting done on time, and our shuttle tray lines are getting the material potted on time," he says. "As we all know, that's a necessity or you don't get your crops out on time." He was able to eliminate several material handling and transplanting jobs as well.

Another major benefit is that his employees love the new space, and it's proven effective for attracting new hires. Phil adds that customers are impressed that they made such a great change, and they can see Ulery's is working to stay efficient.

With the expansion, Ulery's now has enough space to add a third line. "And we're able to maximize our equipment by working longer hours," he adds. "[The workers] aren't as tired. It created a better atmosphere. Running two lines anywhere from fourteen to sixteen hours a day gave us the production that we needed."

Re-Engineer It
A clean, bright, comfortable headhouse is half the battle. How do you make the most use of the space you've got?

Ron Van Der Hengst, South Central Growers, Springfield, Tennessee, wanted to upgrade one of his family's two transplant lines with a faster machine, but he knew they needed help improving the overall efficiency of their cramped 5,000-sq. ft. headhouse. His transplanter supplier, Flier, solved the problem, bringing down a laptop computer and a design program that lets him test different equipment configurations. They measured the headhouse space, put it into the computer, and in just three hours came up with a layout that not only made the two existing lines more efficient, but even found enough space for a future third line.

"The logistics of this setup are 100% better than what they were, just by moving things around," Ron says. One simple change was to replace an inclined conveyor belt on their flat filler with a bucket conveyor, which takes up less space. They now have about 15 ft. between the two lines, plenty of space for moving plants and materials.

"Eventually, we'll have to build more space because the greenhouse structure's getting larger,

South Central Growers can now fit three lines of two into their 5,000 sq. ft. headhouse, thanks to a special computer program that optimized their layout, and to new equipment that takes up less space.
Photo by South Central Growers.

in order to accommodate all of the machinery," he admits. "But for the time being, we can put three lines in 5,000 sq. ft. It will be crowded, but it can be done."

Starting from Scratch

If you have the luxury of building a brand new headhouse, what design considerations should you keep in mind? Experts offer tips in four areas:

What type of building?

The Ulerys actually have two production barns, and their second one isn't a barn at all—it's a greenhouse equipped with hand potting lines for larger containers and ECHOs overhead for two layers of hanging baskets. Phil says that it used to be the employees' favorite because of its good light. He likes that he gets double duty from the space: transplanting and growing.

More growers are turning to greenhouses for some or all of their headhouse space because of that dual-use capability. Metrolina Greenhouses in North Carolina recently built an MXII open-roof house to serve as the headhouse for their latest range. And it's a major trend in the Netherlands, where land is expensive and scarce. But greenhouse builders say another benefit is cost. Greenhouse structures cost less to build than typical steel buildings. And your greenhouse doesn't have to be clear. Even if you cover some or all of the greenhouse frame with metal, the construction cost is still lower.

Another benefit can be in zoning and permitting, depending on your municipality. Growers have told us that in their county they'd need fire sprinklers if they built a steel building, but a greenhouse structure can be exempt from that and other requirements. Check your local laws.

Regardless of the structure you choose, you must be able to maintain a comfortable working environment. That means good ventilation, heating, and light. Don't skimp or your employees will be miserable. Another good addition is several drain points in the floor that will let you water plants, hose down equipment, and do other wet chores without creating puddles.

How much space?

A safe rule of thumb is that your headhouse space should equal 8 to 10% of your greenhouse space, although some manufacturers recommend up to 15%, depending on how labor-intensive your crops are.

However, the Van Der Hengsts have just 5,000 sq. ft. of production space to their 300,000 sq. ft. of greenhouse space—1.6%. And the Ulerys have 21,040 sq. ft. of production space (counting both buildings) to their 650,000 sq. ft. of greenhouse—3.2%. That's because the larger you get, the lower the percentage needs to be. If you're building your first acre of greenhouse, a generous rule of thumb would be to build 4,000 sq. ft. of headhouse—say, a 40-by-100-ft. building. If you added a second or even third acre, your headhouse should still be adequate. The same goes for electric, air, water, and other services: Be generous. You'll never meet a grower who regrets putting in too large an electrical panel or air compressor.

Also consider expandability: The more easily you can add another section to your headhouse, the less you spend down the road when you need more space. This again is where a greenhouse building may come out ahead of traditional steel buildings.

Flow is crucial

The biggest mistake experts say growers make is poor traffic flow. If you have the chance to build a new greenhouse and headhouse at the same time, don't just assume you'll have plenty of space and the traffic flow will work itself out. Plan ahead.

For instance, consider specifying two greenhouse aisles, each with its own access into the headhouse. That will let you bring new plants in one aisle and ship finished product out the other. This loop pattern is very efficient. If you can't do this, at the very least design an extra-wide main aisle that allows easy two-way traffic.

Within the headhouse itself, you should lay out equipment so it's accessible from all sides. Too often a transplant line gets pushed up against one wall or into a corner, making one side of the line difficult to access.

However, it can also be a challenge to provide enough space for the 70-, 80-, or even 100-ft. long production lines growers are now creating. Those can now be shortened using new types of conveyor belts that make 90- or 180-degree turns, allowing you to shorten your production lines.

Program your success

One manufacturer wisely suggests that you "program the layout." Before you pour the first bit of concrete, sit down with your builder and equipment supplier and have them help you plan exactly how you want to use the new space. How many trucks do you want to be able to load at one time? How much storage do you need for pots, carts, cartons, etc. And list everything you need for that building—bathrooms, break rooms, chemical storage, seed storage, a cooler—all the little details that might fall through the cracks. A few hours of planning can prevent costly omissions.

'Tis better to receive

Unless you forgot to designate a proper place for receiving, that is. Do you have a dedicated receiving dock, or will you have to tie up a crucial shipping dock when a springtime media delivery shows up? How far do you have to carry that media to get it to your filling line?

You should put as much emphasis on receiving as you do shipping because excess material handling costs you money, as does impeded traffic flow. There's no secret to doing this. Just make sure materials move as short a distance as possible in as straight a line as possible and without crossing the paths of any other processes. For instance, Powell Plant Farm in Texas has potting conveyors that cross the flow of shipping carts. To keep everything moving, they put the conveyors overhead. Now the cars pass under the flats that are moving into the greenhouse. The slightly longer distance the flats travel is much less costly than slowing carts full of finished plants.

Do What You Do Best

Ron Van Der Hengst has seen first-hand the benefits of working with a machine supplier and/or builder when planning changes to your headhouse, and he wholeheartedly recommends asking for their advice and support. "We grow plants for a living. Let [the experts] come in and set it up for you."

January 2001

Free Concrete for the Asking

Chris Beytes

Jerry Killilea, owner of deMonye's Greenhouse, Columbus, Ohio, estimates he's poured $100,000's worth of concrete in the last six years, and it hasn't cost him a dime.

No, Jerry doesn't have Mob connections. Instead, he wrote letters to local ready-mix concrete companies in the Columbus area, offering his greenhouse property as a dumping site for waste concrete. Jerry knows that small quantities of concrete left over from jobs—usually just a yard or two—are tough to dispose of. Concrete plants have to dump it on their own property, let it harden, then grind it up or they have to find a place to legally dispose of it. His offer of a dumpsite was so appealing that he had trucks pulling in the day after his letters were received.

"They love us," he says of the companies that use his property. Being near the Columbus airport helps, especially when they're pouring runways and a full truckload gets rejected as substandard. "We got forty-two yards one day, forty yards another time, then thirty-five yards," Jerry says. He'd pay $40 to $80 per yard if he was buying it.

Jerry and his sons have poured greenhouse floors, driveways, and plenty of paths. They keep boards and blocks handy to make quick forms, as they never know when a truck might show up. Being zoned agriculture means they don't need permits for what they pour.

A current project is a foundation for a warehouse building. They need to raise it several feet above the floodplain, so the finished slab will be 55 ft. by 96 ft. and a whopping 32 in. thick—more than 500 cubic yards of cement.

We called a few ready-mix companies to see if the arrangement is common and were told it depends where you're located. Some companies have their own recycling facilities; one California company sells excess concrete for $5 per yard. To see if you can swing a similar deal, call your local concrete suppliers and check with zoning officials to make sure you're not breaking any laws.

We checked with an engineer about using small batches of concrete, some of which may have been rejected from other jobs. He said it's fine for walks, paths, or driveways—anything you're not going to build on. If you're making a structure foundation, the pour needs to be done all at once to avoid cold joints, and top-quality concrete should be used.

March 1999

Covering Q&A

Gene A. Giacomelli

Q: Is PAR light the most important factor for choosing a glazing?

A: It's a very important one! PAR, or photosynthetically active radiation, is a measurement of the intensity of a portion of solar radiation that's useful for plant growth. Special quantum sensors are able to interpret the light intensity, similar to a plant leaf. Many other factors affect the PAR reaching the plant, which can be more important than even a 5% difference in transmission among types of glazings.

Q: What factors affect the amount of PAR transmitted to the plants?

A: There are many: the day of the year and hour of day; your latitude; local weather conditions; predominance of direct or diffuse solar radiation; and cover material properties at the time of installation and as affected over time by weathering, air pollutants, moisture condensation, and dust and dirt accumulation.

Other factors include the greenhouse physical structure, including angle and shape of the roof, the number and width of spans (distance from gutter to gutter if multispan or ground to ground if single span), height of end walls, length to width ratio of the structure, and the house's compass orientation.

So don't immediately contact your glazing salesperson when your crop displays a need for more light.

Q: Besides purchase price and light transmission, what other reasons are there for selecting a film over a rigid plastic panel or glass as a greenhouse cover?

A: A continuous film glazing has fewer edges and connections on the greenhouse roof and sidewalls, which reduces the amount of uncontrolled air infiltration. While this can mean lower heating costs in winter, it also means higher inside air humidity resulting from the water vapor of plant transpiration. Also, a "tight" greenhouse can result in reduced carbon dioxide in the air [important for plant growth] when not regularly venting.

Q: Do the specific crops I grow have anything to do with the selection of my covering?

A: The plants have everything to do with glazing selection, as well as all the other greenhouse systems and the structure itself. Consider the relationship within the overall greenhouse crop production system, as well as you and your grower's plant production experience with the potential systems selections.

Q: Glass is traditional—why should I consider new plastic glazings?

A: All of the glazing material commonly sold for the industry offers strength, consistency, durability, manufacturing quality control, and safety in use. Solar radiation transmission and heat-energy conservation should be considered, and ease of attachment is important for glazings that must be removed and replaced as they age. Most plastic coverings are affected by weathering.

Glass is quite inert, in contrast to plastic, and can provide effective use for many decades. Glass is noncombustible, resistant to UV radiation and air pollutant degradation, and maintains its initial radiation transmission throughout its life. The most predominant drawback of glass may be its vulnerability to catastrophic losses caused by hail.

Q: Do glazings perform the same at all locations?

A: The best glazing may still not allow sufficient light in the winter season for some crops. The short-duration, cloud-covered days of late fall, winter, and early spring contribute to the primary cause for reduction of plant growth—too little solar radiation, or "light." Subsequent difficulties in crop production from diseases, nutritional deficiencies, and reduced product quality may also result.

Whatever the amount of natural solar radiation available for the plant, it must first reach the greenhouse and then pass through the glazing and past the overhead structural framework before reaching the plant canopy. Therefore it's important to consider a southerly exposure that is clear of nearby buildings, groves of trees, and other obstructions to light. Note that an unobstructed northern exposure is important as well, because on cloudy, diffuse days, a significant portion of light for plant growth does enter the greenhouse from the north.

July 1999

More Covering Q&A

Gene A. Giacomelli

Q: Which is best: a north-south or east-west greenhouse orientation?

A: In short, a north-south oriented greenhouse is best for year-round production, while an east-west greenhouse is best for winter production.

Greenhouse compass orientation not only affects the total light entering each day, but also the light distribution within the greenhouse. An east-west oriented ridge will have a large south-facing wall and roof area for collecting the low-angle winter sunlight. Thus, it will provide the most total daily light during the winter season. However, distribution of the light may not be uniform to all plants within the greenhouse; plants on the north side may receive less light. Nonuniform light patterns cause irregular plant growth. This is especially a problem for tall crops, most notably if they're grown in rows aligned with the east-west ridge.

A freestanding, single-bay greenhouse generally provides more light inside to the plants than a gutter-connected, multi-bay greenhouse. There is less overhead structure in the single-bay greenhouse, and the relatively narrow span allows for more glazing area. A long, narrow (less than 25 ft. wide) free-standing east-west greenhouse for bedding and potted plants will offer the best light conditions for the winter months.

On the other hand, a gutter-connected, multi-bay greenhouse should be oriented with its gutters (or ridges) in the north-south direction, especially if you will be growing tall crops. The reduction in total light entering the greenhouse is offset by an even more important factor, the improvement of light uniformity to all locations within the growing area. The benefit of the north-south ridge orientation is the "movement" of the shadows caused by the overhead structures as the sun progresses from east to west. No single location of the greenhouse remains in shadow throughout the day. A nonmoving shadow will occur within an east-west oriented greenhouse, and it's most pronounced during the winter months.

Q: Can shading the crop with another movable shade curtain above the glazing help keep the crop cool?

A: Yes. Shading reduces the amount of energy entering the greenhouse, preventing the plant leaves and interior components from increasing in temperature as much. However, there's a potential loss of plant growth from reduced PAR (photosynthetically active radiation). It's best to shade to intensities and/or daily duration that benefit cooling without seriously reducing plant growth. Shade material on a moving system above the glazing is best for cooling, but it is subjected to the weather. Shade systems inside the greenhouse don't reduce air temperatures as well, but they can double as a thermal screen (heat blanket) in the winter. All shade systems should be automated for better control.

Q: Condensation on the glazing: good or bad?

A: Both! Condensation may seem to be an unwanted event in the greenhouse. However, it's an important indication that the greenhouse environment is responding to the plants' transpiration of moisture into the air. Essentially, it can't be stopped, but its potential negative effects can be minimized.

Here are two good aspects of condensation: (1) Transpiration—the evaporation of water from the plant leaves to the greenhouse air—is critical for natural leaf cooling, nutrient uptake, and growth of the plant. The plant won't even stand upright unless it continually transpires water. (2) Condensation of water vapor from the warm, moist air onto the cool surface of the greenhouse covering material is the primary means of reducing the greenhouse air humidity whenever ventilation isn't occurring.

But now the bad news: Condensation is a way that heat can escape from the greenhouse. The change of water vapor to liquid results in a release of energy called latent heat, which is then lost through the glazing.

And, of course, the bad aspect of condensation that we all recognize is water droplets on the glazing. They'll fall to cause potential crop damage by localized overwatering or encourage disease infestation. In addition, droplets remaining on the glazing become another obstruction for light to pass (or to be reflected away) prior to entering the greenhouse.

Efforts to incorporate inhibitors to droplet formation during manufacturing, particularly on plastic coverings, have somewhat reduced this problem. Water movement along the roof surface should not be impeded by the structural supports of the glazing unless at a specific location for the drip gutter to safely carry the water away.

Water vapor from the air can condense inside multilayer film and rigid panel glazings. Where a small fan is used to inflate double-poly greenhouses, it's very important to use outside air, not greenhouse air, for inflation.

Q: Can the open-roof greenhouse become the new "better" greenhouse?

A: The potential of open-roof greenhouse structures has only begun to be explored. Currently, there are several greenhouse designs available where the entire roof can be mechanically opened and closed. The result can be improved plant lighting and air-temperature reduction.

August 1999

Evolution, Not Revolution, in Coverings

Bill Sheldon

The greenhouse covering business might be compared to a germinating seed: Much of the time the grower sees little going on. Then there's a sudden spurt of growth, then a rest period. Meanwhile, under the soil surface, the roots are churning constantly—busier than a one-armed poly hanger.

There's no revolution going on in the greenhouse covering business, but the industry is tweaking good products, seeking a slight competitive advantage as growers across the continent expand their facilities, looking for efficiencies and cost-savings.

The evolution from glass to fiberglass to polyethylene and structural plastic sheets and now to retractable and open-roof greenhouses is circular, not linear, and it's getting more complex.

Here's just a sample of the new products that suppliers are rolling out this year and some thoughts from suppliers on what growers should consider when buying coverings:

"We'll bring out a new 7004 Series polyethylene late this year that will be 25% tougher and 2% clearer," says Tom Grisham, sales manager for Huntsman Packaging, Tampa, Florida.

"Our new Impact Modified Acrylic we brought out last year is virtually unbreakable, is ten times stronger than previous products, and is easier to install and maintain," says Pat Long, sales manager for Cyro Canada, Mississauga, Ontario.

"We're getting ready to introduce an advanced profile corrugated polycarbonate that will give slightly better light transmission and more strength," says Stan Schultz, vice president of marketing for SPS Corporation, San Jose, California. The new product is a modification of the box-rib profile of their existing DynaGlas Plus covering that will let in more light and have improved hail resistance. "We have about 1.5 million sq. ft. installed and will be into full distribution early next year," Stan adds of the new product's extensive field testing.

"Growers need to reconsider light transmission and diffusion. If their roof is covered with water condensation the first four hours of the day, they can't get light in," observes Jim Ralles, sales manager for Klerk's Plastics, Richburg, South Carolina. "Longevity arguments can be absolute garbage," he continues. "Look at useful life (of your covering), not life in a coma. Growers can leave film on a roof too long—until they go broke."

Jeff Warschauer, vice president of sales for Nexus Corporation, Northglenn, Colorado, a greenhouse structure manufacturer, sees glass making a resurgence. "It's good forever, and the price is getting more competitive; it will pay for itself in two or three changes of poly," he says.

Growers have this to say about greenhouse coverings:

"We change crop needs almost every year and our product mix constantly changes, so we put up new plastic every year," says Mark Andrews, supervisor of research and development at Greenleaf Nursery in Park Hill, Oklahoma.

"The biggest difference we've seen with the Huntsman 7000 series [polyethylene] is that it's easier to install, especially to secure into gutters," says Norm White, who has sixteen covered acres in Chesapeake, Virginia.

"The glass we got from Westbrook [Greenhouse Systems] on our 4½-acre open house is excellent; it's just beautiful. We get a better product, especially hardening, before we send it off to the big-box stores," says Jan Barendse of Baker Greenhouses, Utica, New York.

"We've switched from glass to Exolite [from Cyro] because of cost and easier installation. It's clear enough, and there's less heat loss," according to Chris Schenkel, director of horticulture and grounds at Oglebay Park, Wheeling, West Virginia.

"We started with Kool-Lite [from Klerk's] about four years ago. It reduces the heat load giving better worker comfort," says Rick Ouding, owner of Kalamazoo Specialty Plants, Kalamazoo, Michigan. "The difference between 92 and 85°F can mean a lot to workers. We get better productivity. We grow hearty mums all summer, so this is important to us."

Rick ships annuals, perennials, and herbs from Minneapolis in the north to Dallas in the south, and he is constantly broadening his product selection. He feels his poly roof scatters the light, helping bring it down to all the leaves on the plant. "Light isn't a detriment to crop quality. And infrared light is reflected back onto the plants at night. Our crop is excellent; there are no drawbacks."

Common-Sense Covering

Despite the dozens of factors involved in the all-important decision of what kind of covering to choose, growers still depend on good old common sense and logic rather than science and data.

For instance, climactic variability make heating and cooling costs difficult to compare from year to year. Rick Ouding, who has 300,000 sq. ft. of greenhouse, explains: "We can get computerized results on each of our houses, but it's difficult to make comparisons because of weather differences from year-to-year. Maybe all this is not totally scientific."

Jan Barendse feels he grows a better product in his open-roof glass house. "Our customers—40% big-box stores within a four-hour radius—like our crop better than what they get from houses that aren't open. Ours are tougher plants. The stock and snapdragons take the cold much better." Jan grows his bedding plants in the mid-50°F temperature range, and pansies at 48°F.

Individual circumstances also play a large role in covering strategy. Chris Schenkel converted to Exolite from glass after a three- to five-minute hailstorm in the spring of 1998 wiped out two large glass houses. "We wanted impact resistance, and we got a good deal. Maintenance was a factor—we don't need a special workforce to replace sheets," Chris explains. "We have other Exolite houses, and the hail didn't put us out of business in them."

Norm White has been through the gamut in his forty-plus years, growing into one of the country's most-respected growers. His product mix is primarily pot plants—40% mums, along with lilies and hydrangeas—sixty-eight different flowering pot plants.

Norm says he has greenhouses covered with glass, fiberglass ("a devil to heat"), and now is using double poly, including Huntsman's 7000 series. But in Norm's view, "There's not much difference among the polys. All of our houses are about the same on production."

Could Codes Affect Your Cover?

Another focus area, especially for retail greenhouses, is the upcoming major national building codes changes, according to Nexus's Jeff Warschauer. He expects building codes to be unified across the country by 2003. This will affect urban construction relating to building occupancy, retail versus commercial uses, fire resistance, sprinkling, and liability.

"If most cities go by the book, you might never see a greenhouse built," Jeff explains of the proposed new rules. His suggestion: "If you're retail, use a covering that the city won't object to."

Jeff cites a potential customer in Tulsa, Oklahoma, who has been trying for 2½ years to get a building permit. Situations like this have necessitated a Nexus policy of not taking an order without a building permit, he adds.

He says greenhouse size also might dictate that a certain percentage of the roof be covered with a solid material. "This throws out glass and polycarbonates," he says.

Luckily, Jeff doesn't foresee the code changes affecting existing structures.

Retractable Coverings

Another major product area is retractable roofs. John Walters, president of LS Americas, Charlotte, North Carolina, has become the dominant national covering supplier for these roofs in the past five years. "This is not a fad," John says of retractables. "Growers are getting their benefits."

But he says that greenhouse builders and growers have learned a lot since retractables hit the market about five years ago. "There are more choices, and growers have to learn the right application for their circumstances."

Like the other suppliers, John says he doesn't have anything revolutionary to promote, "but we're constantly improving our product and have extensive research and development on-going."

Universities, too, are working to expand the knowledge of growing in retractable and open-roof houses, with both Rutgers University and Oregon State University having built test structures.

Keep It Simple

Summing up the current coverings situation, Jeff Warschauer says, "Plan, plan, plan, especially if you are retail. Don't think the old way works just because Grandpa or the neighbors did something."

Klerk's Jim Ralles, well known for his philosophical condensing of the industry's situation, adds, "The covering is the least expensive but most important decision a grower can make for his greenhouses. It dictates how well he will use the one free resource available to him—the sun."

Archie Vermeer, of Grimsby, Ontario, Canada's Westbrook Greenhouse Systems, sums it up: "The products available are about the same as they have been. Decisions ought to be crop dependent. I don't see much change. Doing the same thing might be your best bet. If your needs are simple, keep it simple."

Summer 1999

Chapter 2

Technology

─────────────────────── 🏠 ───────────────────────

Greenhouses of the Twenty-first Century

Lloyd D. Lemons Jr.

The industry is looking for lower prices, yet labor and equipment costs continue to rise. An insurmountable problem? No, say the experts; it's simply time to explore some very exciting opportunities. And many of these opportunities start with a capital T for Technology. Here's what you can expect to see in the twenty-first century.

Structures

The dust seems to have settled somewhat on the types of structures being used. The basic three designs—freestanding, gutter-connected, and retractable—along with their various design options—cover the needs of a wide range of growers and crops. As the demands of the marketplace force growers to concentrate more on particular crops or niche markets, selecting a type of house will be dictated less by personal preference and more by the need for a strategic solution. Jeff Warschauer, vice president of sales, Nexus Corporation, Northglenn, Colorado, says growers will select the right tool for their crops. "For perennials (a staple of the big-box stores) that like the sun, the retractable-roof greenhouse is great. It gives full sun, it gives full outdoor temperature, and the nice thing about the retractables today is they're peak-type roofs, which means if you're in a hard rain area and the crop is tender, or if you're in a snow area and you're growing pansies, you can close the roof when you see the storm coming."

One thing is for certain. Houses are getting bigger. "We're seeing an increase in height," says John Hoogeboom, president, Agronomico International, Hendersonville, North Carolina. "We're building greenhouses that are 15 ft. high because of spray booms, tables, and all the automation that's going into a greenhouse. On top of that, [growers recognize that] you get a somewhat better climate if you have more air to play with."

Another factor likely to influence the future construction of houses is the building code, an item that hasn't received much attention until now. "Changes are occurring in the energy code, the fire code, and impact codes," says Jim Larkin, Flex Lite Corporation, Boca Raton, Florida. "These are three major areas that the National Greenhouse Manufacturers Association is wrestling with. These changes will increase the quality and safety of the greenhouse facility."

Sun: A Resource to Use Wisely

The desire to improve plant quality has driven research in coverings and has led to some exciting discoveries that are finally making their way into practical application. Basic science taught us that light is made up of colored wavelengths. The trouble is, not all wavelengths are ideal for growing in greenhouses.

Dr. Peg McMahon, The Ohio State University, Columbus, says color in your coverings can give you more control over crop growth. "Plants have built-in mechanisms to detect when they're crowded, based on the quality of light they receive," she says, "specifically, how much of the far-red signal is received in relation to other wavelengths of light." Reduce or remove the far-red signal, and you'll fool plants into thinking they've got more space than they actually do. The result: You'll reduce the stretching or shade-avoidance syndrome of tall, spindly plants trying to reach for the sun, and you'll get plants with a much more robust appearance.

The covering industry's response to this phenomenon has been to develop plastics that absorb or reduce the amount of far-red light that gets to plants. You'll see this "photo-selective plastic" first in polyethylene products.

Poly manufacturers aren't the only ones working on light transmission. Polycarbonate companies are working on photo-gray technologies. When the sun hits one of these panels, it turns gray, similar to the polycarbonate eyeglass lenses that are widely available today. "One version of polycarbonate I've seen has microscopic glass beads impregnated throughout the sheet," says Jim. "This serves to lower the yellowing of the product and enhances its resistance to scratching. It also improves light transmission initially and over the long haul."

"We're going to be looking more and more at how plants relate to the environment and how we can more rigorously control the environment to control plant growth," says Peg. "Those two things are the biggest changes I see. Growers are going to be presented with some very revolutionary techniques, not just in the area of photo-selective plastics, but in temperature manipulation, nutrition, watering strategies, and many other things."

This new focus on plant environment is evident as more growers turn to computers for environmental control. The basic functions of heating, ventilation, irrigation, and fertilizer injection systems—all standard equipment originally controlled by simple thermostats or analog controllers—are being integrated and controlled by computer. Merging all of these functions has brought much more stability to the greenhouse environment.

Automation

Think of the automotive industry: vast, peopleless facilities, filled only with products and the machines building the products. Robot welders, computerized transport systems, and laser-guided equipment hum about. Too futuristic for the growing industry? This type of technology already exists in Holland and is receiving increased interest in the U.S.

As labor costs rise and technology costs drop, the prospect of sophisticated automation gets closer to home. One greenhouse on the East Coast plans to have a twenty-four-acre operation run by only six people by the end 1999. That's an almost completely automated facility—and a substantial investment that's affordable to only the largest growers. Will smaller growers be left out in the cold? "Now that so many of the theories have been proven, the technology has become cheaper," says Robert Lando, Flier USA, Oberlin, Ohio. "The smaller growers will finally be able to afford automation that wasn't available to them before."

Automation such as tray fillers, drum seeders, needle seeders, potting machines, and automatic transplanters is finding its way into houses as small as 20,000 sq. ft. Labor savings and the need to produce more plants out of the same square footage are making this technology irresistible. Additionally, fewer houses are growing crops on the floor. "They grow on tables," says John, "where they can bring the crops to the workers, not the workers to the crops." He sees rolling benches, automatic planters, and plant spacers continuing to gain acceptance.

Automated Transport

The challenge of efficiently transporting a greater number of plants around the greenhouse has become the latest focus of medium and large growers. The twenty-first century will likely see manual overhead cranes, which are used to move benches, giving way to robot cranes that are navigated by programmable logic controllers. Unmanned robots on the ground will move with the aid of laser-guided systems, not rails. Even today, Hamer Plant, a large grower in Holland, uses five robots that run in the same area, crossing one another, meeting one another, and opening doors automatically. This system includes a computerized "traffic leader" that directs traffic via radio frequency transponders that are read by the robots. The robots are integrated with computers that monitor the growing environment. They move plants from station to station to different climates as needed, and they work twenty-four hours a day, taking the place of dozens of workers. Moreover, this equipment often moves above plants, allowing for maximum use of the growing area.

In Holland, most growers are working to minimize the number of times plants are touched by human hands. The Dutch look at it this way: If you can turn over a crop four times a year instead of three times a year, you have an extra crop per year. That pays for the automation, reduces labor costs, and makes you much more efficient.

With all of this automated transportation, how do you keep tabs on any particular crop? Inkjet bar-coding of benches and plant containers is one popular method, but another way is to mount inexpensive receiver chips on growing trays. These small chips, explains Larry Salone, E&B Developments, Cary, North Carolina, "can locate and capture a complete history of the tray contents. When the grower goes out to make a check during the day, he carries a small hand-held gun. He aims it and picks up data off of any tray via a digital readout."

Machines Watch Plants Grow

"If you want to control plant production, the best way to tell how plants are doing is to look at them directly," says Dr. Peter Ling, a researcher at Rutgers University, New Brunswick, New Jersey. The high-tech way to monitor plant growth requires a digital camera, a computer, and some very sophisticated software. As a plant rolls by on a conveyor, the digital camera captures its image and feeds that information into the computer. The computer records a variety of information, which may include plant height, width, number of flowers, color intensity, and other characteristics. This information can then be used to grade, sort, or otherwise process the plants according to established parameters. To Peter, there's a fine distinction between computer vision and machine vision. To greatly oversimplify his definition, computers give people information with which to make a decision, but machine vision makes the decision without human intervention. And that's what's beginning to happen in this country.

Machine vision is a sophisticated operation that's effective at different levels. The basic system looks for the absence or presence of plants, as in plug transplanting inspections used in Holland and now at a few U.S. plug producers. They use a camera to look at plug trays and see where the vacancies are, then use robotic transplanters to refill those vacancies. The next level looks at plant quality from a uniformity point of view. It measures plant sizes, number of flowers, intensity of color, and uses this information as grading criteria. The third level is monitoring. Digital cameras can see nutrient deficiencies, water stress, temperature stress, or other problems. And the fourth level (still in research) will be used to control plant growth. At some point, machine vision systems will be linked to environmental control computers to change the greenhouse environment according to plant requirements.

All of this high-tech gadgetry will be used to increase production, improve quality, and control labor costs by requiring fewer employees. Future advances in vision technology will likely connect it to inventory, planning, scheduling, and cost analysis. "If you want to look at the future, we shouldn't limit ourselves to higher plants, we should also look at possibilities in the areas of tissue culture and the embryo genesis," Peter adds.

Computer "vision" systems, such as this one at a Dutch foliage production facility, use a video camera (located in the box to the right) to quickly determine plant height, thickness, stage of bloom, color, or any number of other factors to help growers more efficiently grow, sort, and ship their crops.

Planning for Tomorrow

The future promises to deliver a variety of technologies that will allow growers—large or small—to build the best system for their needs. The question "Where do I want to be in five or ten years?" is an important one because it seems that the only limits to greenhouse technology are money and the grower's imagination. There are technical solutions in existence, or on the horizon, for virtually every challenge that arises.

As the dynamics of the industry continue to evolve, growers will have to be ever vigilant as they watch over their businesses. The bottom line, of course, is to be able to grow, grow well, and be profitable.

Summer 1998

Tool Time

Chris Beytes

Why do we spend the time and money to fly to Amsterdam every year for the NTV show? Because the Dutch floriculture industry is ahead of everyone else technology-wise, due to the high land and labor costs they face and the tough government regulations they're required to meet. Much of the technology that meets their needs can be adapted—either right away or at least in a few years—to the less stringent but nonetheless ever-expanding demands of North American growers.

Labor Efficiency

European growers in general are seeking to reduce their workforce while increasing output, the same as you are. You'd be amazed how many Dutch pot plant greenhouses are almost totally automated, with one exception:

There are always one or two people standing at the output end of the pot filling machine planting liners by hand.

Mayer, a major German equipment manufacturer, was one of several companies showing transplanters (photo 1) that connect directly to circular pot fillers, rather than the in-line designs we're used to here. They're specifically designed to plant large plugs or liners into various sizes of pots and can work on pretty much anything grown in a liner tray, from large bedding, flowering, and foliage plants to woody ornamentals.

Mayer's machine uses push pins to dislodge and lift the liners and three grippers to grab the liners from the sides and plant them. It can plant 4,000 to 4,200 plants per hour. At about $78,000, Mayer projects you'd need to plant 250,000 to 500,000 pots per year to make it pay. The Belgian company Demaitere has had a similar machine on the market, but this year they added a third gripper to their Demtec transplanter to increase its speed. One difference between it and the Mayer unit is that the Demtec has interchangeable gripper styles: needles for plugs or large paddle grippers for liners.

Now that you've automated the transplanting, why not speed up your pot filling, since you don't have to worry about your machine outpacing your workers? Javo showed a very cool new pot filler (photo 2) that will fill and drill 7,000 pots per hour compared with 3,000 or so for their standard machine. The secret is three drills that move in concert with the rotating table to dibble three pots at once without the pots having to stop. Its soil hopper is removable and uses belts instead of chains to move the soil, which results in quieter operation and no crushed soil.

Fine Tuning

We asked one manufacturer at the NTV what he noticed about the latest products, and he replied, "Mostly what I'm seeing isn't brand new ideas, it's fine tuning and tweaking existing equipment to make them even better."

That was obvious in many stands. Along with their new high-speed filler, Javo showed a new spacing fork—these are the devices that will pick up a row of pots from a Dutch tray bench or conveyor belt and put them onto another bench or belt. The mechanism is complicated, but the fork itself is just an aluminum sheet with cutouts that the pots fit into. There's one problem with that idea: Top-heavy pots tend to tip when picked up and swung by the fork. So Javo has come up with a new fork that works hydraulically to gently grip the pots when it picks them up. That way your heavy begonias or hydrangeas aren't tossed around.

We saw a very simple addition to Flier's drum seeders while visiting Novartis's young plant production facility out in the Westlands. Novartis's Hans Olsthoorn told us that when plug trays pass through the filler, media often winds up clogging the small air holes between the plug cells. So Flier drilled holes between each dibbler point (photo 3) and added a compressed air fitting so when the tray gets dibbled, air blows any media out of each hole in the tray.

Even lowly motors and gears are getting more attention. As one manufacturer put it, "A gear drive on your greenhouse is like the transmission in your car: You never give it a thought until it doesn't work."

Lock is a German company that makes industrial motors and drive systems. They displayed a very impressive new line of rack and pinions for Venlo roof vents (photo 4), featuring sealed bearings, milled and hardened steel racks, and a sculpted housing that looks great—and they say it casts less shadow than a typical housing.

Ridder is another popular manufacturer of motors and gear drives. They've incorporated a frequency controller into their motor/gearbox combination for curtain systems. This allows the curtain to start and stop very slowly (for accuracy) and then move four times faster to open or close quickly. We saw it in action in the stand of greenhouse builder P. L. J. Bom, where Bom showed off special slipping clutches on their curtain system that prevents damage even if the curtain hits a ladder or other obstruction.

Quiet Please

Workplace noise levels are another target for improvements. Javo (and we've heard of other companies as well) made a simple modification to the collector unit that pots pass through when heading for the spacing fork. This is the device that clacks noisily as the pots pass through its metal fingers. Javo replaced the metal stops with plastic, which quiets the metallic plinking to a softer ticking.

Another noisy area of the modern, high-tech greenhouse is the bench washer. A high-pressure spray of water against the thin aluminum tray really makes a racket. Alcoa Agro showed drawings of a new washer that has much more sound insulation and also is expected to operate at double the speed because it doesn't tip the bench on its side—it passes through horizontally.

These are just a few of the interesting innovations we saw in and around NTV. In the next article, we'll take you out into several Dutch greenhouses where the machines and the technology are so new, you'll be among the first on the planet to read about it.

January 2001

Greenhouse Tech

Chris Beytes

GrowerTalks is always on the lookout for growers who are using new and existing technology to keep their production costs down, cut their labor needs, and improve their crop quality. We've encountered four such growers in recent months. Two have invested in new automation—one is building a new greenhouse range, and one has developed a complete production system. All four expect their investments to help them stay competitive.

Moving Flowers

Delfgauw, the Netherlands, near the famous Westlands, is home to Lansbergen Gerberas' impressive Moving Flowers system, probably the most automated cut flower range in the world today. Future plans are to reduce their labor needs to almost zero.

Co-owner Hein Lansbergen told us the best way to reduce labor is to bring the plants to the workers. "Like a car factory," he explains. "People stand still and the cars come by." Except at Lansbergen, the gerberas come by.

With the help of internal transport specialist Hawe Systems, Hein designed aluminum tables equipped with two gutters to hold the plants and a self-contained irrigation system that feeds the plants through drip tubes.

The Venlo-style Greentex greenhouse covers more than 720,000 sq. ft. and is divided into twenty bays, each 26 ft. wide and an incredible 1,378 ft. long.

The production area is divided into ten two-bay sections, each with two rows of roller track and nine hundred tables. The tables roll toward the back of the greenhouse in one bay, cross over to the next bay, and then roll back to the front of the greenhouse, all automatically. The 2,600-ft. round trip takes two days.

As the tables travel, the irrigation reservoirs are filled as needed with about 1.3 gal. of water and fertilizer by outlets along each bay. Hein says designing this was the most difficult part of the project—he likens it to refueling a jet in midair.

To harvest flowers in their old system, workers walked up and down between the plants to cut flowers. With the new system, where the plants come to the workers, Hein has cut his labor force from forty to twenty because they're more productive, each harvesting eight hundred stems per hour compared with six hundred per hour the old way. The next big labor saver will be harvesting the flowers by machine instead of by hand. Hein hopes to have a prototype harvester built within two years and to be doing all harvesting by machine within five years.

Total investment is about $4.3 million. Hein says that costs him about $0.50 per sq. ft. per year to payback. However, he says he's saving $0.60 per sq. ft. a year on labor, so the system is actually earning him $0.10 per sq. ft. per year. An added cost benefit is realized in space savings: He gets 8% more space in the greenhouse, which equates to about 2.5 million more stems per year.

A third way he hopes to realize payback is by selling the Moving Flowers concept to other growers. Lansbergen has formed a new company, Friendly Flower Systems, which provides Hein's knowledge and technology from

Hawe and three other partners to any interested grower, worldwide. Several cut rose growers are interested, and while he hasn't tested the system with any other crops, he's convinced they can realize the same benefits. The system can be retrofitted into older greenhouses, and the benches can move fast enough for twice-daily harvesting, if needed.

Perfect Transplants

Chris van der Voort grows spathiphyllum liners and finished plants in Honselerskijk, the Netherlands, just a short drive from Lansbergen. Their finished product goes through the auction, which means it must be consistent, uniform, and dependable week in and week out. And it means they have to control costs any way they can.

The Van der Voorts plant some 25,000 pots per week into 9-cm (3½-in.) pots with three plants per pot, and 2,500 17-cm. (6½-in.) bowls with six plants per bowl. They also do some 12-cm (4½-in.) pots on special order.

Chris's son, Olaf, told us that planting is the most labor-intensive part of their business since it must be done year-round. The repetitive nature of the job makes it difficult to find employees, plus there's the threat of repetitive-motion injuries from doing the same task all day long.

The obvious solution was an automatic transplanter. The only problem they saw was that their young spathiphyllum plants vary a bit, depending upon germination. Olaf says they try to sow three seeds per cell (six seeds per cell for plants destined for 17-cm pots), but sometimes only one or two will germinate. Workers can grade those substandard plugs out by feel. But how would a machine do it? Visser, one of Holland's leading machine builders, came up with the answer: a prototype transplanter that would grade each plug before planting it.

The plugs, which are grown in Styrofoam Star trays, enter the center of the machine. Forks push up ten plugs at a time in front of a bright light. A video camera looks at each plug and a computer evaluates its height and thickness based on predetermined size standards.

Next, grippers reach down, grab the plugs, carry them sideways to one of four pot lines—two on either side of the plug conveyor—and plant them into pots. Once planted, pots come out of the machine and are carried by conveyor to a fork that automatically puts them out pot to pot on moving tables. The entire operation can be supervised by one employee who monitors the transplanter, replaces any missed plugs, and makes sure the tables get loaded properly. Olaf says the machine can plant 25,000 plugs in seven hours.

Originally, the concept was to grade the plugs with up to four different standards and plant similar plugs together—small ones with small ones, full ones with full ones—and then put each different grade into a different greenhouse zone where they would be given growing conditions that would create one uniform finished pot size. But they found they can't create uniform quality when working with a range of different plug sizes, so now they use the machine to grade for A-quality plants, which are the top 80% or so of all plugs. Any B-grade plants get discarded. Also, in the three years since first installing the machine, their sowing and germination process has improved considerably, so they get better plugs to begin with.

The Van der Voorts now have two grader/transplanters. The original prototype (described above) is now three years old. A second machine that's been in place for two years works similarly, but the plugs enter the left side of the machine and the four transplant lines are all to the right. Olaf says the designers originally thought having the plugs in the center would be more efficient, but plug tray location doesn't actually affect machine speed.

Ten seedlings at a time are held in front of a light panel so a video camera, linked to a computer, can judge their height and thickness. The best 80% of seedlings make the grade; the rest are thrown away.

The newer machine is primarily used to bump up seedlings into twenty-eight-count liner trays for resale to other growers. It can grade up to four different sizes and plant into four different trays.

"High, but worth it," is how Olaf characterizes their investment. Payback comes in several ways. First, they get their transplanting done with fewer employees. Second, finished plant quality is better and more uniform because the plants are all potted to the same depth and without being squeezed or damaged by human fingers. Third, they have virtually no plant loss in the greenhouse.

Olaf says their next investment will be in the upgraded software that comes on model that's now available commercially (called the Select-O-Mat) to increase its speed.

The Cutting Edge

One of the most labor-intensive jobs in horticulture today is sticking unrooted cuttings. Automate that task and you can write your own ticket. Chrysanthemum breeder and propagator Cees Dekker has done just that, but not quite the way you'd imagine. Cees has found a way to take cutting sticking out of the high-cost Netherlands and move it to low-cost Tanzania and Brazil.

Dekker Chrysanten, based in Hensbroek, the Netherlands, is a world leader in chrysanthemum breeding and propagation, producing some 300 million cuttings annually. According to company Director Mark Hilberts, for the past five years Dekker has been growing at an annual rate of 15 to 25% in a market that's been growing only 3 to 4% per year. They accomplish it with a vigorous and innovative breeding program and through a very aggressive approach to efficiency.

They do their breeding and rooting in Holland, but the vast majority of their cutting production occurs at two offshore production sites co-owned by Dekker, one in Brazil and one in Tanzania. The Brazil facility produces for a large and growing internal market as well as for export, while Tanzania produces only for export to Holland. That's where the new technology comes into play.

Dekker's traditional way of sticking cuttings in Holland involved hiring contract laborers to stick cuttings by hand into peat moss cubes. Workers are paid by the piece; most can stick from 2,200 to 2,400 cuttings per hour. Typical hourly wages averaged $15. In Dekker's new system, cuttings are still stuck by hand, but into special plastic strips developed by Cees Dekker and

Heli Plastics. And they aren't stuck in Holland, they're stuck in Tanzania and in Brazil, where labor costs just a fraction of that.

After cuttings are stuck into strips, they're shipped to Holland, 3,000 cuttings per box. One worker takes the strips out of the box, dips them into a liquid rooting hormone and places them into special plastic trays. They travel by conveyor into a prototype Visser transplanter, which is equipped with special grippers that pull the cuttings from the strip and plant them into peat blocks. The grippers make a hole slightly larger than the cutting, but the natural elasticity of the peat block closes the hole around the cutting to hold it firmly. Conveyors carry the finished boxes of peat blocks to a stacker for transport into the greenhouse, while the empty strips and trays are carried away for cleaning and reuse.

Dekker's prototype cutting transplanter has been in the works for one and a half years. Cees came up with the idea for the plastic strip while watching a soccer match on television and snipping some thin plastic with scissors. A sculpture in the Dekker lobby shows the stages of development of the strip, from that first idea to the finished product (which will be available for licensing to other cutting propagators).

While their machine is a prototype that sticks 7,000 to 7,500 cuttings per hour, the commercial model will do 20,000 per hour, replacing ten workers. Eventually, they'll have just one hand sticking line for small or special lots. Cost for the machine itself? About $100,000, which will easily be repaid in labor savings.

We first publicized this machine back in July, and based on some of the phone calls, many other vegetative plant producers hope to adapt this technology to their particular crops. It could change the cutting business considerably.

Blending Technologies

Weatherford Farms, located near Houston, Texas, is blending the best of old and new greenhouse technology in their new range. Their system proves you don't have to abandon an old system if it works.

Weatherford's street frontage has become too valuable to use as wholesale greenhouse space. The existing houses (some forty years old) require constant maintenance, and the older facilities were making it tough to keep up the quality of their weekly potted plant program (the majority of their business). Plus, they needed more production space. So they plan to sell the street frontage and move to the back of the property.

Weatherford's choice for new structures is Venlo-style glass. Why a typically northern-style greenhouse in hot, sunny Texas? "We went with glass because the [original] glass houses are forty years old and the glass is still up there," replies company president Jack Weatherford. He adds that they have to run fan-and-pad cooling most of the year anyway, regardless of the glazing material.

The two new Rough Brothers houses just over 60,000 sq. ft. each. Bays are 24 ft. wide and 256 ft. long, with 14-ft. high gutters. HAF fans keep the air moving, while Rough Brothers shade and blackcloth systems and Wadsworth controls provide temperature, light, and photoperiod control.

There are two unique aspects of Weatherford's new houses. First, Jack chose to install probably the oldest form of greenhouse benching known to man: boards and blocks. So again, we have to ask, "Why?"

"If you're doing smaller pots or a bedding crop, [rolling benches] work," he answers. "We use the aisle. When these [mums] are all ready to bloom, the plants are out in the aisle. To grow the quality of plant we grow—a big plant—we put the pot on the edge of the bench and use that space." Plus, he adds, when they grow baskets over the aisles between the benches, he doesn't want them dripping on the plants below. An added benefit of cinderblock legs is that he can lay his under-bench hot water heat tubes (standard home baseboard heat pipe) in the holes.

But why not at least go with the stationary aluminum benches? What's another buck or two per foot in a nice house like this? "Do you recoup it?" Jack asks in reply. "If I was going with rolling benches, I probably would have put in a much more elaborate bench system. But as a stationary bench, I don't think I'd ever recoup the cost."

The second unique feature is the enclosed 24-ft. wide area between the two sections with a concrete walkway and roof bows that support insect screening. The pad systems face into this walkway. All the incoming air is screened, cutting insect problems to almost nothing. A shade curtain lets them use the space for foliage in the summer. Jack calls the difference in pest problems between the new and old houses "phenomenal."

Weatherford Farms is planning on finishing the project with thirteen total acres of useable growing area using this style of house. That should let them focus on growing their business, rather than keeping it from falling down.

March 2001

Equipment and Mechanization Tips

Debbie Hamrick

It's easy to fall into the trap of thinking that adding equipment and mechanization to automate your greenhouses begins and ends with writing the manufacturer a check. In reality, successful automation means research and planning. Flier USA's Robert Lando has more than twelve years experience in mechanizing American growers. Here are some of his tips to help you consider all angles of automation and ensure success.

Replace worn out equipment. It's tempting to keep using a paid-for, fully amortized piece of equipment until it falls apart. Be warned. Old pieces of equipment begin to work inconsistently. A worn out potting machine for example, will result in crop losses. A good rule of thumb is that you should discard equipment after ten years. Used production equipment almost always has a market. How much will a used piece of equipment sell for? The question to ask yourself: Would you pay the price you're asking? If the answer is yes, it's likely that someone else will too. If you're a larger grower, you can't afford the inconsistency of an old machine. (If you're buying a used piece of equipment, call the manufacturer and ask about that machine's history before you buy.)

Know when to mechanize. If you're producing 10,000 or more bedding plant flats, you need a flat filler. You can justify seeders at lesser volumes such as only 2,000 trays because you can buy less-expensive models. To justify a high-volume drum seeder, however, you'll need about 40,000 plug trays. If you're small- to medium-sized, you may never mechanize soil mixing but instead choose to buy soil premixed. Why make the investment when you don't have to? Unless you want to mechanize simply to spend money, think first about what you're doing and what you need before you buy.

Is leasing right for you? Almost every company offers the option to lease many pieces of equipment. However, if you're not able to get regular financing or to pay cash, you likely won't qualify to lease the equipment either. Some growers prefer to lease, setting up payment terms more favorable to their cash flow cycles. Ask about all financing options.

Check references. Before you write a check, call growers who have purchased the same model you're considering. Ask them not only about the machine, but also about how long they've had it, their opinion of how it's working, and their opinion the company and of manufacturer support. Also, visit one or two growers with machines like the one you're considering—especially if you're buying expensive machines.

Be leery of pay later offers. Some growers take equipment on a "try it and pay later" basis. A cost is associated with using a piece of equipment that doesn't integrate into your production line or greenhouse system: You'll be tied up using that system until it's taken away. Again, rather than getting caught up in the romance of mechanization and a deal, think about what you need to do the job.

Think about how to organize your production line. For example, you'll need to put a conveyor belt in front of the flat filler—fifteen feet or so for assembling inserts into trays or putting pots into shuttle trays. The person doing this job won't be busy all the time and can walk the transplanting line, helping to keep production flowing. But asking this person to also remove finished trays would be too much.

Avoid extra steps. Many growers prefill flats, palletize them, then feed them into an automatic transplanter or transplanter conveyor. However, these growers have added extra steps—having to stack filled flats and unstack filled flats when a flat filler could be synchronized to run with the transplanter or transplanting line. Compacted media is also an issue to consider: Stacking flats on top of one another compacts media, taking air out. This can result in problems with root disease. Avoid stacking filled plug trays onto each other, as compaction is even more serious in tiny plug cells.

Put buffers in the system to avoid work stoppages. A system is only as good as its weakest link. To avoid slowdowns, accumulate a store of flats on a conveyor belt, for example, before they're fed into a transplanter or transplanting line. This way if the flat filler stops for a couple of minutes, the transplanter can continue to work.

Look at your weekly volume to determine capacity. Too often growers get stuck looking at how fast a machine will operate in a given hour. It's better to look at what you need to get done by week, then size the equipment. You can then look at how many hours a day you'll run the equipment. For peak transplanting, most growers today run two shifts because it just isn't practical to gear up to transplant everything in just a few hours a day.

Think flexibility. When you're looking at any single piece of equipment, ask yourself, "What else will or can it be used for?" Will the flat filler work with pots? Can hanging baskets pass underneath the watering tunnel? Can the flat or pot filler operate at variable speeds to accommodate different pot or container sizes? Machines sized for one company's 512 plug tray won't necessarily work with another company's 512 plug tray.

Go for 100% soil return. When you're looking at a flat filler or pot filler, spend the extra money on a machine that returns all of the soil. You'll save in the long run in labor and soil costs.

Retrofitting new with old. Don't hesitate to ask about integrating your existing production equipment with new pieces of equipment. Just because you're buying a transplanter doesn't mean you also have to get a new flat filler. Machines can be synchronized to work together.

Set up new equipment before the rush. Work the bugs out of equipment before you need to rely on it totally. No piece of equipment is going to come of off the truck and work perfectly from the first minute. You'll also want some time to work with the equipment to test your original assumptions. Perhaps when a piece of equipment is running, you realize you need another ten feet of conveyor belts or that you need to change insert sizes. When the manufacturer delivers the machine, be sure to have the exact products you'll be running with the machine available for set up. For example, make sure you run seventy-five or a hundred of the plug tray sizes you plan to use through the transplanter before the manufacturer leaves.

Put in a drain in your headhouse. Watering tunnels are standard on seeding lines and on many transplanting and pot filling lines. You'll need to be able to handle the water runoff.

Allow plenty of space. A production line can be a hundred feet long by the time you put conveyors going in and conveyors going out in front of pieces of equipment and add buffer conveyors, patching, tagging, watering, etc. Allow plenty of space for the line itself and for carts or trays to take planted pots or flats.

Don't skimp on the air compressor. Today's production equipment is pneumatic and has to have high quality, dry air. It's better to oversize your compressor than to undersize it. You'll need a minimum of 15 cu. ft. per minute at 100 psi. You may spend $1,500 to $2,500 for a compressor large enough to supply air to a complete transplanting line.

Install three-phase electricity. You can use single-phase power, but you'll need phase converters. It's best to go with three-phase, 230 volts as standard, even if you have to do some rewiring.

Seeders are special. Make sure your seeding room is dust free with low or no humidity and no wind. Also, make sure the seeder has some sort of counting mechanism so you'll know how many trays have been sown without stopping the seeder and counting them manually.

Good roof. Machines don't like rainwater. While temperature isn't a problem for the machines, you'll need to ensure worker comfort.

Breathable covers. When the machine isn't in use, cover it with a breathable material to avoid condensation and humidity build up.

Install a phone in the headhouse. It may only be a port for a portable telephone, but having a telephone near the equipment so you can troubleshoot problems or make adjustments with the manufacturer on the line is very helpful.

Keep an emergency tool kit in the headhouse. Ask the manufacturer to provide you with a stash of parts such as valves, sensors and cylinders that will wear out, bend, or break during normal operation. The manufacturer can provide you with a list of recommended spare parts.

March 1997

Power Tools

Don Grey

Many of today's innovations in greenhouse automation and technology come from researchers who are working not just on theoretical projects, but on specific applications that can benefit the industry today. Here are three such projects that growers soon will be able to use to make managing their crops easier.

Sensing the Environment

Today's environmental control technology can monitor many climatic factors in greenhouses. In the near future, new tools should help growers monitor the actual plants and their responses to the environment.

Peter Ling, an assistant professor of food, agriculture, and bioengineering at The Ohio State University, Wooster, is researching sensing technology and how it can be adapted for use in greenhouses. The Ohio Florists' Association and the Ohio Agriculture Research and Development Center are funding Peter's work.

Sensing technology, such as camera visioning systems and infrared thermography, has been around for years and is used commercially in a number of other industries. The National Aeronautics and Space Administration (NASA) became interested in monitoring plants in order to develop life-support systems for manned space missions to Mars. Peter is currently working with New Guinea impatiens as a test crop and is concentrating on water stress detection, using sensing technology to check turgor pressure in plants.

By using sensing technology, Peter says, growers can control a greenhouse's environment based on how the plants themselves respond to various conditions. The technology can monitor the plants' physiology, and the feedback can help adjust climatic controls. The four stages of application are:

Stage 1: Visioning can check the presence or absence of a plant, say in a plug cell.

Stage 2: It can inspect the size of a leaf or cotyledon as a grading method. For example, visioning can inspect an African violet crop for canopy, size, and color. It can be used in vegetable crop production, Peter says, to check the size of lettuce heads.

Stage 3: Visioning can monitor the health and physiological development of plants for temperature or water stress.

Stage 4: Once the system detects a problem, growers can take measures to correct it.

Stages 1 and 2 are gaining use in greenhouses today, and Stage 3 is nearing application, Peter says. He anticipates completing a working prototype by the end of 2000, and a system could enter commercial production soon after.

How is the visioning technology applied? Peter is using a highly sensitive camera that "scans" a plant or block of plants and provides feedback to a computer. Peter is also studying infrared thermography, which measures the temperature of a plant under sunlight. When the environment heats up, the only way for plants to cool is through transpiration. As a result, the amount of water movement in a plant can be measured, along with any temperature changes, which can help determine stress levels.

Peter says sensing technology can be easily implemented. The simplest way would be to put a sensing unit at a greenhouse's driest spot, say near a vent. Another would be to mount a unit on a boom, which could then scan a bench or bay of plants.

Transporting Plants

Monitoring plants is hard enough, but moving them in and out of the greenhouse can be another problem. Research in the Netherlands, however, is showing growers how best to plan for and control the movement of plants.

"Internal Transport Control in Pot Plant Production" was a recent project conducted by the Institute of Agricultural and Environmental Engineering, a research institute of Wageningen University, and was funded by the Netherlands' Ministry of Agriculture, Nature Management, and Fisheries. The project's leader and senior researcher was Engelbertus (Bert) Annevelink, Ph.D., a specialist in information technology and operational research and how each applies to horticulture.

Bert's research, which formed his Ph.D. thesis, focused only on internal transport of flowering and foliage plants, two of the main floriculture crops in the Netherlands. The research "not only attempts to find new ways of supporting the internal transport control process, [but] it is also concerned with developing a new control approach." He looked mainly at a greenhouse's operational planning level.

Bert says the two main production systems used in the Netherlands today are the transportable bench (Dutch tray) and the concrete floor. Fixed benches are on their way out because up to 30% of a greenhouse's space, such as aisles between the benches, is nonproductive, he says. He estimates that a full transportable bench system can have a "high technical space utilization rate" up to 90% or more.

With more growers using transportable benches, internal transport of plants can be a logistical nightmare. That's because crops have to be moved throughout greenhouses several times during their production cycle, from potting and spacing to growing and harvesting. With multiple annual crop cycles and differing growing conditions, these highly complex systems can be difficult to manage.

Managers, however, often use rules of thumb to make daily decisions about their crops and when to move them. For his research, Bert compiled rules of thumb from eleven nurseries and ran them through computer simulation modeling (TRANSIM) analysis. Using a "local search method" (an algorithm to test and improve upon a solution to a problem, specifically simulated annealing), Bert developed a transport system sequence of input and output benches that showed how to make use of "parking positions," areas where benches that need to be moved in the near future are temporarily stored.

An automated guided vehicle (AGV) loading a transportable bench at a Dutch greenhouse. In the near future, high-tech automation such as this can be made even more efficient through the use of software that plans the most logical movement and placement of benches.

Bert says the most important practical aspect of this research is that growers should pay attention to their amount of internal transport—the number of movements and the transport distance—to avoid bottlenecks and delays when harvesting and delivering potted plants. They can do this by scheduling the sequence of the transportable benches.

Growers can use the methods described in Bert's research to calculate optimal transport sequences based on their own operations. Sound complicated? It is. But Bert says that ultimately a "completely automatic support system for internal transport in pot plant nurseries" is within reach—probably in the form of planning software that can be used to plan bench movement through the greenhouse.

Handling Plants

Another project under research in the United States is using true "rocket science" to help improve labor and production efficiencies in nurseries.

The National Robotics Engineering Consortium at The Robotics Institute, Carnegie Mellon University, Pittsburgh, Pennsylvania, is developing a container-handling robot that can move and space nursery pots more efficiently than can be done by hand. The consortium is a joint project of Carnegie Mellon and NASA, whose mission is to transfer NASA technology to industry through collaborative projects. The robotics project has received funding from NASA, the USDA's Agricultural Research Service, and the Horticultural Research Institute of the American Nursery and Landscape Association.

A goal of the project is to develop a machine to automate the way nursery pots are picked up, moved, and spaced in outdoor beds. The machine also must be affordable for large and small growers. The prototype currently under development will be able to handle between 30,000 and 45,000 pots per eight-hour shift, with only two workers to operate it. The machine, nicknamed Trident, is expected to cost between $50,000 and $75,000.

The Trident project was launched in early 1999. Robotics scientists first toured several container nurseries to learn more about the industry's production systems and needs. Then they went to work on an initial prototype, which was unveiled in July 1999 at the ANLA convention in Philadelphia. After critical feedback, the scientists went back to rework and improve the prototype.

"We basically improved on the design and what was shown in Philadelphia," says Hagen Schempf, senior system scientist at The Robotics Institute and lead scientist. "We've changed a lot of things from that prototype; we're now working on a new prototype."

Hagen says the machine's new design was to have been completed by the end of April, ready for testing at various nurseries by August. After further trials and refinement, a prototype is expected to be unveiled at the Mid-Am Trade Show in Chicago in January 2001.

The new Trident prototype is twice the size of the old. It's a stand-alone machine, not an attached implement. Robotic arms pick up a row (6 ft. long) of twelve pots at a time and move them to the side until all arms are full. Trident then can be directed to space the pots neatly, row by row, either "pot tight" or spaced out. It can pick up and drop pots from a bed or from a nursery trailer. The prototype works ideally with No. 1 containers (1 gal.) and to a lesser degree with No. 2 (2 gal.) nursery pots.

Hagen says the prototype to be demonstrated in Chicago will be a full-scale machine. If such a robust machine proves to be overkill, a scaled-down, cheaper machine could result. Even at its projected cost of at least $50,000, he estimates a grower's payback could be as few as one to two seasons.

If the Trident prototype proves successful, the consortium hopes a manufacturing company will license the technology and build and sell the machines to growers.

May 2000

Image Is Everything

Peter P. Ling

Have you ever dreamed that someday robotic eyes will hover over your crops to tell you when to water or when to spray? While this sounds like science fiction, this technology is called imaging, or machine vision. Imaging is an automated process that uses a computer to analyze digitized pictures captured by cameras. The technology can be used on plants in many different ways.

Growers are already using imaging technology to measure size, shape, color, and canopy structure of plants. Imaging can be used to sort potted plants based on their flower colors or even to detect nutritional problems, as is usually done by experienced growers.

But what makes the imaging technology even more exciting is its ability to see beyond human vision. The technology offers the capability to "see" near infrared (NIR) and infrared (IR). Furthermore, machine vision technology can be used to accurately determine growth and development of plants. While experienced growers can tell if a crop is roughly on schedule or lagging behind, imaging technology will be able to provide much more precise information. For example, imaging can show that a plant grew 10% in size and 5% in height over the last two days. Armed with superhuman capability to gather NIR and IR information and able to quantify a plant's growth and development, growers will someday be able to pinpoint plant health disorders before their eyes can observe them.

What does the supersensing technology mean to you? You'll be able to use it to improve your bottom line at different levels. Some levels of imaging application are already commercially available, while others are being developed in research laboratories. Machine vision applications for plant production can be classified into four levels.

The first is to simply detect the presence of plants. A good example is plug tray patching, where the patching machine determines the locations of empty plug cells by shining light through them from underneath.

The second level of sophistication is to grade plants based on their size, shape, and color. The first step in plug grading—sensing and removing undersized or ungerminated plugs—uses size and color to decide which plugs are good and which should be blown out. Another example is separating smaller potted plants from larger ones to improve greenhouse space use and product quality. Plants may be graded by size several times during production, and again just before shipping to ensure uniform size and quality. Growers will likely adopt more and more level-two imaging applications in the next few years.

The third level of imaging is monitoring plant health, and we're just at the juncture of research and development with this one. At The Ohio State University, we've had excellent results determining plant stress. For instance, water stress of New Guinea impatiens could be detected one day before the symptom was obvious to human eyes. This type of information could help growers get a better handle on irrigation scheduling while improving disease prevention.

Level four of imaging may be a system that recommends control strategies based on findings by the plant health imaging system, such as adjusting nutrient levels if a deficiency is detected.

The first two levels of imaging applications for plant production are commercially available and are already making positive impacts on growers' bottom line. Level four is still in the future. What about the level three? We predict that plant health monitoring packages will be used in commercial production greenhouses in three to five years. It's actually very practical to mount cameras on watering booms to acquire plant images. In Europe, growers already bring plants to a centralized image chamber using movable benches.

Imaging technology for plant production is here to stay. It's already a useful and affordable tool for plug production and potted plant grading operations. As the price of computer hardware drops and imaging technology matures, using imaging technology for plant growth monitoring will no longer be far-fetched science fiction.

October 1999

Mechanical Hands, Electric Eyes

Bob Johnson

At Bell Nursery in Burtonsville, Maryland, the future is taking shape. Seedlings are put into pots not by hand, but by an automatic transplanting machine. The flats then move to the production area on rolling aluminum tables. Once in the production area, the plants are irrigated through an ebb-and-flood system that filters and recycles all irrigation water. Hanging baskets, suspended overhead on motorized cables, glide past automatic waterers. When ready for shipment, the baskets travel to the workers, rather than workers having to go to the baskets.

The future hasn't come cheap, however. The internal transport system totals more than $2 million. The fully equipped automated transplanting line cost $300,000. And, so far, only half of the eleven-acre nursery has been retrofitted.

Owner Gary Mangum figures the investment will pay for itself in four years, however. A crew of eleven or twelve people used to do the transplanting; now only four people do. The internal transport system makes it possible for one worker to roll ten tables holding 450 flats rather than carry 2 flats by hand. Gary has seen a 40% reduction in the labor needed to move product through his range, and irrigation time is a quarter of what it used to be. All of this improved efficiency has allowed Gary to get one more turn from his production area in the spring.

But just as important as the efficiencies is the higher-quality product that has come with mechanization. "We're producing more consistent crops than we were before," Gary says. The improved consistency comes in part from more dependable irrigation, which avoids the problems that can result when water from overhead plants drips onto lower plants. "Everything we're doing today is different than we were doing five years ago," he adds. Gary's only regret? "We might have started sooner," he admits.

Plants Come to People

Faced with competition from low-cost production areas, shrinking margins, and cutthroat buyers, growers of the new millennium are turning increasingly to automation. From sowing the seed to carrying the finished product out the greenhouse door, machines are bringing to every phase of the process an efficiency that was unimaginable just a decade ago. But it's not enough to simply invest in expensive, modern greenhouse machines and sit back and wait for the efficiency to kick in.

Ask Kerry Herndon. He invested an additional $7 per ft. in modern mechanization when he rebuilt Kerry's Bromeliads in Homestead, Florida, after his range was completely destroyed by Hurricane Andrew in 1992. "Just buying stuff isn't going to help you," Kerry says. "Just having automation doesn't mean anything; it forces you to develop new processes around the equipment."

Kerry's new machinery allows him to produce more orchid plants with a remarkable increase in efficiency: While it took 500 people to operate the 1.4 million-sq. ft. facility before mechanization, the work can now be done by 230 people.

But Kerry figures he wasted two or three years using old processes that didn't take advantage of the new equipment. In order to make good use of the new and expensive machinery, Kerry had to rethink the entire operation around a simple, basic principle: "Plants come to people; people don't go to plants."

Today at Kerry's, a machine puts soil into pots, which are then picked up by another machine and placed on a conveyer belt, which carries them to the machine that picks them up and places them on the internal transport benches, where workers plant by hand. Conveyer belts and rolling tables move all the plants. The increase in efficiency is astonishing: "Now we have a guy pushing a table with 700 plants rather than carrying a tray with 15 plants," Kerry says.

Half of the plant movement through the greenhouse range is accomplished with no human muscle at all. The aluminum tables, which roll on horizontal rails in each bay, are pushed into the bays by a mechanical ram capable of pushing a row of a hundred 5-by-14-ft. tables. A cable system can pull an entire row of tables. An automated train can pick up as many as three benches at a time and carry them to another bay designated by a computer.

Leider Greenhouse, a twelve-acre greenhouse north of Chicago, retrofitted their existing greenhouse range way back in the late 1980s with the same type of internal transport system Gary and Kerry use. As with their ranges, Leider uses conveyor belts, and machines are used to fill and empty the tables. Although the system has allowed the firm to drastically reduce their labor costs by 20%, it works best when dealing with relatively few varieties of plants. "Every time you start and stop these machines, you lose your efficiency," said General Manager Mark Leider. "It only works efficiently if you reduce the variety of what you grow."

For Leider, the process of learning to use the mechanized tools has led to the development of a greenhouse production software program that takes much of the guesswork out of the operation. According to Mark, the grower puts in the information about how much of which plants need to be ready for sale on what date. The software then works back from that information to tell the grower exactly when to plant, when to pinch, when to space the plants—every detail of production. The software is now being marketed through FMI Technologies, a division of Florist Mutual Insurance.

Even with the automated equipment and software that can plan the growing process, there's still no replacing the value of experienced growers and hands-on attention to your crops. "It's management by walking around—you'll never get away from that," says Mark. "We come up with these recipes, and we've been growing for a hundred years. But you can't tell if one year you'll have forty days of no sunshine and the next year forty days of nothing but sunshine."

And Mark cautions that with the efficiency of automation comes vulnerability. Maintenance becomes more important—and more expensive—because when a key piece of equipment goes down, the greenhouse is filled with workers doing nothing.

Mechanical Snowball

As mechanized greenhouses come of age, new technologies are constantly creating the need for new tools.

Ratus Fischer of Greenlink, in Asheville, North Carolina, has installed fifty flood-floor irrigation systems in the past few years. Irrigation labor is virtually eliminated as plants take their water up from the flooded cement greenhouse floor. Runoff, too, is virtually eliminated as the excess water is captured in pipes beneath the floor, filtered, and then recirculated. The plants are watered evenly, and disease control is improved because the foliage never gets wet.

But aside from the cost—flood systems run about $5 per sq. ft.—the system also involves the potentially backbreaking scenario of putting the plants on the floor and picking them back up by hand. The Dutch firm Visser has already come up with an answer to this problem—a forklift called the Space-O-Mat specifically engineered for the greenhouse. A variety of fork attachments are designed to allow easy access to the plants; with adjustments, they can lift rows as wide as 10 ft.

"This is the only one that's on the market—there have been other attempts," Ratus says of the Visser machine. "They are one of the technologically cutting-edge machines. In many ways, they are the company that sets the benchmark." Several are in use in the U.S., both in greenhouses and in outdoor production areas.

Henry Huntington is using the Space-O-Mat as part of Pleasant View Garden's new two-acre range in Louden, New Hampshire. The machine, at a cost of $40,000 plus forks, can pick up 36 flats at a time. With thirteen forks, it can be custom set to fit the dimensions of the flats. In one year, one worker using this forklift was able to lay down 50,000 flats of cuttings.

"[The Space-O-Mat] is perfect for floor irrigation," Henry says. "You're not doing all that back-breaking work of putting things on the ground [by hand]."

Electric Eyes

There are machines to fill the pots, plant the seeds, move the flats, and water the crop. And these machines that replace hands and muscle are now being joined by tools that do the work of the eyes and mind.

Cameras are already widely used by citrus and potato growers to grade their harvest by size and shape and to detect imperfections. Golden State Bulb Growers in Watsonville, California, has been using this potato-adapted technology since 1998 to sort bulbs into different size categories, send bulbs of each size down the appropriate chutes and into storage cartons, and count them to ensure that each of the storage carton contains three hundred bulbs. Now this type of camera technology is beginning to appear in greenhouses for grading and sorting everything from seedlings to finished plants.

Bruce Knox of Knox Nursery in Orlando, Florida, is just one of numerous U.S. plug growers who've purchased one of these new video tools for detecting and removing unacceptable bedding plant plugs. After the operator sets parameters for acceptable amounts of leaf surface, the video camera takes a picture of the plug tray, a computer determines which plugs fail to meet the standard, and blowers use a puff of air to jettison the rejects. Knox paid about $80,000 for this labor saver; a separate machine that automatically refills the empty cells can be had for a similar price.

The question of which, if any, of the greenhouse mechanization systems are worthy investments is an individual decision that depends on the relative availability of capital and labor and, most important, on a willingness to commit to learning how to do everything differently. Even the most forward-looking greenhouse growers with capital to invest are discriminating in their choices of which of the new automated greenhouse systems make sense for their operation. For example, even with millions of dollars invested in upgrading Bell Nursery, Gary Mangum has seen no need to further invest in equipment that would mechanize the moving of his rolling tables. And at Kerry's Bromeliads, workers still plant by hand. "We're orchid growers," Kerry says of the decision to not use automatic transplanters. "Our plugs don't cost six cents [the price of a bedding plant plug]; they cost a dollar."

And even the grower who sinks an additional $7 per ft. or more into equipping the greenhouse of the new millennium had best be prepared to be behind the times not long after his new equipment is up and running. Kerry recently returned from a trip to Denmark, where he saw some of the world's most automated greenhouses, equipped with the very newest quiet, efficient, smooth-operating machinery. That eye-opening trip led him to conclude that "the guy who has the latest automation has the best."

December 1999

Cutting Labor in the Greenhouse

P. Allen Hammer

When *GrowerTalks* asked me to write an article on labor and step savings in the greenhouse, they e-mailed me. I faxed a questionnaire from my computer to growers, then e-mailed the article to *GrowerTalks*. Would that have been possible only ten years ago? Not a chance! As Jack Schmidt Jr. added to the bottom of his response, "Fax machines are great!" This is just one example of how technology is impacting our business. Our world, and our industry, continues to change at a pace that is unbelievable.

Thanks to all of the growers who responded to my fax. With very little editing, I have simply listed their responses, which require few additional comments because they are so clear. What is so interesting to me is that greenhouse size and greenhouse location didn't affect most answers.

Production costs have been reduced in many ways; however, growers most often mentioned automatic watering and materials handling. Several growers wrote about the need to invest in concrete floors, walks, and driveways to effectively use carts and material handling equipment. All agreed that concrete was a good investment that saved money in the long run. Who would have guessed that concrete would be listed as a laborsaving material?

Responses to the question about factors that make the greenhouse job easier were the most interesting to me. Two growers commented that nothing has made their jobs easier. Labor- and step-saving items had simply increased productivity, kept them competitive, and changed employee challenges to mechanical challenges. This response was somewhat different among greenhouses depending upon the amount of hands-on managerial responsibility. Conveyors would make your job easier if you were the person loading the plants, while an environmental computer would make the job easier if you were the one responsible for environmental control. So, as you read the grower responses to that question, keep that connection in mind.

Shipping and watering by far have the greatest need for labor- and step-saving approaches in the greenhouse. Shipping is an area that the industry has spent the least amount of effort in improving. This isn't a real surprise because growers usually say growing, while shipping is just "something we have to do." Growers' responses to the greatest need question would, however, suggest that that attitude may be changing. I suspect shipping will receive a great deal of attention in the next five years.

As Van Wingerden International's Robert Milks said in his response, "OK, you made me say it: The computer is the new 'tool' that has made the most impact in the greenhouse in the last five years." There is no question that the computer has made and will continue to make a very large impact on the greenhouse. Computer technology has changed the greenhouse operation in numerous ways. But I also agree with the counterpoint that in some ways, computers have made my job more difficult. On the other hand, the new computer technology has increased my productivity. It has also greatly improved the quality of the things I do. This article would have been five times more difficult without e-mail and the fax machine. So, life must be easier!

What greenhouse work area do you think has the greatest need for labor savings or step savings?

Shipping
- Reducing labor is job No. 1, all aspects of shipping are very labor intensive and very time critical, this is our least mechanized task
- Shipping area
- Shipping and packaging systems
- Packing

Watering
- Better irrigation
- Springtime watering of plants

- Watering, more booms for table, and ECHOs for basket watering
- Watering large numbers of plants on benches and floors with crop diversity

Plant handling
- Plant/material handling in Quonset greenhouses
- Potting and planting areas
- Potting and transplanting system for the small grower
- Vegetative propagation (cutting, sticking, transplanting), materials handling (moving plants)

Miscellaneous
- The office, to better plan the movement of products
- Computer system to organize greenhouse, inventory control system, greenhouse space utilization, costs accounting
- Logging and inventorying chemicals for Worker Protection Standards
- Organized headhouse used for production, shipping, and storage—we're always short on room

What laborsaving or step-saving change have you made to your greenhouse business operation in the last five years that has made your job easier?

Production automation
- Low-volume sprayer that starts and stops automatically
- Rain Bird clocks for watering hanging baskets and pot plants on tubes—can be started manually or programmed to water automatically
- Automatic watering and environmental control
- VPD (vapor pressure deficit) control for propagation, booms for misting and watering
- Drip irrigation, flat filler
- Automated moving table system, improved Flier and Blackmore seeding equipment, Flier transplanter
- Automatic seeding machine
- Computer environmental control

Production management
- Set up teams for production and rotate tasks among teams
- Planting in the greenhouse saves steps and time
- Taken more hands-on control of crops

- None—you just trade employee challenges for mechanical ones
- None—they allow us to do more work and to stay competitive

Shipping
- Trolley system to help move 14-in. geraniums, racks
- Conveyors

What laborsaving or step-saving change have you made to your greenhouse business operation in the last five years that has reduced your production costs?

Shipping
- Carts to move products
- Rental trucks for peak delivery instead of purchasing additional trucks.
- Conveyors
- Consolidated two greenhouse locations into one. (Shipping out of two locations was a spring nightmare.)
- Cart and tagger systems, concrete walks and driveways—I only wish I had done it ten years ago

Production
- ECHO hanging basket system, Cannon carts added 20% additional shipping space, Cravo houses for hardening off plants instead of moving plants
- Transplanters, taggers, pot and flat dispensers, complete sowing lines, ebb-and-flood floors, computer (environmental control, production programming), potting machines, boom irrigators
- Automatic watering: water-holding trays for 4-in. pots
- Automated transplanter, ebb-and-flood floors
- Using true 1020 flats for 1801 landscape material to give more production in same space
- New Holland fork lift, concrete isles, small seeder, inventory control
- Transplanter line, water tunnel, tagger, rack (cart) system, trolley system
- Drip irrigation for garden mums and hanging baskets, concrete walks and floors for shipping, automatic flat and pot filler, bench-level heating for propagation
- Installed ebb-and-flood tray system, shipping conveyors
- Q-Com computer environmental control

- Changed from double poly to Lexan
- Boom watering, permanent conveyor system, long-day lighting on boom reduced electrical costs by ten times, hot-water ground heat
- Replacing old greenhouses with new structure
- Creating production manager position, using early evening team of high schoolers, using a computer to control shipping orders, creating a production incentive system

What new "tool" has made the most impact on your greenhouse operation in the last five years? What is the impact?

Automation
- Rain Bird clocks and solenoids
- Drip irrigation, flat/pot filling machine
- Overhead sprinkler system in Quonsets
- Automatic seeding machine that reduced plug costs and improved quality and consistency of plugs
- Select-A-Feed Jr. for granular application
- Double-head spindle transplanter by Flier has doubled production
- Dramm Autofogger has automated pesticide application, reduced employee exposure to pesticides and controls insects
- Automatic low-volume sprayer

Shipping
- Rack (cart) system allows centralized transplanting and the ability to move greater quantities of plants with less labor
- Conveyors
- Cart delivery of plants and having enough carts to ship a load and collect a load for staging—it's wonderful!

Computers
- Computers, both environmental control and production scheduling, implementing team concept with increased productivity, requires less supervision and makes work more fun for employees
- Computer for record keeping and crop programming
- Computer to calculate cost of goods sold
- OK, you made me say it: computers
- Office computer
- Computers—could not do without them

Miscellaneous
- Interest rates are good for building—new 40,000-sq. ft. warehouse and 8,000-sq. ft. greenhouse holding area

Special thanks to these growers for their input. They're the ones who really wrote this article: Wayne Crowder, Crowder's Greenhouse; Bruce Danhauer, Danhauer Greenhouse and Garden Center; Bill Davis, Sandpoint Greenhouses; Dennis Deibel, Deibel Greenhouses; Jim Dickerson, Dickerson's Greenhouse; Tim Galema, Galema's Greenhouse; Dan Gibbs, Krueger Maddux Greenhouses; Billy Hardin, Hardin's Wholesale Florist Supply; Ken Hensch, Hensch Brothers Greenhouses; Dave Jones, Buren J. Jones and Sons Inc.; Jeff Mast, Heartland Growers; Tom Miksich, Mayday's Greenhouse; Robert Milks, Van Wingerden International; Jack Schmidt Jr., Timbuck Farms Inc.; Ron Shelbourne, Gardner's Ltd. Greenhouse; Louis Stacy, Stacy's Greenhouse; Jim Leider, Leider Greenhouse; Dave Wiesbrock, Mid-American Growers

April 1998

Precision Growing: Tools and Techniques for Better Crops

Don Grey

When you combine modern greenhouse technology and a quality-oriented mind-set, you can produce the most consistent, uniform, cost-effective crops possible—call it "precision growing." Here's how six growers are making the best use of the tools and techniques at their disposal to improve their finished products.

Start with the Crops

"To be a precision grower—a consistent, quality grower—you need to look at the demands of each crop," says Mike Gooder, Plantpeddler, Cresco, Iowa. "What are the demands of that plant? You can't treat all plants equally. That's the biggest transition I've seen in growing over the years. [TrueLeaf's] Jim Rearden calls it 'plant-centric' growing."

Plantpeddler specializes in a wide range of potted plants such as mums, hiemalis begonias, and poinsettias for Iowa and surrounding states. They've got thirty different blooming crops shipping weekly from two acres of gutter-connect ranges—a mixture of double poly, polycarbonate, and wide-span glass, and a few Quonsets.

Mike looks at the specific crop's requirements before looking at the facilities and equipment. He micro-zones his greenhouses where possible with interior curtains to better control each zone to each crop's needs.

An environmental control system helps maintain climates in those zones. "I find it to be an amazing tool to fine-tune the environment," Mike says. "To me, it's the final piece of the puzzle that makes a grower successful."

For precision growing, Mike also relies on crop modeling and graphical tracking. "Our crops have changing cycles," he explains. "You can't use the same recipe in January that you do in July." Data is captured weekly, and a history of the crops is plotted and tracked in an Excel spreadsheet. That data is a valuable tool to gauge how and when a crop grows and finishes.

For Mike, precision growing is as much about philosophy as it is about the tools that make it happen. "The ultimate goal," he says, "is replication of a consistent product fifty-two weeks of the year, year after year."

Labor and Precision

Dan Busch, Busch Greenhouses, Denver, Colorado, believes escalating labor costs often point to inefficiency.

"We need to continue to work toward automation, streamline, create more precision in our crops and more predictability," Dan says. The fifth-generation business propagates spring bedding plants year-round, shipping to all fifty states through distributors, plus finishes a range of crops.

Dan points to his new transplanter as one way to increase precision. "The transplanter is consistent," he says. "It performs at a specific rate and a specific time. We know how many trays it can produce per hour and with what number of people. At certain times of the year, you need to be in a position to run more than one shift a day."

Adding the transplanter forced Dan to examine other parts of his operation. He changed the size of his plug trays and finished plants to work better with the transplanter. He also changed the way he schedules plants for transplanting. The line is now set up to transplant more of one variety before someone has to reconfigure the machine.

"Don't look at automation strictly as dollars and cents—there are other tangibles," Dan suggests. "[With automation,] a smaller crew can transplant and keep up production. And uniformity is important. Automation takes away a lot of the uneven human element. Uniformity and less shrinkage go hand in hand with consistency. This year we've sold more trays of bedding plants because of uniformity—there's less shrinkage."

Dan also believes a precision grower needs to keep an eye on labor costs, especially areas such as material handling and transplanting by hand. "Keep questioning what you can do to cut labor. Be sure to set up goals for workers to achieve and set parameters."

Dan's rule of thumb is to keep labor costs below 22% of gross sales (excluding taxes, insurance, and benefits). That's the biggest single cost you have," he says. "And it's not the price of labor so much as its quantity and quality."

Smart Space

For Pleasant View Gardens, Loudon, New Hampshire, precision means wringing as much productivity from its greenhouses as possible by improving working conditions. Head grower Mike Goyette calls this "smart space" thinking. For example, Pleasant View Gardens equipped some older stock houses with smaller benches so workers could better access the plants for cutting production. Hanging baskets that were double-cropped overhead are now benched so workers can take cuttings faster and easier. That sacrificed greenhouse space but with better end results. Plants are also grown on tighter spacing to cut fuel costs.

A new 100,000-sq. ft. range under construction features flood floors, and wider aisles will give even better access to the plants and faster shipping. "Labor is definitely more expensive in the old facilities," Mike says. Pleasant View plans to add another shift to stick cuttings on their Visser and Flier transplant lines, and a Visser Space-O-Mat system allows one person to move and space thirty-five trays at a time, solving a major bottleneck.

Space Wars

At Brookside Greenhouses, Langley, British Columbia, Will Van Baalen gets 95% space use. The grower of cyclamen and orchids achieves this largely through a multiple-spacing regimen. Crops start out pot-tight, then go to half-spacing and then to final spacing. Growing the crops so tight lets Brookside produce more plants per square foot.

Cyclamen and orchid production are high-labor crops. He can't bench-run his finished crops, and hand picking plants adds up. "Labor is our biggest expense, by far," he says. They try to keep repotting (necessary with orchids) to a minimum, and delay or eliminate repotting whenever possible.

Brookside automates as many processes as possible. An environmental control system helps maintain even temperatures. Their irrigation and nutrition program are automated. Moving tables use a subirrigation trough system that recirculates water, and computer monitors preset EC and pH levels.

Growing Panes

How does a company maintain precision as it grows? Dallas Johnson Greenhouse in Council Bluffs, Iowa, is one good example. From just one acre under glass fifteen years ago, the bedding plant grower has thirty-two acres today and still is growing, with 100,000 sq. ft. under construction.

"It's extremely difficult to be precise the larger you get," says Todd Johnson. "With thirty-five to forty acres, you can do a good job, but any larger you worry. You also need to have a good staff. If you have a good foundation the business will run itself, if employees are well-trained."

Todd is automating as much as possible. Four automatic transplanters have cut labor costs while improving production to 14,000 trays, 8,000 to 10,000 hanging baskets, and 60,000 to 80,000 4-in. pots per eight-hour shift.

Internal transport is the next frontier. "We're handling the product three to seven times," Todd says. "It takes me more people to move the product around than any other part of the business."

With automation cranking high output, greenhouse space use becomes critical. "I don't like benches for finished product," Todd says. "The floor gives us more room and easier access to our product." Three-foot-wide aisles in bays provide ample room for workers to access the plants.

With hanging baskets, Todd says you essentially get one good turn per season, so you need to maximize production and space. He estimates his ECHO systems have increased overhead space use by as much as 100%. He's installing eighty-five more in his new range.

He also has a very efficient picking and shipping area: "The most efficient system I know of in our industry today," Todd says. Greenhouses are equipped with an inverted roller track and conveyor system that can transport up to 1,000 trays in twenty minutes. Four people pull orders, and with twenty more in the shipping area, they can ship 30,000 trays per day. The 54,000-sq. ft. facility also accommodates up to 17,000 hanging baskets overhead. As Todd says, "You've got to have the flexibility or you're losing money."

Simplify

For Tom Fessler, Woodburn Nursery & Azaleas, Woodburn, Oregon, precision begins with simplicity. "We try to take the thinking out of it for the employees," he says. "Anything we can do to make it simpler for them, we will. Our philosophy is that we'll continue to expand, but not expand our work force."

Woodburn grows a wide variety of nursery stock and potted dormant and finished floral azaleas, which account for 65% of its total business, in fifty-four acres of greenhouses. "The ultimate goal is to produce the most No. 1 plant material you can," Tom says. "We'll never get 100%, but high 90s is our goal." The space costs the same for good and bad plants, he says, so why not get the best plant possible?

With just one turn of azaleas per year, Woodburn doesn't need much technology. There's no need for Dutch trays because transport isn't a big issue. But they're installing large numbers of retractable-roof greenhouses for the most flexible growing environments.

Little changes add up, too. Tom now buys premixed fertilizer, eliminating one worker. They're also developing a central mixing system for media, which will be distributed to other ranges as needed, simplifying and speeding production.

Like Todd Johnson, Tom is moving from benches to flood floors. Not only can workers quickly move the plants using trailers, but Tom feels he gets a better quality forced azalea from ebb-and-flood floors compared with overhead irrigation.

He's also experimenting with Palm Pilots—small handheld computers that will give his growers instant access to crop information and inventory figures when they walk their greenhouses.

"Customers are getting more demanding," Tom says. "They want better quality and cheaper prices, and if you want to play the game, you'd better find a way to get there."

December 2000

Flat Filler FAQs

Jim Fowler

Third in our series of frequently asked questions, this month we look at pot and flat fillers. These are probably one of the very first major pieces of "automation" a grower will buy to save time and labor. Bouldin & Lawson has more in service than anybody else does, so we asked Sales Manager Jim Fowler for the answers to the most common questions he gets from customers.

Q: Can I fill flats and pots with one machine or do I need two separate machines? And what about plug trays?

A: It really depends on the size of containers that you're running and production numbers required. For example, if I have a customer who wants to fill flats of jumbo 606s and 1204s but also needs to fill several thousand 10-in. hanging baskets, I would probably recommend a Maxi Flat Filler (approx. $10,000) for its versatility. This would allow the grower to fill the flats at rates of twenty per minute or baskets at rates of twenty-two per minute.

If you also need to fill plug flats, I'd recommend you purchase a Vibrating Kit for the Maxi (approx. $1,000), which helps to reduce air pockets in the cells while increasing compaction.

Q: I use nine different pot sizes, from 3 in. up to 16-in. color bowls. Can I do this with one machine? How long does changeover from one size to another take?

A: Yes, you can. Our Maxi will accommodate containers up to 12-in. tall and 18-in. wide. But do you run your smaller pots—lets say 3 in., 4 in., and 6 in.—in shuttle trays? If you don't, you might need to purchase a special pot transfer device to move these smaller units on to another conveyor after filling. This will also mean the machine will have to work harder to return unused soil in the filling process. This will reduce life expectancy for parts used in handling the soil. With shuttle trays, production numbers are drastically increased and life expectancy of some parts of your machine is extended.

As far as changeovers go on a filler, five minutes is normal, as long as containers fit within the height restrictions of the equipment. And again, since there are no standards on baskets and bowls; each type has to be addressed separately.

Q: Do I have to change my soil mix to run it through a pot filler?

A: Machines that will be running a basic greenhouse mix have no problems. It's when you want to run one machine with both a heavier nursery mix and a greenhouse mix that you encounter problems. Always alert the manufacturer's salesperson to this so he can set the machine up for the heavier mix, then the lighter mix won't be a problem. Adding a variable speed soil chain lets you fluctuate soil amounts on demand, which will make a single machine that is much more versatile.

Q: How many pots per hour can I expect to fill?

A: What size pots? We have machines that will fill twenty-two 10-in. pots per minute to machines that will fill and drill 1-gal. containers at speeds of nearly one hundred pots per minute. What are your preference or production requirements. You can fill thirty bedding plant flats per minute on a big flat filler, but that's faster than any transplanter on the market today. You get the greatest savings by reducing handling. Speed isn't always the biggest benefit.

Q: Do I need any other special equipment—compressors, a new electrical service, etc.?

A: That depends on the type of equipment you're purchasing. Normally all that's required is that the correct breaker size be added to your main disconnect box to handle the amperage required by the machine. If any air or special requirements are needed, we'll let you know up front.

Q: How much should I budget for maintenance? Is it something that I can do myself, or do I have to call your technicians?

A: A lot of people are concerned with maintenance. Scheduled maintenance for a piece of equipment may include cleaning it out at the end of each working day, giving each bearing a shot of grease, or even just a visual check for potential problems. In most cases, a factory tech isn't needed but is available, depending on the job.

Q: Once I decide what I need, how do I calculate payback on the equipment? How do other customers do it?

A: The simplest way is to look at what it cost you to produce something last year using hand labor for filling pots. Then figure what it might cost you to do it with automation, based on production numbers that the manufacturer says you can expect. For instance, suppose you hire two college students for minimum wage to fill pots for two months. They'd earn roughly $4,000. That's about half the cost of a Mini flat filler. With the machine, your existing staff could probably fill the pots themselves, paying back the cost of the machine with just four months' worth of labor savings. This is oversimplified, but you get the point.

Q: I'm also considering a transplanter, but from a different manufacturer. How can I know my new pot filler will be compatible, and will be able to keep up?

A: Let the various manufacturers know what you're planning. Most of the people in manufacturing know and understand other manufacturers' equipment and how it operates. By letting us know what your intentions are, we can address any problems or concerns before arriving on site. We may all use different brands of components, but we all have the same outcome in mind.

Q: I don't have a main potting shed. What do I have to do to be able to move a pot filler from house to house?

A: Tires, casters, a trailer, or a wagon—it really depends on the terrain, how far a piece has to be moved, and what type of equipment it is.

Q: This is a big investment for me. How long can I expect my pot filler to last?

A: Taking care of your equipment is vital to its longevity. We've had identical pieces delivered to different locations, and one may run more than thirty years while the other might not last five years. It's very important that you maintain your investment.

Summer 2000

Sant's Helper

Chris Beytes

The cutting business is big business, thanks to the tremendous growth of vegetative varieties. That means that propagators are looking for their niche. Canada's George Sant & Sons have invested in an interesting piece of Danish technology called Ellepot to give their liner business an edge.

Ellepots are simple paper cylinders with no bottom that are filled with potting media. Ellepots let you root right in a potting medium that's loose for easy root penetration, accepts water and fertilizer just like a pot of media, and, after transplanting, adapts to the surrounding medium quickly. Also, they pop out of trays easily. These are a few reasons that Ron Sant says he and his brothers, Rick and Dan, went with the Ellepot.

Ron says that in Europe, where there are more than 250 Ellepot machines in operation, Ellepots are becoming extremely popular among growers, many of whom won't buy a young plant if it's not grown in one. "We felt that it's probably going to be a few years, but that might happen over here, where [propagators] will have a bit of an edge by growing in an Ellepot."

The Ellepot machine (manufactured by Ellegaard AS; Blackmore Co. is the primary North American distributor) is like a giant cigarette roller. The potting medium of your choice is fed from a hopper into a metal tube. (The Sants use a fine plug mix with a starter fertilizer charge.) Biodegradable paper is fed from a roll and wrapped around the tube, then is heat-sealed at the edges to form a continuous cylinder. The metal tube stuffs the paper cylinder with medium, and then a saw blade cuts the paper cylinder into individual lengths. Voilà—Ellepots!

The Sants started out a couple of years ago with a small Ellepot machine, but as their liner production has expanded to account for close to 30% of their total business, they've had to upgrade to a self-loading, double-head machine that loads the Ellepots into 105-count trays at about 8,000 an hour. This will let them make the estimated 5 million pots they need this season.

Ron says cuttings root great in the Ellepots, especially those with really fine roots such as *Brachycome*. He says that customers think Sants' cuttings are a week to ten days ahead of cuttings in other rooting systems.

But can a machine like this pay? Well, when we visited in March, the Sants' Ellepot had been running for just one month, but it had already cranked out more than a million pots—that'll mean pretty quick payback for the $55,000 machine.

Summer 2000

Getting Hooked

Chris Beytes

This year, U.S. growers expect to produce some 37 million hanging baskets, and every hanger on every basket will have to be put on by hand. And that's not even counting the 25 million foliage baskets or Canadian production!

Your fingers may be saved, however, thanks to an inventor who has designed and built a machine that automatically clips plastic hangers onto baskets. The machine not only works, it's set to make its debut at the Ohio Short Course in July. Reportedly capable of "handling" 1,200 pots per hour (with more speed on the horizon), the Hook-On, as it has been dubbed, will be a boon to basket growers.

Mac Winsor and his amazing Hook-On basket hanger attacher.
Photo by Altamont Corp.

Malcolm "Mac" Winsor, a forty-year veteran inventor and machine designer, runs Altamont Corp. in the tiny southern New Hampshire town of Mont Vernon. There he runs a small but efficient machine shop where he and his staff create prototype machinery for some of New England's largest corporations.

Mac says the idea for the Hook-On came about over breakfast last year with an old friend who happened to be in the horticulture business. On a whim, Mac asked if there were any machines that plant growers needed. "A machine to put hangers on hanging baskets," the friend answered.

"The challenge piqued my interest," Mac says, "but there was no thought of actually doing something in metal. It started as a fascinating 'what if,' but as it started to take shape on the sketchpad, it got more and more doable."

First, Mac acquired some common hanging baskets to examine their design. Research revealed that most high-volume basket growers use pots from two manufacturers, Dillen and ITML. Their rim and hanger designs are similar enough that Mac felt he could build a machine that would handle both.

"The next step was a simple working model of one of the operators to slide the hooks off the supply rod," Mac continues. "It worked well and seduced me into more experiments for the next stages of the process, which were pretty well formed in my mind. Finally, there was nothing to do but put together a frame to hang all these models on, and there I was, fully committed, and the Hook-On has turned out to be a real product in the growers' world."

It will be a real product thanks to Flier USA, which has been involved in the project, providing real-world experience with greenhouse automation. At press time, Flier's president, Robert Lando, told us that they were making some final changes to the prototype and were planning to get it running in a greenhouse environment for a thorough testing, to have it ready to show to the industry at Ohio. But other than a few minor changes, Robert says that the Hook-On "definitely works," adding that it will be a perfect complement to transplanters that plant baskets.

The Hook-On works with Dillen and ITML baskets from 6½ in. diameter and 4½ in. tall to 12 in. diameter and 7½ in. tall. Mac says it might be possible to retrofit for other brands, but he's focused on perfecting the current setup.

As for the cost, Robert says it's too early to know. But if the Hook-On survives its real-world testing, you can bet that sore-fingered growers will be lined up to get their order in.

Summer 2000

FAQs: Seeders

David Steiner

Q: There seem to be so many types of seeders on the market. Which is right for my business?

A: There are five basic types of seeders: wand, plate, semiautomatic, reciprocating, and drum/cylinder.

Wand or plate seeders are typically used by smaller operations and by researchers. Wand seeders, such as Blackmore's CAN-DUIT seeder, use needle tips to handle raw seed as small as petunia or as large as watermelon; pelleted petunia and begonia are recommended. Hand operated, it sows one row of seed at a time. Rates of operation vary from a tray per minute for round seed to a row every five seconds or so for more difficult seeds. Plate seeders sow an entire tray at a time, excelling at round or pelleted seed, but they have more limited use on odd-shaped seeds such as marigold. Prices start at about $600 for a wand and go to $2,000 or more for a plate seeder with a full range of seed and tray sizes.

Semiautomatic machines have a handle to move a manifold mounted on a framework, picking up seeds on needle tips and depositing them into the tray. Cost is in the $3,500 range. They're basically reciprocating seeders without a motor.

Reciprocating seeders (sometimes called needle seeders) are the most common and handle a wide range of seed, as small as raw begonia or as large as marigold, dahlia, and zinnia. Typical throughput is 75 to 100 512-count trays per hour. Most growers using reciprocating models sow 2,000 to 10,000 plug trays per year. Blackmore offers a double-row attachment that permits rates of 300-plus trays per hour for seeds as large as pepper going into 288-count or larger trays. Cost of a reciprocating seeder is roughly $10,000, including compressor and vacuum pump, for Blackmore models.

The top-of-the-line is the drum or cylinder seeder. This type uses a revolving drum to pick up and then deposit seed into the plug tray as it passes beneath. Expect a drum or Blackmore's cylinder type to cruise along at about 500 trays per hour on most seeds. A two-option cylinder gets you to 800-plus trays an hour, requiring a palletized benching system to take the trays away. Marigold? Expect to slow down to 350 trays per hour with a two-option head.

Blackmore's cylinder seeder operational features set it apart from drum seeders. You can change from single to double sowing with just the push of a button or by "clicking" the head to a double hole setting. Change from sowing raw petunia to geranium just by clicking to a different setting on the cylinder head. The four-option head sows a wide variety of seed without requiring hardware changes.

Cost? Well you don't get Ferrari speed for a Neon price. The cylinder seeder starts at about $23,000. The most popular model—a stretch chassis with the PLC controller and Top-Coater—goes out the door at $30,000.

Q: Do I need pelleted seed?

A: We recommend using pelleted begonia seed for ease of operation, altough two of our models (gear and turbo) are capable of sowing raw begonias using an exclusive counter-bore manifold and seed wipe-off brush. Today, most of the best seed (petunia and begonia) is being pelleted, so many growers choose that type.

Q: What about extra-large seeds—marigold, dahlia—and direct sowing?

A: These seeds are sown on reciprocating machines with large needle tips and special large drop tubes configured for a plug tray or direct sowing into bedding plant trays. The CAN-DUIT wand seeder uses the same large tips. Many growers choose the two-option head for a cylinder seeder when doing marigolds to keep the speed up. The cylinder may require special holes on the head and larger vacuum pumps for cucumbers and melons. Alyssum performs better when directly sown, and the cylinder handles it at 600-plus trays per hour.

Q: Do I need a dibbler?

A: A roller/dibbler is a good investment because making sure your seed is centered increases the number of usable plugs. They cost about $800 or so, but if you get 2 to 3% more plugs, there's the payback. A high-speed drum or cylinder seeder sows a row of seed in just a 15/100th of a second. You'd better give that seed all the help you can to get it to land in the right spot in the tray.

Q: What plug tray(s) should I use?

A: The most popular plug trays are the 512 CE (common element) and 288 CE, which incorporate design parameters for ease of seeding, transplanting, and dislodging. A popular in-between size is the 384 tray. When making the switch to a new seeder, choose one of these more popular trays; you'll have to make the switch at some point anyway, and you might as well pay now rather than pay more later.

Q: Will I need a tray filler?

A: You can get by without a tray filler if you're operating one of the lower-volume machines. However, almost as important as sowing seed accurately is making sure the tray is filled uniformly. That helps to determine how good a stand you actually have and, if you have an automatic transplanter, how well it will transplant.

Q: Should I buy new or used? Are there lease programs available?

A: Used cylinder seeders are almost nonexistent, but reconditioned reciprocating models are available. Some lease companies are willing to write leases on new or used machines. Blackmore has a short-term lease with an option-to-purchase program for reciprocating models. A one-season lease is prepaid; at the end of the season, you can buy the machine with the lease payment applied to the price or send it back.

September 2000

Sowing Seeds of Change

Bill Sheldon

"We're going through an Industrial Revolution in horticulture right now. This is our biggest year for new products," is the easy response from Robert

Lando, president of Oberlin, Ohio-based Flier USA when asked about automatic seeder technology. "Small and medium growers can have an integrated [seeding] line for less than $40,000."

McMinnville, Tennessee's Bouldin & Lawson is also on the cusp of change. Engineer Graham Goodenough hints at that, saying, "There's a good deal of secrecy this time of year. We're working on several new machines. We'll have revolutionary aspects and some surprises."

David Steiner, vice president of Blackmore Company, Belleville, Michigan, a pioneer in automated seeders, is equally succinct: "What growers have now is a plant factory. And this means the smaller grower is getting more flexibility at lower cost."

Seed Technology: People Are Key

The focus seems to be on technology, but people remain the key. Growers are absorbing expansion with equipment, not more personnel. Or they're seeding faster and more accurately to use people more wisely.

Two growers with different operations stress the people portion of the technology formula.

Tim Raker, an owner of C. Raker & Sons, Litchfield, Michigan, has seven acres of houses at his twenty-two-year-old plug production business. "The labor issue is tough," Tim says. "You have to be progressive, offer good wages and benefits. Find people who are interested in what they are doing. We have to teach people to manage the equipment. Don't try to replace people with equipment, just get more efficient."

Martin Stockton is head grower of two-year-old First Step Greenhouse in Orange County, California. He has a highly automated 70,000-sq. ft. facility. "From the beginning, we underestimated the key position of the seeder," Martin recalls. "The operator controls our profit and success. We have to dedicate time and effort to train and reward this person. There's an art and finesse to seeding," he explains. "We need a person we can trust more and pay more to get us uniform and consistent production. This is hard to pencil. What's uniformity worth to you?"

One of the country's largest growers also points to personnel, but with another twist. Sim McMurray is the head grower at Metrolina Greenhouses, Huntersville, North Carolina, a few miles north of Charlotte. This year Metrolina will have sixty-eight acres of greenhouses and 300 peak-period workers, and will grow 100 million plugs, all for their own use.

"Finding help is the challenge of the industry. We've had a problem with that," Sim admits. But he adds that personnel needs expand into maintaining the line. "You almost need a factory rep on site," he says. "If a production line goes down, you'd better have quality maintenance people there to minimize your down time."

Roger Styer, an internationally known plug specialist, consultant, and author of *Plug & Transplant Production,* sees the people/technology conundrum from two perspectives: "Growers make the mistake of not having good enough maintenance or a trained operator," he says. "Good equipment and poor training hurts."

Roger says that where the seeder is located can be as important as what kind of seeder you use. Growers also don't seed in as protected an environment as they ought to. Cold, wet, hot might mean machines don't run as well. This also is important for the operators, who need more creature comforts.

"More education on equipment is needed. There's not as much of an off-season anymore, and machines or parts can't be sent back to the distributors as conveniently. This means service has to go to the machines."

Roger puts some of the burden on manufacturers. "Seeder companies need to do better. There is too much limping along; they need to provide better help." He adds that he thinks growers are ready to pay for necessary maintenance and training, and that they're looking for better, faster, more flexible machines. "The growers are pushing a lot of technology back on the distributor and manufacturer. There's also a lot of pressure coming from Europe. There's need for more accuracy and for machines to handle a wider range of seeds."

Cylinders Roll On

"Speed is not as important as efficiency," says Dave Koranski, possibly the plug industry's best-known spokesman and champion. "Labor costs sometimes make 'faster' important. But the critical issue is the number of useable seedlings. The proper seeding operation can make the difference between 95% and 99% useable seedlings, and that can mean a lot of money. This is a bigger issue than anybody in North America understands."

Dave explains that the issue is not just about equipment, "but instituting processes and procedures to do seeding right. You want consistent operations hour by hour."

Which gets Dave to the grower's decision-making process in buying a seeder. "Analyze the payback for your own operation, not for something that doesn't fit your greenhouse. Decisions should be based on your [business] and your costs, not your emotions. You have to look at the short- and long-term paybacks. Travel. Ask questions. Be critical. Do your homework."

While precision is an essential element of a seeder, growers are definitely looking for speed and efficiency in their sowing lines. The answer seems more and more to come from cylinder seeders, which combine the versatility of needle seeders with the speed of larger drum seeders.

Scott Swift has 100,000 sq. ft. of plug production at Swift Greenhouses, his family's Gilman, Iowa, business. They grow liners of six hundred varieties of perennials and herbs. Scott has moved from a turbo needle seeder to a cylinder seeder.

"We're phasing out the turbo because we have several people who can run the cylinder," Scott explains. "They can do in part of a day what it used to take all day on the turbo. This frees them up for other tasks."

Martin Stockton's California operation has grown 70% in its two years, and he, too, has moved from needle to cylinder seeders. "We should have bought the cylinder in the beginning," he says of his decision. "We didn't because we were relating equipment to what we were doing at the time, and we were worried about spending twice as much. But with the cylinder we're not looking at payback. We were at sixty-hour weeks, but with the cylinder we get back time and get better seed placement, which reduces our error percentage—a vital, key situation."

Tim Raker has also made the transition over to cylinder seeders. "We've had drums and needles and went exclusively to cylinders a little more than five years ago. We wanted versatility and easy changeover. We often do four different jobs on the same cylinder head. We're into our second generation of cylinders. Now we have three Blackmore cylinders that do all our seeding." Roger Styer says this isn't uncommon. For the plug growers he's visited, "Blackmore cylinders have become the high volume seeder of choice."

Manufacturers, such as Blackmore's David Steiner, spend a lot of time evaluating how their customers can get the most from their seeders, whether needle, cylinder, drum, or simple plate seeders. David suggests that the best seeder is the one that lets you spend the least time using it. "Especially for the smaller grower, time is getting more valuable. Why have your best people standing around all week on a seeder? Have them seed two days and actually grow plants most of the time. That's where grower value is."

Another consideration is greenhouse space use. "The faster equipment also makes better use of greenhouse space," David says. "When you're heating to 75°F in January to seed only a couple of days a week, you're saving money."

While these growers are now using cylinder seeders for virtually all of their production, Robert Lando of Flier USA is more cautious. "We make drums and cylinders and sell a lot of them. But they each do not necessarily work on every seed," he says. "Growers teach me that each machine has a reason. Large growers, especially, use each machine that's better for certain things. The grower decides which way to go by looking at the job as just one corner of the day, not just what has to be sown. Varieties change; how many seed sizes are involved, what short runs do you have. They want to reduce changeover time. "Seeding alone might be only 20% of the total production time," Robert concludes. "Make sure the seeder can perform all the tasks you need."

Graham Goodenough of Bouldin & Lawson urges growers not to invest in excess capacity, and to increase speed only as their business increases. "A typical three- to five-acre grower can build his business properly with one fully automated precision needle seeder for about $16,800," Graham says. "Distributors shouldn't quote silly production numbers. Six hundred flats an hour is enough for most people. Accuracy is the key. It's of no value to have big speed when you aren't going to or can't use it."

Graham adds that there are lots of changes coming on needle and drum seeders. "We're increasing the range of our seeders. I think we all may see something radical in a couple of years."

David Steiner says Blackmore sells roughly an equal number of cylinder and needle seeders. "But this includes selling a lot of used seeders from the 1980s that are available. We probably sell two-to-one used to new turbo seeders. If you look at new cylinders compared to new needles, it's about three or four to one."

For a fully automated, in-line system like Metrolina's, they use cylinder seeders for everything except marigolds, zinnias, daisies, and some perennials. Sim McMurray estimates these products are about 5% of their total workload. Sim also says he expects equipment costs to come down in a few years, opening opportunities for smaller growers.

These growers, distributors and consultants clearly believe in what they're doing and have opinions that conflict with each other's experiences, which probably reinforces Dave Koranski's comments on growers being careful to look at the seeding process for their own needs.

And, then there's one other highly scientific analysis suggested by Robert Lando: "Maybe it's just because growers like their toys?"

Summer 1999

From the Ground Up

Chris Beytes

Few businessmen are as innovative as growers are. And few growers we've met are as innovative as Bob Ondejko. This Canadian bedding plant grower who, with his brother, John, runs Seacliff Greenhouses in Leamington, Ontario, has successfully designed and built a machine that the industry has been needing for years: a flexible, relatively low-cost machine that puts plants down on the ground and picks them back up again.

Bob's invention is an electric Plant Truck equipped with a 5-by-15-ft. tilting conveyor belt on the back that Seacliff uses to fill their 500,000 sq. ft. of concrete flood floors. Similar systems have been used in Europe, primarily to handle vegetable transplants grown in rock wool cubes, but nobody has adapted them to floriculture production.

Like all other growers who produce on the ground, they knew they needed a solution to the heavy, time-consuming labor it takes to place product down on the ground. "I've watched all my people bend down, and they all swear at me," Bob jokes, "so we had to make something easier."

Bob, despite his lack of engineering training, went to the Netherlands in October 1998 to see what was being done there. Many of those systems operate on rails or tracks, which limit their flexibility. He didn't want that. And forklift-style systems don't have the flexibility to carry a wide range of containers without costly, slow changeovers.

The Seacliff system relies on wide conveyor belts and electric trucks. The belts start right behind the transplant line. Containers are transplanted by hand or with one of two transplanters. They're then moved onto wide belts, where they're staged until the transport cart is ready to load.

To do that, the truck operator backs up to the belt, which is the same width and height as the truck's belt. The truck is lined up using an infrared sensor, and a drive mechanism from the truck links into the staging belt. The driver flips a switch, activating both the truck's belt and

Bob Ondejko's Plant Truck sets the plants right where the driver wants them.

the staging belt to feed the pots or flats onto the truck. In just ten seconds or so, the driver is ready to head into the greenhouse.

Once in the proper section, he backs into the bay where he wants to set out the product, then lowers the rear of the belt down to the floor. Thin metal plates smooth the transition between belt and concrete. He then engages the belt and drives forward. As he does, the belt rolls backward at the exact same speed, feeding the product right onto the floor. If the truck changes speed, the belt does, too, ensuring that pots wind up right where the driver wants them.

Picking up works the same way, except Bob is designing a fork device to handle pots because the metal plates won't slide under them like it slides under flats.

The photo above shows the truck setting out fifty-six 12-in. patio pots, the most difficult container to unload because they're top-heavy. One person can space about 600 an hour. Most other containers—bedding flats, shuttle trays (for 4- and 6-in. pots), 10-in. baskets, window boxes—are moved at about 1,000 per hour, which Bob says was their goal, to keep up with the production lines.

The battery-powered trucks are fairly simple. The battery pack slides out for recharging, and a fresh pack slides in—the carts never have to park for recharging. An electronic controller coordinates the speed of the belt to the truck.

So far, Bob has built three trucks. The plan is to have two trucks available for each loading belt for filling the farthest points on the nursery. That will let them maintain the 1,000-to-1,200-container pace they need. The two acres closest to the production area can be handled by just one truck.

The best news is that the Ondejkos aren't keeping their invention to themselves. Flier USA has already started to produce the Plant Truck and the entire system and plans to show it at the Ohio Short Course in July. They're also helping out by finishing up the design work on the final bits, such as staging belts for pots and the forks for picking pots up for shipping.

Why don't the Ondejkos keep the technology to themselves, for the competitive advantage? "We're growers," John replies. "This is a sideline."

Summer 2000

Better Sprays

Kurt Becker

Your old sprayer's pump is wheezing as you fill the solution tank for possibly the final time. Maybe you're concerned with the time it takes to spray your greenhouse. Or you may be wondering if you're making the most effective applications possible.

All of these are reasons to consider a new sprayer. However, spraying is much different than it used to be, with many different types of chemical applicators available and many decisions you must make about your needs. Certainly, you could make use of almost any sprayer available, but the most efficient use is your goal. However, just one type of sprayer usually won't be enough. You should view your sprayers as tools in a toolbox. A wrench works well on bolts; it's not much good for pounding nails.

What's Available?

There are three basic types of chemical application equipment used in greenhouses: high-volume hydraulic sprayers, targeted low-volume sprayers, and ultra low-volume applicators. Each machine has its place. And they all have advantages and disadvantages.

High-volume hydraulic sprayers

The standard hydraulic sprayer has been around forever. Often it's the most effective treatment for an out-of-control pest problem. Because it's a useful, flexible tool for general application, spot treatments, and the best option for applying plant growth regulators, a hydraulic sprayer is still a must.

Standard hydraulic sprayers usually operate at pressures between 100 and 300 psi, output between 2 and 4 gal. per minute, and have average particle sizes between 200 and 400 microns. Some hydraulic sprayers offer lower volumes, usually less than one GPM, and higher pressures, over 500 psi. These are useful because they don't overwet the plants but create a finer droplet spectrum and allow a more deliberate, controlled application.

Targeted low-volume sprayers

Caught somewhere between hydraulic sprayers and true aerosol foggers, the targeted low-volume sprayers offer flexibility with better coverage. Typically characterized by lower flow rates (generally less than a liter per minute) and smaller particle sizes (between 30 and 100 microns), targeted low-volume sprayers are intended to be directed at their target. This allows for spot treatment and focused application to problem areas. Because the particle size isn't too small, these sprayers can be used in shadehouses or even outdoors in light winds. They allow the flexibility of spraying one bench or the entire house at a quicker pace than with standard hydraulic sprayers. Plus, they offer the benefits of low-volume chemical application: little to no runoff, more even coverage, and greatly reduced amounts of water. Types of equipment in this range include high-pressure cold foggers, electrostatic sprayers, mist blowers, and rotary disk atomizers.

Ultra low-volume sprayers

These machines are most commonly called foggers. ULV equipment generally uses very small quantities of water (2 liters per 10,000 sq. ft. of greenhouse) and generates spray droplets smaller than 25 microns in diameter. Because of the small particle size, ULV sprayers typically need to be used in an enclosed space to contain the spray solution. For best results, proper air circulation is necessary. Generally, ULV sprayers reduce application time by operating quickly or even automatically. Even though they use dramatically less water, they create billions of small particles that cover plant surfaces evenly. ULV foggers can be very effective as a preventative tool. They're easy to use and because of time savings, they get used more regularly. ULV equipment includes timer-controlled stationary foggers, total release aerosol canisters, and thermal foggers.

How to Choose?

With a basic understanding of each type of sprayer, it's possible to determine the best machine for any greenhouse. For example: While a grower with a garden center containing tomatoes, herbs, and geraniums may prefer a ULV approach, it wouldn't be as practical as a targeted sprayer. Because the ULV fogger treats everything in the house, the grower would be limited to the pesticides available for use on the edible crops. A targeted low-volume sprayer would allow the flexibility of using different pesticides with the benefit of low-volume spraying and a reduction in application time over hydraulic application.

It's important to consider your entire greenhouse—structure, environment, and crops—when choosing a sprayer. While there are more choices than in the past, each type is focused on specific benefits. By understanding these benefits along with their corresponding disadvantages, you can better choose the right sprayer for the job.

October 2000

Benching Today: Beyond Boards

Paula A. Yantorno

No one ever said it would be easy. But with new technology and innovative systems, today's growers are finding the perfect bench systems to fit their growing needs. While many are the standard bench choices that have been on the greenhouse scene for years, some growers are making the change to less labor-intensive systems. Benches now tend to maximize the available growing space, reduce physical handling of product, eliminate watering with hoses and emitters, and meet mounting water conservation requirements.

Greenhouse owners calculating square footage costs and yields for their greenhouses know every inch of space is valuable for turning a profit. With start-up or retrofitting expenses and labor costs increasing, bench systems play an important part in the number-crunching game.

Making Your Choice

Which bench system you choose can also depend on what crops you're growing and where you're located. For example, the labor market in Colorado is much more open than in the New England states, where growers find it hard to hire people willing to do "stoop labor."

Overall greenhouse size also often determines bench choices. Bob Riney, American Clay Works, Denver, Colorado, says that few wooden benches are being built these days—many small growers starting out with just a 30-by-90-ft. greenhouse begin by building simple wood benches with chicken-wire tops, then advance to metal benches later, as their businesses grow.

David Johnson, United Greenhouse Systems, Edgerton, Wisconsin, says a lot of growers still make their own benching, spending their own time to create "economical benches" out of materials such as concrete, fencing, and lath, but he has seen an increase in rolling bench and containerized systems. According to David, more sophisticated growers are using containerized benches with built-in ebb-and-flow watering or rolling bench tops made of expanded metal Bench Mesh.

Rolling benches are real space savers with configurations that can create a single aisle wherever it's needed. By using rolling benches and eliminating wasted aisle space, growers maximize their available growing space. Standard aisles with stationary benches can use up to a third of available greenhouse space, but palletized and rolling systems can be 90% efficient.

At Center Greenhouse Inc., Denver, Colorado, owners dismantled the original raised redwood carnation benches when they switched to a bedding range in 1975, removing the soil and laying side boards flat in the aisles to create a giant redwood deck. Now, these benches have been replaced with movable benches by Nexus Greenhouse Systems, with about 25% of the entire greenhouse range in rolling metal benches. They're used as an intense growing environment for seedling germination and vegetative cutting propagation. Using rolling benches has increased growing space by 25% . They're set up in a peninsula-type layout (one aisle with benches sideways down the house) with two 50-ft. greenhouses each sharing an 8-ft. walkway in the gutter. Heating and irrigation lines are stationary beneath the bench structure, and the bench top moves above them.

Bartlett Bench & Wire Inc. specializes in "galvanized after welded" wire mesh that's sold in rolls or panels for bench tops. Because it's galvanized after it has been welded, this product has a thicker zinc coating and longer life than mesh that's galvanized before it's welded. The rolled Bench Mesh (primarily 1½-in. square mesh) is mostly used by growers with wood frame benches, while Bartlett's sells panels (mostly 4-by-1-in. mesh) to growers for both standard metal frames and movable benching.

In April, Bartlett Bench & Wire Inc. began production on their new Channel Bench Top, which should prove valuable to growers fighting the tangle of heat pipes or irrigation tubing under their moving benches. The Channel Bench Top is a standard bench top with wire mesh channels attached to the underside in place of steel tubing cross supports. The channel is U-shaped and is 3 in. wide and 3 in. tall. The 1½-in. square mesh allows most heat or irrigation tubing to slide through the channels, keeping all of the heat or irrigation tubing right where it should be—under the top but above the rollers. The tubing is incorporated inside the bench frame and moves with the bench.

Ebb and Flood: Time and Labor Savings

Anyone who has ever had to drag heavy hoses around a greenhouse can appreciate the benefits of the ebb-and-flood method of irrigation and growing. These growing systems can be stationary, rolling, palletized, or flood floor types. Subirrigation systems put water below the roots, hold it there for a predetermined time, then drain it away, sometimes into a runoff recovery holding tank.

Growers who use ebb-and-flood methods and manufacturers such as Midwest GROmaster Inc. are singing the praises of this type of bench (and floor) system. Henry Huntington, owner of Pleasant View Gardens, Loudon, New Hampshire, uses a combination of bench types, including rolling benches with expanded metal tops and ebb-and-flood benches. "Pleasant View is probably one of the first greenhouses in the Northeast that's doing ebb and flood," says Henry, who suggested that the New England trend seems to still be in rolling benches. He also added that a lot of smaller greenhouses with minimal capital investments still have traditional, wooden benches with metal tops.

"Ebb and flood is a great system, a huge labor savings," says Henry. With a fully automated system, one person can water an acre or more in only twenty to thirty minutes. Findings by Midwest GROmaster cite additional savings of 30 to 95% on water and fertilizer, depending on the previous methods used.

One of the disadvantages of ebb-and-flood bench systems, according to Midwest GROmaster, is the slightly higher up-front costs compared with other benching systems. Most customers have said they had a ten-month to two-year payback period in savings. As an example, a typical 6-ft. wide expanded metal rolling bench costs $2.80 to $3.40 per sq. ft. for good quality, to which you would add $.50 to $.75 for a typical drip irrigation system. This compares to $4.20 to $4.95 per sq. ft. for a typical ebb-and-flood bench system, depending on factors such as types of controls and plumbing.

Henry, who grows about one million 4-in. pots each year, is building an expansion range this summer, which will have a flood floor system. While flood benches would be ideal, he says, "Flood floors are less expensive to install, and there are added benefits." Flood floors offer versatility, without locking you into any specific container size. Also, you don't have permanent aisles. Henry also notes the advantage of being able to move carts directly to the product. The biggest downfall, he says, is the problem of "stoop labor," but he's trying to minimize that with conveyor use.

At McClish's Plants Plus Greenhouses, Washington Court House, Ohio, Brent McClish practices water-saving methods on a small scale. About seven years ago, he switched from wooden benches to a trough system. Much like gutters, the aluminum troughs (from Westbrook Greenhouse Systems in Canada) are about 7 in. wide and ¾ in. high on the sides. A 4½-in. pot fits into the trough. Each trough is set up on a slight slope, with a tank at one end to recirculate the water. Fourteen troughs are positioned across each 8-ft.-wide metal bench.

Karen Panter, Colorado State University extension agent (commercial greenhouse), is quick to point out future issues of importance for greenhouse owners and the need to look into ebb-and-flood methods of growing, especially in relation to water quality and quantity. The EPA and the Colorado Department of Public Health and Environment (Pollution Prevention and Water Quality Divisions) are beginning to target nonpoint source pollution. (Point source is where a pollutant can be traced to a specific business.) In agriculture, however, pollution is considered non-source because there isn't one spot where fertilizers and pesticides can be seen entering the environment. Because of this emphasis on non-source pollution, there will be more focus on the importance of water quality as it leaves the greenhouse. "We'll see more water reuse, so there will be more ebb-and-flood arrangements," she warns. "Unfortunately, most growers will probably be regulated into it rather than being proactive."

The Future Is Automation

Automation in any form seems to be the way of the future in greenhouse benching systems. Back in the late 1970s, American growers were fascinated with the laborsaving mechanization of Dutch tray systems. Today the Dutch tray system, also known as palletized or containerized benching, is becoming more and more common.

At Busch Greenhouse, Denver, Colorado, Dutch trays by Intransit are used in a one-acre system of planting, growing, and shipping. Benches are moved from the planting area into the greenhouse, then back into the packing area for shipping. Employees manually push benches along stationary rollers. Owner Dan Busch says the benches are great for specialized, single crops but that the system becomes inconvenient when used with a variety of crops. The Dutch trays require a certain level of management to control what moves into and out of the greenhouse. "During the first year when using the system for propagation, we realized a labor savings of 60%," he says.

Efficiency—with Any Bench

Efficiency is the buzzword for systems like the one at Greiling Farms, Orlando, Florida, where computerized, motorized benches move product throughout the greenhouse with little human effort. Some automated setups use electric, computer-controlled container trains that move pallets off of benches and down aisles on rail tracks.

In addition to using palletized benches by rolling them along the tops of bench frames, some can be used as the name suggests. Pallet-style bench tops can be moved using a forklift or a pallet jack. Automatic stackers also make storing movable benches a possibility. A new pallet bench, the Wing Pallet, created by Len Van Wingerden, V. W. Systems, Somers, Connecticut, is a plastic bench that can be stacked in many configurations and can be used for growing and shipping, as well as for retail merchandising.

While stationary bench systems are the least expensive when compared to ebb-and-flood and Dutch trays, using no benches is probably the least expensive method of all. Center Greenhouse Inc. grows more than 100,000 sq. ft. on the ground inside glass greenhouses, using 1 1/2-in. round river rock over a clay base and landscape fabric weed barrier. The large rocks and groundcover keep any plants from rooting into the ground. For half of the year, the area becomes a finish area for perennial liners; for the other half, it is used for bedding plants. "The system is just more economical than benches," says owner Paul Yantorno. "Denver enjoys a large, inexpensive labor pool that other parts of the country don't have. But if the labor situation changes in the future, we plan to go to a movable tray system. Plus, our place is built so that runoff collects in one spot. If it ever becomes an environmental necessity, we're ready to do that."

When selecting landscape fabric for groundcover use in the greenhouse, Landmaster Products, Englewood, Colorado, offers several points to consider. The fabric should be just strong enough to withstand the most vigorous stresses of application and should have a consistent, even distribution of fibers that's tight enough to keep weedy grasses from coming through. It should also be porous enough to allow water and air to pass freely to the soil. Marshall Hogan recommends using Polyspun Landscape Fabric.

The porous polyester fibers, along with the special patented spunweb construction, "make Polyspun landscape fabrics the most water- and air-permeable spunbonded landscape fabric available."

Most growers take advantage of all available space when planning greenhouse configurations. Many have devised innovative solutions to maximize space, such as the two-layer system of rolling benches that Tagawa Greenhouses uses on a range at its Brighton, Colorado, facility. Another option is the ECHO System, marketed by Cherry Creek Systems, an overhead automated cable system for hanging baskets that uses above the bench space without compromising the crop below. No matter how greenhouses achieve it—with hanging systems, double layers, rolling, or movable benches—more growing area equals more dollars in greenhouse currency.

The consensus of manufacturers and growers seems to be that greenhouse benching system trends are leaning toward methods of growing that both reduce labor and increase production square footage. Growers are taking advantage of easier irrigation methods with ebb-and-flood systems and rolling benches that allow more growing area and better use of aisle space. The philosophy of Cherry Creek Systems says it best: "Our industry is approaching the end of an era . . . the end of labor-intensive, low-producing, and low-profit greenhouse operations. But with every end comes a new beginning . . . a new way of doing things. As labor costs increase along with all other costs of production, greenhouse owners are faced with no other option but to automate!" Automation with palletized systems and subirrigation features seems to be the future. And, the future is now.

Summer 1998

More Space from the Same Space

Chris Beytes

Danish growers, who use as much sophisticated greenhouse automation as you'll find anywhere, also make widespread use of a simple and relatively common benching system: rolling benches. Why? Because rolling benches provide the greatest compromise between space use and labor efficiency of any type of greenhouse bench. The Danes, facing some of the highest land, labor, and energy costs in the world, have crunched the numbers and tell us that, in many situations, rolling benches are the way to go.

For those who haven't seen them, rolling benches are much like standard stationary benches, except that they sit on a pair of long pipes that allow them to be moved from side to side. A 6-ft. wide rolling bench might move 2 ft. left or right. This means the benches can "share" a common aisle, rather than having to leave one on each side of every bench. (Don't confuse them with moveable benches, often called Dutch trays or container benches, that can be moved throughout the greenhouse range on rollers.)

Let's try some math: Suppose your greenhouse has 21-ft.-wide bays, each with three 5-ft. wide benches and three 2-ft. wide aisles—that's 15 ft. of benches and 6 ft. of aisles, which means 72% of the bay is benches, 28% is aisles.

Now, lets make those benches 6 ft. wide and leave one 3-ft. aisle (you could make them 6 ft. 4 in. wide, with a 2-ft. aisle, but that odd bench size wastes material). Now we have 18 ft. of benches and just 3 ft. of aisles, or 86% growing space and 14% aisles—an increase of 14%. That's like adding 6,000 sq. ft. of growing space to a 40,000 sq. ft. greenhouse!

Granted, there is a cost, primarily in retrofitting the greenhouse with new or modified benches. If you're handy and are growing on lumber benches with concrete block legs, changing over might be as simple as nailing on an extra foot or two of bench to one side, and fitting pipe rollers underneath.

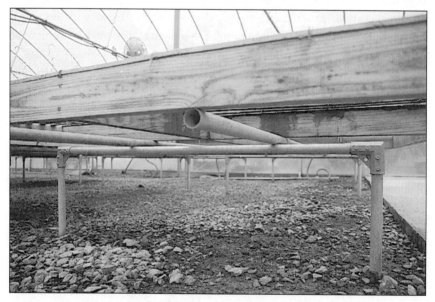

Roller detail of a homemade rolling bench.

It's been done in many an old greenhouse (just make sure the bench legs are sturdy enough to avoid toppling when you push the bench).

Most growers, however, opt for manufactured benches constructed of steel or aluminum because poorly designed benches can "walk" out of line. Plus, you want a lightweight bench that glides from side to side fairly effortlessly—especially if you don't want employees throwing their backs out.

If you're considering expanding, look into rolling benches for your new and existing greenhouses. Industry sources say the square-foot cost of stationary versus rolling benches is very similar—the biggest difference is that with rolling benches you're buying more square feet of bench. But the per-square-foot cost is a fraction of what new growing space costs.

February 2000

Bench Racing

Chris Beytes

In the good old days, the purposes of a greenhouse bench were simple: to keep plants out of the dirt and keep growers from throwing out their backs.

However, growers quickly realized that a bench could do much more: It could provide airflow, water—even transportation. Plus, they calculated that benches were cheaper than greenhouses, so they started squeezing more bench space into their houses.

Today, you've got a dizzying array of choices for growing your crop: on the ground on plastic or cloth, on stationary wooden benches; on commercial stationary metal benches, on rolling benches (again, wood or metal, homemade or commercial), on concrete ebb-and-flood floors, or on a mobile bench system.

Let's stick with the basics: the pros and cons of stationary and rolling benches.

It's All about Compromise

Bench design is always a compromise between space use and labor efficiency. The closer you squeeze your benches together, the more difficult they are to work around.

Rolling benches are a good example. They allow you to eliminate all but one aisle per greenhouse bay by rolling the benches from side to side. This increases your growing space, but limits crop access to one aisle at a time. If you're growing a labor-intensive crop such as pot mums that requires disbudding, this could be a problem. Also, if you plan to sell at retail from the space, your customers will have a tough time getting to plants.

Stationary benches, on the other hand, give you more access to your crops, but you sacrifice space-use efficiency. On average, you'll get 60 to 70% space use from stationary benches. Rolling benches can increase that to 70 to 85%. Increasing your bench space—and production—by 15% can help pay for your bench system. In today's highly competitive marketplace, rolling benches are almost an essential.

Size Wise

What about bench dimensions and aisle width? Again, that's entirely up to the grower. Five to 6 ft. wide is standard; with benches wider than that, workers can't access the middle of the bench. And keep in mind potential worker's compensation claims for back injuries! Bench height should be 26 to 36 in. Container size can also play a role in choosing a bench width: Measure your flats and shuttle trays to make sure you won't be wasting space by leaving 6 in. of empty bench.

Bench length usually is dependent on the structure and the grower. You have to decide how far you want your employees to walk. One 100-ft. bench is more efficient, space-wise, but two 50-ft. benches with a center aisle are easier to work around.

Aisle width also depends on employee comfort—18 in. is the minimum that manufacturers recommend, but they've seen growers go narrower. Retailers, of course, should allow ample space and height for customer access and comfort.

Main aisle width depends on the type of plant transport you use. Again, it's a compromise between space use and labor efficiency. Allow 4 ft. as a minimum for handcarts and at least 8 ft. if you plan to use motorized vehicles.

Homemade or Store-bought?

Cinder blocks, two-by-fours, and snow fence or welded wire make good benches. Cost is roughly $.75 to $1.00 per sq. ft, but that doesn't include labor to build them. A 5-by-50-ft. bench would cost $200 to $250 for materials. They last reasonably well, but are difficult to set up level and straight.

For long life and durability, commercial benches are usually built of galvanized steel and aluminum. Most have built-in leveling systems so they can easily be set level. Cost is roughly $2.50 to $3.00 per sq. ft. of bench space. Interestingly, commercial rolling benches usually don't cost much more than commercial stationary benches—you just have to buy more square feet of rolling bench.

Another consideration with commercial benches is whether the legs are sunk into concrete or attached to a concrete floor. In-ground legs are more rigid and may require less bracing than freestanding or bolted legs.

Like everything else in the greenhouse, benches come down to what you want, what you need, and what you can afford. But, as with any equipment decision, plan for the long haul.

January 1998

Bar Codes Solve the Plug Inventory Dilemma

Chris Millar

Knox Nursery's new state-of-the-art six-acre plug range in Winter Garden, Florida, is definitely a showcase of the latest greenhouse technologies. In planning and developing this new greenhouse, Bruce Knox's goal was to take advantage of any technology that was available and practical that would reduce labor costs. From the seed sowing lines, which are capable of producing 1,800 plug trays an hour, to the high-tech Argus environmental control system, this theme is evident throughout the greenhouse. Automation and technology are used at every level.

One key area, however, lagged behind the rest: inventory control. While every other system was in place when production began more than a year ago, Bruce hadn't settled on a system for tracking inventory, which resulted in some fairly serious growing pains the first season.

That problem is behind us now, thanks to a bar code–based system that tracks every table and every tray through every step of production, from sowing to shipping. And best of all, 80% of the system uses off-the-shelf software, saving us time and money. Our total budget was $40,000. Here's how it works.

Too Many Plugs, Too Much Movement
Knox Nursery produces almost 1,500 varieties of plugs in five different tray sizes. Most of the orders we ship out include several different plant varieties.

One of the prominent features of the new plug range is the Dutch table system we grow on. Each table holds forty-two plug trays and can move easily throughout the greenhouse on a system of tracks. While these tables make it easy to move product they also present a liability: In a greenhouse equipped with Dutch tables, plants tend to be moved around considerably more than in a range that has fixed benches. Since it's practically an effortless task to move several tables, our growers take advantage of this to shuttle the tables into different growing zones in the greenhouse during each crop's growing cycle. However, this creates a challenge when it comes to keeping track of where the product is at any given time. The logistics of pulling multiple orders that all have dozens of varieties are complicated enough—pulling orders is even more difficult if you don't know where the plants are in the range! To put our situation in perspective, we currently have a capacity for 3,500 tables and 147,000 plug trays—and our future plans for expansion could more than triple our capacity.

The main challenge was to come up with a system that would track each individual plug tray from sowing all the way through production to shipping. We wanted to keep an accurate inventory of what quantities were on hand as well as the location of each plug tray.

Our first two seasons in the new range demonstrated a need to have a better handle on our inventory. We had used manual counting and verifying, which gave us fairly accurate numbers on what we had in the greenhouse. But that didn't tell us the specific locations of anything. We tried to group similar crops with the same finish times in the greenhouse, although at times these groups could consist of several hundred tables. To search through that many tables for one specific tray can be time consuming and tedious, to say the least. One of the most frustrating things that can happen to a plug producer is to spend several weeks growing a tray for a specific customer and then not find the needed tray at the time of shipping—only to have the tray in question show up weeks later, ready for the dump! We wanted to make sure that never happens at Knox.

Our Requirements

We decided early on that bar codes would be at the heart of our inventory system. Bar codes are widely used today, and there is a variety of equipment that can read or scan them. We were already using custom-made label printer/applicators to label our plug trays; adding a bar code to our existing label presented no extra cost and was fairly easy to do. Plus, we found no practical alternatives to bar codes for identifying our plug trays, Dutch tables, and various growing locations in the greenhouse.

The first and most important step was to record what was being sown at the beginning of production. In seed sowing, we had two main concerns. We didn't want to slow down the production lines in any way. If possible, we wanted to record what we produced in a totally "hands-free" fashion.

After each tray is sown, it's laid onto a table with an automated table loader. We first needed to associate each plug tray with the table on which it's placed. Then, as each table is moved into the greenhouse, we needed to be able to record its location. Plus, all table movement from this point until the product is shipped needed to be recorded as well. By keeping track of table movement, we'd know exactly where each plug tray was when it came time to ship it.

Prior to shipping, we wanted to be able to print picking tickets that include the products' specific locations. When a tray is ready to be boxed, we wanted to remove it from inventory. In addition, Bruce thought we should use the system as a final quality control check, making sure each tray is actually needed for the order being boxed. Finally, we wanted to print our FedEx labels with the contents of the box printed on the label.

Warehousing Provides the Answers

Once our requirements were outlined, we began our search for ways to make it happen. The first place we looked was commercial inventory software designed for the horticultural industry. This software uses handheld wand or pen-type scanners. This wasn't the solution for us, as handheld pen scanners would require too much labor. Next, we looked to warehouse inventory and "plant floor data collection" specialists for help. After all, in theory, our needs aren't that much different than a typical warehouse. Just like most warehouses, we store our product in containers that can be moved from one location to another.

We invited four companies that specialize in inventory and data collection to review our requirements and put together proposals on how to meet our needs. We received four very different solutions. Here's what we chose.

The solution in production

This application, especially in production, could be called "data collection." IBM makes a line of data collection terminals that are capable of collecting data from a bar-code scanner. The backbone of this system is the IBM 7526 Data Collection Terminal. We have four of these connected to a PC using an Ethernet network. There are two of these small units in seed sowing—one on each of our two lines in production and another pair in shipping. Each of the terminals in seed sowing has two bar-code scanners connected to them. Both of these scanners are "raster" laser scanners, which are the best type for reading bar-code labels that are moving. One scanner reads the labels on the plug trays as they move down the conveyor line. The other scanner reads the bar codes on our Dutch tables as they move out of the table loader machine.

The solution in the greenhouse

Every growing location (a row of twenty-four tables) in the greenhouse also is labeled with a bar code. As the tables leave seed sowing, we have a record of which trays are on which tables. To track the movement of the tables in the greenhouse, we use Symbol handheld laser scanners. By scanning the table and its location, we now have the complete inventory of what was sown and where it is.

Managing the inventory in the greenhouse requires some discipline. We had to make certain that anytime there is table movement it's recorded with one of the three handheld scanners. Anytime there's any inventory shrinkage, it needs to be recorded with the handheld units. These handheld scanners record the information you scan until put in a docking station that uploads the information to the PC. We could have invested in Radio Frequency scanners that would automatically update the computer, but they're more expensive (although coming down in cost) and only save a small amount of time.

The solution in shipping

The first thing that's done at the beginning of a ship day is to load into the PC a list of all orders to be shipped. Next, we print picking tickets that detail each customer's order and the product's location in the greenhouse. Employees assemble these trays and push them up to the shipping warehouse for packaging.

We have two data collection terminals in shipping that each have two handheld scanners attached. There's a scanner located at each of the four packing stations that are used to scan the plug trays as they are being packaged. Once a tray is scanned in shipping, the first thing that happens is a check for accuracy. Does this plug tray belong to this order? Next, the tray is removed from the inventory database on the PC. Finally, we print the required shipping label, which also shows the box's contents.

As mentioned before, we have a network of four data collection terminals connected to a PC. The actual inventory is maintained on this PC using Microsoft Access, a popular database program. The total software solution was about 80% off the shelf and 20% custom written. IBM provides a program called DCC Connect with their data collection terminals. This keeps the network running and records what the terminals report. The custom-written software moves information from DCC Connect to Access verifies the orders and creates the shipping labels.

Benefits

The first obvious benefit of our new system is accurate information. We now know the exact quantities we have on hand, as well as the location of every plug tray, including the table it's on and the specific greenhouse location it's in. Plus, using bar codes to manage the inventory beats manual counting any day. We expect to see a big payoff this spring when we start shipping large numbers of trays, as the labor spent on pulling and assembling orders should be drastically reduced.

Customers benefit, too. By having a better handle on our inventory, we can avoid last minute cancellations. And by printing the contents of the box on the shipping label, our customers can identify the material they want to unpack first without opening every box in their order.

Advice to Other Growers

We experienced long delays with our programmers for various reasons. When entering in to any type of contract, specify a bonus or penalty for making or missing deadlines. Break your project up into sections that make sense. This may be easier than trying to tackle a big job all at once.

What's Next?

The next step for this inventory system is to tie this database in to our company's mainframe. We have future plans to upgrade our main computer, as well as the software we use to run the company. When we're ready to do that, we will certainly want to link the two systems together.

Knox even has a Web page under construction (www.knoxnursery.com) that will be linked to our inventory system. With a better handle on inventory, we'll be able to post availability lists much earlier than at present, giving us more time to sell anything that's not sown for a precommited order.

And one other use for the system may be with finished bedding production. There's no reason we can't track flats and pots using the same bar-code system, although with more hand scanning, bringing some of the same efficiencies to our finished plant business that we expect to realize in our plug business.

September 1998

Chapter 3
Transplanters

The CE Tray: Savior or Threat?

Chris Beytes

The idea of uniform container standards has been argued for years, and the topic has become especially critical with the advent of automated plug sowing and transplanting equipment. Finally, the industry has its first container standards, which came out of a meeting initiated by Flier USA President Robert Lando. (Flier manufactures seeders, transplanters, tray dispensers, and other container-handling equipment.)

Back in August, Robert invited the major plug tray manufacturers to a meeting to discuss the idea of creating standard dimensions for plug trays. "We didn't think it was our place [to set the standard]," Robert explains. "We just thought that if this meeting could be the vehicle to get there, then that would be great."

The group had no problem agreeing that the industry would benefit from common elements, and that it wouldn't be difficult to agree on the elements needed to be standardized: cell spacing, tray width, drain hole size and placement, height, and minimum tolerances of each dimension.

These standards would still allow enough design flexibility so that each manufacturer could still create unique products. "It's the only thing that makes sense," says David Steiner, vice president for Blackmore Company. Blackmore not only is a leader in trays and seeders, they also distribute Harrison and Rapid transplanters, so they understand the mechanical benefits of a plug tray standard. "When you have a $500 dislodger, it's not that big a deal," says David. "But when you have a $100,000 transplanting machine that you can't use because somebody didn't make the right kind of trays, then it becomes an issue. That's what has forced the standardization in the industry."

Jeff Kissenger, marketing manager for Landmark Plastics, agrees with David. "We view it as a benefit to the industry." Jeff wouldn't reveal when they'll begin manufacturing and promoting CE (common element) compatible trays;

other manufacturers say they'll have CE trays available this spring or as customers begin to ask for them.

Like Flier, Bouldin & Lawson, which builds transplanters, sees the standard as "an excellent idea." Says Marketing Manager Jim Fowler, "After we adapt to [the new] dimensions, it will actually make our jobs as manufacturers a little bit easier because we won't have such a variety of setups to do. We won't have to custom-build every machine."

Possibly the biggest benefit of the standard is for growers buying in plugs and using an automatic transplanter. Right now, you have to make sure any supplier you use is growing in a tray that's compatible with your machine, or else you have to spend $800 to $5,000 or more adapting your transplanter to a different tray. With the CE tray, you can configure your transplanter to that standard (if it isn't already). Then, any CE tray you buy from any source will run through your machine. Plug growers we've talked to say they haven't yet started discussing the trays with their customers, but they think a standard is long overdue.

"I think everybody would be better off to conform to a standard configuration that still allows flexibility and interchangeability between plug sources," says David Wadsworth, owner of Suncoast Greenhouses.

Speedling's Barry Ruda sees the new tray as a marketing tool: "There are some definite advantages to going to [a standard], because it's a real problem to sell to new customers because of transplanters [and their need for specific trays]."

Changing over to CE trays could require some more investment in your existing equipment. You'll have to make sure your existing plug popper or transplanter fits the new tray, or else have it modified. If you're buying a new machine, just specify that it be set up for CE trays, and you'll be able to transplant from any source without any additional costs.

If you grow your own plugs, you don't have to do anything: Tray companies assure customers that they'll continue to make their existing trays as long as there's demand for them.

A bigger issue than cost is that standards are fine—as long as we're the ones setting them. What if chains decide on a standard pack, for instance? Some in the industry express that fear. However, there's never been any evidence that chains are interested in those types of standards. If anything, we have too many containers because of the chains' interest in always being different from their competition.

In fact, standards for finished packs and pots would go a long way toward reducing equipment costs and increasing innovation. The CE meeting came about through an earlier meeting between Flier and two hanging basket companies. The topic: Could they agree on standard rim and hanger designs that would let Flier design a machine for automatically attaching basket hangers?

However, Robert emphasizes that the CE movement has no intention of impacting finished plant containers, except to make growers' lives easier. "There's always a place for variety in the finished plant marketplace," he says.

February 1999

Full Circle

Chris Beytes

Few growers have invested in the industry the way Green Circle Growers has this season. The Oberlin, Ohio, plug and finished plant producer is the first to sell 100% of their plugs in reusable CE (common element) plug trays. The big benefit to Green Circle's customers comes from the trays' ability to run very dependably through automation such as transplanters.

To do that, Green Circle made a multimillion dollar investment, including 700,000 Dillen injection-molded trays, two plug poppers and six plug fixing machines (fixers are roughly $80,000 each), and a new high-speed sowing line that runs trays through sideways instead of lengthwise. They even had to add two inches to every one of their 3,000 growing tables to fit the new trays. Oh, did we mention the additional five acres of open-roof greenhouse ($22 per sq. ft., fully loaded) they added to accommodate their increased production?

Green Circle's David Van Wingerden, who took us on a tour of the upgraded facility, told us that the entire investment is built around the CE tray, a concept Green Circle has championed since its conception. CE trays, regardless of the manufacturer, share several common dimensions that allow them to fit most automated equipment—such as transplanters—set up to CE specifications. Rigid trays go one step further: They don't get bent out of shape in handling, so they fit machinery perfectly even after many uses. And they're "endless," which means that when they're end to end or side to side, there's equal spacing between every plug in all trays, essentially allowing you to transplant from one, continuous plug tray.

Green Circle has tested rigid trays in their own production for four years precisely because they work so well in their own seeders and transplanters. That's why they decided to pass those same benefits along to their customers. (Green Circle's plugs are available through Express Seed).

Because each tray is reused, it gets its own permanent bar code label (from the car battery industry), which stays with the tray for life. The bar code is used to track each tray from sowing to shipping. They can even track the tray's history and what's been in it. A human-readable label is printed on the opposite side to identify the variety in the tray. It's cleaned off after each use.

If the tray is the star, then the new one-acre fixing greenhouse is center stage. Here, Green Circle can now accurately grade their plugs to a guaranteed minimum count of 490 for a 512 and 280 for a 288. The industry standard has been around 450 for a 512.

Trays come into the fixing greenhouse on tables. Workers feed them to one of two Flier plug poppers, which use cameras and computers to identify and blow out any missing or weak seedlings. The trays are put back on tables and are moved to one of six patchers, which works like a transplanter to fill any now-empty cells. Then they go back onto tables and into the greenhouse. This manual tray handling is temporary while they decide how to automate the process.

Linda Kyer checks plugs from a patcher while David Van Wingerden looks on.

In fact, logistics is now Green Circle's biggest challenge, says Production Manager Dan Reed, because there's a very narrow window (as little as forty-eight hours) when plugs can be mechanically graded. So they've had to adjust their sowing schedule to accommodate a grading schedule. They also run into challenges keeping production lots together as they move from sowing to germination to grading and into the greenhouse. Tables are numbered to help workers keep them together; Robert says they're exploring electronic table and tray tracking methods.

High-count plug trays in the volumes that Green Circle produces (some 300 million total) are impossible without automation. David calculates that one fixing machine will replace 32,000 to 40,000 plugs per eight-hour shift. An employee might do 4,000. Each machine needs two operators, so he figures he's saving eight people per machine per shift, or ninety-six people a day in the peak season. Still, a few sizes and varieties, such as dahlia, marigold, and 512 vinca, are popped and fixed by hand because they're almost impossible for the popper's cameras to accurately grade.

So if you buy your plugs from Express and get reusable trays, what do you do with them? Are they clean? Are you paying more? David says that every tray is thoroughly cleaned and sterilized. In four years of in-house use, they've had few problems with chemical residues or diseases.

As for cost, Green Circle hasn't implemented a deposit, even though the trays are nearly triple the price of traditional trays. On small orders, growers can ship them back, postage-paid. Green Circle's trucks pick up large rack orders. So far, about 95% have been returned (the bar code also helps them track trays). David hopes other plug growers will adopt the same technology so the recycling concept will become more widespread.

So if you're thinking about a transplanter and you've specified CE, there's at least one plug grower out there who's committed to helping you get the most out of it. Just don't forget to send your trays back!

Summer 2000

The Need for Speed

Chris Beytes

When the typical transplanter that pulls 32 plugs at one time just isn't fast enough or efficient enough for you, what do you do? If you're Tom Van Wingerden, you call your friend Frank Van Dijk in the Netherlands and order up a one-of-a-kind transplanter that will plant three trays of jumbo 606 packs—108 plants—at one time!

Tom, owner of North Carolina's Metrolina Greenhouses, helped pioneer the modern transplanter with the MetroPlanter, which he and Frank designed and sold for a time in the 1990s. The notable feature of its design is corkscrew-style grippers, which spin down around the plug to grab it, then quickly spin in the opposite direction to plant it. The design is easy on plugs, especially crops like begonias, which don't like to be bent or mishandled by the transplanter system.

Since giving up on the commercial transplanter business, Tom has owned a range of machines. He currently runs three TTA machines and at press time had another TTA on order. But they don't satisfy his need for a big, fast machine that has his patented screw grippers. So he called Frank, owner of FW Systems, and together they designed a MetroPlanter for the twenty-first century.

The centerpiece of the design is again the screws, which are identical to those on the original model. Frank redesigned the mechanism that rotates them to work with much less horsepower, and the machine takes advantage of all the latest computer technology.

A dibble unit is built into the transplanter's frame. That's one of the reasons this unit is so big: roughly 25 ft. long, 8 ft. wide, and 7½ ft. tall. And as for the weight of the behemoth, Tom's son, Art, says it's a whopping 2½ tons!

Metrolina grows all their own plugs in rigid, endless Winstrip trays—288 and 216 count. Tom says the endless design is what allows the new MetroPlanter to pull from three plug trays at the same time. And handling that many plugs at once gives a major speed advantage. Tom says it will do 1,300 606 flats an hour. "But, of course, we can't get the ink-jet printers to run that fast yet," he adds, "so we get it down to 800 or 900 an hour, and it runs smooth. We don't need more than that right now, but we do have the extra capacity."

When we visited, Tom's crew ran it long enough for us to shoot photos and video, "but because it is its first year, obviously there are still some changes yet to be made on it to be sure it runs smoothly," he explained. A call to Art a couple of months later revealed that it was now working "decently, but it's not yet where it should be." They're still trying to find the perfect size screw so they don't have to change them when they change plug sizes.

A major change that Metrolina will be making to their plug production is moving to one plug size for everything—a 200-count tray. Right now they use the 288s for early production and 216s for later, fast-turn crops such as ten-day impatiens. The new 200-count Winstrip tray will still give them quick turns late in the season, and Art says that it's specifically designed for mechanical transplanters. Plus, having just one plug size means they never have to change any automated equipment from one size to another, especially important if they invest in plug grading automation, as they plan to do. Tom's not worried about the added space they'd take up. He says they're going to work toward irrigating mature plugs with ebb and flood because it gives less cross-rooting on top of the plugs and helps develop more roots low in the cell.

But what about the new MetroPlanter, Tom? Is there any chance you'll decide to get back into the transplanter business? He shakes his head and says with a laugh, "This is for home-use only."

Summer 2000

Growers on Transplanters

Chris Beytes

Today, perhaps the only excuse for not owning an automatic transplanter is that you don't grow plants. Otherwise, the old excuses—labor is plentiful, you don't grow enough flats, you can't afford the high cost—have been thrown out the window by growers who have found many reasons for owning transplanters and by manufacturers who make transplanters for nearly every budget.

To take a fresh look at the transplanters currently on the market in North America, we asked growers who have been using the different machines for their opinions on quality, service and performance.

Transplanter: Harrison Transplanter Corp.
Grower: Jay Guild, Jay W. Guild Wholesale Grower, Peconic, New York

Jay Guild has nearly five years of transplanter experience, beginning with a small Harrison. That machine would transplant about 200 flats per hour. He quickly decided that he needed more speed, so he traded it in for a larger, faster Harrison, which he's been running for three years. It does 300 to 320 flats per hour from 512 plug trays and about 450 per hour from 288s.

Why Harrison? Because they're based less than half an hour from Jay's Long Island business. He says that was the biggest factor in his choice, especially considering that four years ago most transplanters were in the developmental stage. Harrison's location meant quick service and convenient training. He also likes the way the extractors work, picking up the plugs from the top without using dislodging pins, which Jay feels can disturb the plug's root ball.

Setup was relatively easy, he says, with no unexpected problems or expenses. The biggest equipment challenge has been occasional computer crashes due to operator error. Harrison is updating his software this winter. Their new machines use programmable logic controllers (PLCs) instead of PCs. This type of computer stands up under heavy industrial use and is common in most modern greenhouse automation.

Changing from 512s to 288s takes "minimal downtime," Jay reports. His biggest production challenge has been with plugs. He buys them in and has to make sure his supplier ships the same tray every time.

Maintenance-wise, the parts most likely to break are the extractors, usually after hitting a tray that wasn't quite the right size. He stocks spares, which can be quickly replaced.

Jay was growing about 40,000 to 50,000 trays per year when he first bought his transplanter. Now, he's up to about 90,000. And he's cut transplant labor from eight people down to four.

But the biggest benefit comes from efficiency. "At the height of the season, shipping the last week of April, we can fill the greenhouse up quicker," Jay says. "In other words, we can get that extra turn." He transplants 512s for the early crop and switches to the faster-to-finish 288s for the end of the season.

Jay says he didn't try to calculate payback when investing in his transplanter, but he's seen tremendous benefits from automation. "My help is happy. They're happy with me; everything runs smoother—that's priceless."

Transplanter: Rapid Automated Systems
Grower: Jim White, White's Greenhouse, Godfrey, Illinois

Jim White owns two Rapid 500 transplanters, one purchased in 1995 and a second bought in 1998. That's the best testimony to his satisfaction with Rapid's machines.

What's unique about Jim's setup is that he moves his transplanters through his greenhouses, rather than bringing the plants to the transplanters. His land is hilly, and transporting the flats after transplanting is difficult. Moving a transplanter only takes about twenty minutes, Jim says, "but we really don't want to lose [transplanting] a hundred flats in that time when we're busy." So, they'll move them during breaks or before or after a shift. They've equipped the houses with air connections to let them set up the transplanters anywhere.

Surprisingly, moving the transplanters hasn't caused any special maintenance problems. They bought the second Rapid so they'd always have a backup, but they'll run both this spring. "Rapid has been wonderful about support," Jim says. He can get parts shipped to him the next day. Last year, Jim sent the old transplanter in for a tune-up. Cost was minimal, he says, and Rapid went through the whole machine, making numerous upgrades.

White's transplants about 100,000 flats per year. Before automating, they were doing 175 per hour. Now they can do about 300, which Jim admits isn't as fast as many automated transplant lines. One major benefit, however, is that output is consistent. "We know how many flats we're going to put on the ground every day," Jim says. That makes planning and scheduling much easier.

The biggest problems they've faced? Flats. Jim says consistency in flats and plug trays is essential—he wastes a lot of time adjusting for various flat configurations. In fact, that's his best advice to growers considering transplanters: Decide what size packs and trays you want to use, and stick with them.

Also, invest in a tagger, Jim says: "You'll lose two people tagging all day, versus half a person with an automatic tagger."

Transplanter: Flier Holland
Grower: Gary Mangum, Bell Nursery, Burtonsville, Maryland

Gary Mangum and partner Mike McCarthy bought their Dutch-built Flier Model 32 in the spring of 1997, even though they were transplanting less than 40,000 shuttle trays of 4- and 6-in. pots a year and growing almost nothing in packs.

"I think when we made the purchase decision, we had no business buying one," Gary recalls. But he says they recognized that the future of the business lies with efficiency. He was right: Bell now grows 1.6 million 4-in. pots and 120,000 6-in. pots, most of which go through the transplanter.

Why Flier? Gary says they were comfortable with the people from Flier USA, especially company president Robert Lando. Naturally, they looked at machines at trade shows and talked to growers using Flier transplanters. "We liked what we heard," Gary says.

The biggest problem in adapting to the machine has been their lack of experience with the equipment. In the first season with the new equipment, it took three to four hours to change container sizes, which really cut into their efficiency. Now they have changeovers down to two hours and are running two shifts. Flier quickly resolves problems, when they occur. Gary says, "We've really been happy with the service and with the follow-through."

As for cost, Gary says they spent $105,000 for the transplanter, "and we keep adding to it." They've added a tagger and a faster pot filler. And in 1998, they spent $30,000 for a Flier pot destacker (the first one in the U.S.). Seven or eight employees used to fill shuttle trays during December and January, and Bell had to store all of those filled trays. "[The destacker] paid for itself the first year," says Gary.

Speed is of the essence for Bell Nursery, so without a transplant line "we could never refill the greenhouse the way we do now," Gary says. Last year, when they added the destacker, they gained an extra half turn from their greenhouse. This year, they added a Dutch tray system and expect to achieve another full turn. Gary expects they'll add a second transplanter next year.

Transplanter: Cherry Creek Systems
Grower: Glenn Wolter, Boven's Quality Plants, Kalamazoo, Michigan

Introduced at the 1997 Ohio Short Course, the Revolta transplanter, built in Holland by TTA and distributed in the U.S. by Cherry Creek Systems, Larkspur, Colorado, made a splash with its immense size and unusual swing-arm action. One of the first to buy a Revolta was Boven's Quality Plants. Head plug grower Glenn Wolter says the installation and setup went "pretty smoothly," considering how complicated transplanters are. A crew from Cherry Creek handled installation, and the designer also traveled from Holland to assist with setup and training. Glenn adds that the Revolta isn't as complicated as it appears and is pretty easy to run once you know how to set it up and use the computer.

Most of the problems they've had have been computer-based. Sometimes it would shut down the machine completely, or the swing arm, which is supposed to slow down before reaching the pack or tray, would go in at full speed, moving the tray around. The designer had to come over from Holland to solve the problem.

Boven's was smart: They started early by installing the machine in November, which gave them two months to set it up and train their employees. They even grew some plugs just to "test drive" the transplanter.

Because they were already growing 512s and some 288s, they didn't have to change their plug production. Glenn says it's pretty simple to change the Revolta for different finished containers; just push a button, and the computer makes the changes. Changing plug trays requires moving the grippers, which takes 30 minutes to an hour.

Why the Revolta? Glenn says they had a Flier at their other location. They liked it, but it was showing its age. "It was tough to decide which to go with," he admits. One thing that sold them on the Revolta was its unique swing-arm motion—they thought it looked like it would be easier on the plugs.

Boven's transplants about 150,000 spring flats and 40,000 fall pansies, so labor savings was a major issue. The transplanter will handle 3,500 to 4,000 flats "on a good day," says Glenn. With fewer people transplanting, he can put employees onto more important jobs.

"[The transplanter] allows us to use our people more efficiently," he says. "We still have to have people downstream from it, patching and labeling, but it isn't as many people."

Transplanter: Visser
Grower: Kathryn Tatterson, Tatterson Greenhouses, Mathews, Virginia

The Tattersons bought their Visser transplanter back in 1994, and they still run it every season. In fact, they have no plans to put it out to pasture. "We'll be running it forever," Kathryn Tatterson predicts. As proof, she mentions that they still use what may be the oldest Javo pot filler in the country.

When they bought their Visser, transplanting labor was getting harder and harder to find at their coastal Virginia greenhouse. "We knew we had to go to automation," she says.

They chose Visser after reading a *GrowerTalks* article on transplanters and looking at some at the Ohio Florists Association Short Course and making a fact-finding trip to the Netherlands. "It was the best one out at the time," she recalls, adding that they liked how solidly it was built compared with the competition.

Setup was a challenge only because the machine and the crew had to come from Holland. Once it was running, any problems had to be resolved long distance. Parts availability occasionally slows production, but being linked with a modem means that software and computer problems can be resolved over the phone. Having a good distributor to work with (Edwin

Hoenderdos, president of Hove International, Marietta, Georgia, sells Visser in North America) is a big plus, Kathryn says.

Tatterson's Visser machine uses special Star Trays patented by Visser, which means that their entire sowing and transplant line is built around these custom polystyrene trays, and they can't buy in plugs from outside sources. But Kathryn says Star Trays grow great plugs: "The roots go straight down rather than going around the edges."

Their best investment, other than the transplanter itself, was a tagger, as employees tagging by hand couldn't keep up with the transplanter's output of 200 to 220 flats per hour. Overall transplant labor has gone from sixteen people to just four.

Transplanter: Bouldin & Lawson
Grower: Kevin Childress, Jordan's Plant Farm, Henderson, Texas

Talk about confidence in a product: Kevin Childress bought not one, but two Bouldin & Lawson (B&L) transplanters in January 1998.

Jordan's Plant Farm does 600,000 flats per year, running three or four manual transplant lines, so the idea of two machines isn't so absurd. Kevin explains that having two transplanters gives them a backup in case one breaks. And having one model lets them interchange parts.

Why B&L? "I like the way it grips the plugs," Kevin says, adding that it handles begonias better than any other machine he's seen. Plus, they already had B&L soil handling equipment, so he knew the company. B&L did an excellent job integrating the two transplanters with their existing flat filler, Kevin adds.

The biggest challenge Jordan's has faced has been with plugs. They grow 50% of what they use and had to make some changes to how they grow them. They buy in plugs from Tagawa Greenhouses in Colorado, so they switched over to the same 512 and 288 trays Tagawa uses.

They also improved their growing methods. "You've got to be better in production," Kevin stresses. You don't want empty cells in trays, and you can't afford to time your production wrong and let plugs get overgrown. He says their Starcom Plant Partners planning software is essential for maximizing production.

Jordan's installed their transplanters in the beginning of peak transplant time in Texas. Kevin's advice to growers is to bring in a new transplanter several months before you need it, to have time for setup and training.

Labor savings have been "significant" since they've added the transplanters, Kevin says, cutting transplant labor from thirty-five to thirty-eight people down to fifteen to seventeen. They've increased production, and while there are now more people loading carts and moving plants into greenhouses, the automation has reduced the cost to transplant each flat.

"We're very happy," Kevin says of his investment. "When you get them rolling, you wonder how you managed without them."

It's a safe bet that other transplanter owners would agree.

March 1999

Transplanter Tribulations: Keep a Long-Term View

Chris Beytes

Based on comments from the growers we interviewed for the article "Growers on Transplanters" (above), buying and setting up an automatic transplanter is an exercise in patience. If you expect to just plug it in and go, you might be overly optimistic.

Ben Miller, owner of Stutzman's Greenhouses, Hutchinson, Kansas, is a very patient man when it comes to transplanters. His story is a good example of the very common stumbling blocks you might encounter when making any kind of major equipment investment.

First, the Bouldin & Lawson (B&L) machine he ordered for January 1998 arrived about four weeks late, cutting short the time he and his employees had to get it set up.

Second, they discovered that the plug trays they'd been using, Blackmore 406s, had inconsistent drain holes—they weren't all centered in the cells. The transplanter's extractor pins, which are supposed to poke up through the holes to eject the plugs, would sometimes miss the holes, wreaking havoc with the plug trays.

To solve the problem, B&L machined the extractor pins to a smaller diameter to give them more leeway for finding the holes. But now, instead of pushing the plugs up neatly, they'd often spear right through the plugs instead. Granted, it handled plugs with solid root systems, such as portulaca and dianthus, like a dream, Ben says.

Realizing he'd have to change trays, Ben flew to Tagawa Greenhouses in Colorado to look at the 512 trays they use, which have larger drain holes. They also checked Tagawa's soil—B&L had suggested that they might need to compact their plug soil a bit more. Instead, they switched to a Blackmore soil mix (which Ben says made a big difference in overall plug quality) and to Landmark 512 and Blackmore 288 trays, which B&L said would perform best with their transplanter.

This solved the plug-tray issue, but the problems weren't quite over. When B&L reconfigured the machine for the new 512s, Stutzman's didn't have any plugs ready to test it. When they finally had a chance to run some plugs through, it still didn't quite work. B&L came out one more time to finalize the hardware and software setup.

Reaping the Benefits

Despite the challenges, Ben is happy with the quality of the machine and with B&L's service and follow-up. "Their customer service has been tremendous," he says. "They're committed to the industry."

One of the things that Ben likes about the B&L transplanter is its unique water extractors, which keep the fingers clean and help set the plugs into the soil while giving them a preliminary watering. However, he still uses a water tunnel at the end of the transplant line for a final watering.

Ben also likes the machine's quick changeover from one size of finished pack to another. "We can go from 1206s to 1204s on the fly—no mechanical changes." He adds that it takes very little time to switch over to jumbo 606s.

When Stutzman's got the machine going, they cut transplant labor from thirteen people down to six. Ben expects a two-year payback on labor savings alone, but that isn't the reason for the investment. He says, "It's in increasing capacity, meeting customer needs, and in the ability to come back quicker with an extra turn."

Staying Positive

Ben's story applies to any investment you make in technology that's still new enough that a relatively small number of growers are using it. In fact, the more pioneering you are with technology, the more time and money you'll spend getting everything working. For instance, Powell Plant Farm, probably the world's first greenhouse to adopt SAP software, will invest several years and millions of dollars before it's all up and running. The second grower to try SAP will benefit greatly from Powell's investment. And Tom Van Wingerden had to scrap thousands of dollars' worth of aluminum racks built for his prototype crane system because of one minor change.

In spite of his travails and having spent a fair chunk of change on modifications to his plug production (B&L didn't charge extra for any of the changes to the transplanter), Ben doesn't regret his investment. He knows the payback is worth it and that the lessons he's learned will be applied toward his next. He's quick to look back and laugh at problems that would have had other growers looking for someone to blame.

And while Ben admits wishing he'd waited another year because of some of the new equipment he's seen coming out, his motto keeps him looking forward: "He who waits too long is always going to be last."

March 1999

Chapter 4
Environmental Controls

Control Choices

Bob Johnson

The continually growing menu of greenhouse environmental control systems makes for challenging choices. At the simplest, there is the thermostat, similar to the one that controls your house's temperature, that can be had for fifty bucks. Or for $10,000 or more, there are high-end computerized systems that can control the heat, light, humidity, CO_2, and, for hydroponic growers, nutrient solution in numerous greenhouse zones at once—and even keep a reliable record of the changes.

"Somebody who opens a greenhouse without automation is going to fail," warns Hugh Roberts, general manager of Connellsville, Pennsylvania-based Oglevee Computer Systems. "There's more to life than working in a greenhouse, and computer control can bring more to your life."

What Questions to Ask
The breathtaking control capacities of the most advanced computerized systems can be mesmerizing. But insiders caution that it's important to choose the right tool for the job.

"A lot of growers are buying things they don't need," says Tom Piini, president of Temecula, California-based Micro Grow Greenhouse Systems. "Some control systems are extremely complex and take a lot of computer experience to operate. Most of the growers don't have that luxury; they want to throw a box on the wall and forget about it."

The choice of a control system is a financial decision that has much to do with your volume of business. But there are enough exceptions to shred any attempt to devise a simple rule basing the choice on spending a set percentage of annual revenues on the climate control system.

"Gross revenue is the last thing I would look at—the control system is a machine just like a tractor, and I would ask, 'What can this machine do for me,'" says Alec McKenzie, manager of White Rock, British Columbia-based Argus Control Systems. "Some growers don't want complete control. If you're growing petunia [plugs] in a greenhouse, you don't want the trans-plants going from a completely controlled environment to somebody's backyard. I've got people doing millions of dollars [in sales] who don't want anything more than thermostats, and I've got people doing tens of thousands of dollars who want complete control systems."

A better crop
First on the list of questions to ask, according to Alec, is whether a more sophisticated and more expensive control system will help you produce a better crop. A superior crop can quickly recoup the cost of a control system through higher sales volume, better prices, and easier marketing.

Labor, energy
Labor or energy savings are next on the list of reasons that would justify investing in a higher end control system. Tom Piini seconded the importance of energy savings, saying, "One of the places the [cut] flower growers, who are being hit by the imports from South America, can save is on energy costs."

Record keeping
Centralized computer systems can also keep superior records of all the inputs into the greenhouse growing process and of the resulting harvest. That's a major plus of computer controls, if maintaining this information is valuable to you.

Time savings
Finally, the more-sophisticated systems can also save management time by allowing for far greater flexibility in setting the alarms that alert the grower that something needs to be corrected in the greenhouse environment. A computer-controlled system, for example, can raise the threshold for a fan alarm on hot days to avoid the exasperating experience of being summoned to the greenhouse to learn that when it's 100°F outside on a hot summer afternoon, it's also pretty warm inside the greenhouse, even when all the fans and vents are functioning perfectly.

The Choice of Systems
Thermostats have the virtue of low cost, at a price as low as fifty dollars apiece. They'll save the elbow grease expended in opening vents or closing curtains by hand. They're the oldest and most rudimentary of controls and, for a few growers, they may still be the most sensible choice.

"If you're happy with thermostats, a complete system will give you a lot of bells and whistles that you're probably never going to want," advises Scott Shelton, Midwest representative for the Q-Com Corporation, which offers high-end computer-control systems running $10,000 or more.

But most greenhouse growers are weary of the unreliability of thermostat controls or with the lack of flexibility provided by this most rudimentary of control systems. "They finally get fed up with the unreliability of thermostats—they have their heater set for 65°, their fan set for 70°, and they're both on [at the same time]," says Scott Murphy, a systems analyst for Arvada, Colorado-based Wadsworth Control Systems, which offers the full range of control systems, from thermostats to integrated computer controls.

Thermostats can be unreliable, however, because even out of the box they are only accurate to within a few degrees. And over time they wear out, and even that modest accuracy deteriorates. The result is an unpredictability that may be acceptable in controlling the furnace heating a home, but that can cause expensive snafus when mismatched devices are controlling systems that work in opposite directions. And even if the relative imprecision of thermostats can be endured, there are jobs they simply will not do.

At Murray Greenhouse and Farm, outside Concord, New Hampshire, the temperature of the greenhouses is deliberately shifted to suit the needs of the plants at different stages of their development. The 50,000 sq. ft. of greenhouse space at Murray Farm is used to grow poinsettias, Easter lilies, and a variety of spring bedding plants. The lilies, in particular, thrive at one stage of their growth on a lower temperature during the day than at night—a temperature control job that thermostats can't handle.

Thermostats can't tell the time of day, which can create exasperating problems if you want to adjust the greenhouse climate as the sun rises and sets. "If you're heating, you might get an override and your fans are blowing that heat out at night," said Dave Murray, Murray vice president.

The solution: an integrated system. "Today, everything is integrated anyway; it's a good thing that the left hand knows what the right hand is doing," said Richard Hiebendaal, general manager of Vineland Station, Ontario, Canada-based Priva Computers Inc.

Step controllers solve the most exasperating problems of simple thermostat control, and they can be had for as little as $800. To begin with, a step control system integrates the functions of numerous thermostats into a single unit, thus eliminating the problem of having climate devices work at cross-purposes. The fans, vents, and heaters, for example, are all controlled by a single unit programmed to maintain a certain temperature. Step controllers can also be set to maintain different greenhouse temperatures depending on whether it's nighttime or daytime. And they can be programmed for DIF—dropping the temperature a few degrees before sunrise, for example.

They're called step controllers because they change the temperature by triggering a series of steps. When the greenhouse is too hot, for example, the first step would be to open the vents. The next step would be to turn on some fans, and the final step would be to turn on the rest of the fans.

While they solve most of the problems that come with thermostat control, there's much that basic step controllers can't do. They're limited to being able to control a single climate zone. And they're also limited in that they control just the temperature. "A step control system doesn't have flexibility," suggested Priva's Richard Hiebendaal. "And a step controller makes adjustments after the fact, while a computer control makes adjustments ahead of time."

"Once you want to control not just the temperature but also the humidity, light intensity and CO_2, then a step controller won't work for you," suggests Wadsworth's Scott Murphy.

In order to achieve greater flexibility in setting the entire greenhouse environment, the next level, at a cost of around $2,000, is a computer zone controller. Zone controllers are capable of breaking the climate control process into many more steps, as many as two dozen. But more important, they bring the greenhouse into the computer age and can give you a level of climate control that until a few years ago was unimaginable. "It's easier to add on wind sensors, rain sensors, even light sensors," said Argus's Alec McKenzie.

They don't, however, offer the flexibility of maintaining different climates in numerous greenhouses. The number of different climate zones to be maintained goes a long way toward deciding whether it makes economic sense to upgrade to integrated computer control. "When you get to about four or five [greenhouse] zones, it makes sense financially to go with central point computer control," agrees Q-Com's Scott Shelton.

Once this final step has been taken, it becomes possible to enter a world of extraordinary control of the greenhouse environment and beyond. An integrated computer system can, for example, maintain records, which can be important in analyzing the effect of climate changes on the quality or quantity of the crop.

Oglevee's Hugh Roberts suggested that the level of sophistication of your integrated computer system will depend greatly on the region. California growers, for example, would do well to achieve greater control over irrigation, while Florida growers need control over both irrigation and cooling. In the northern states, however, efficient heating and cooling are more important than irrigation.

Q-Com has an integrated computer control system for around $10,000 that will handle two or three zones. This system can be run on a lower-end computer that many firms have stored in the closet, such as a 486/66.

Consider Your Future Plans

Most control system industry insiders agree that the size of the greenhouse operation is not the predominant issue in choosing a system.

"A greenhouse in a research facility no bigger than my office has just as much equipment to control," Priva's Richard Hiebendaal pointed out. "Certain systems are developed for bedding plants while others are developed for the vegetable growers and are usually much more complicated. We usually start with the question: What are you growing?"

At www.argus-controls.com, Argus Controls offers a synopsis of the four basic control systems. For each of the control systems, the Web site provides price range information, capabilities, and advice on what to consider in making a choice.

Growers who are building new greenhouses would do well to consider future expansion plans in choosing a control system, according to Q-Com's Scott Shelton. "If you're building new, you might want to ask how many zones do you think you're going to build down the line," he says, advising that it's more economical to invest in the right control system at the beginning than to continually upgrade as the operation is expanded.

"You've got to be very careful who you shop with; you've got to go with someone who's been in the business for a while and has a track record," recommends Oglevee's Hugh Roberts. Five years ago, Oglevee began orienting itself toward serving growers who are starting with relatively small operations but intend to expand later.

But when all the details are sorted out, the choice of a control system comes back to the practical thinking that's familiar to every grower, be it field or greenhouse. Says Scott Shelton, the questions to ask of your current environmental control equipment are: "Is it doing what you want it to now?" or "What isn't it doing for you?"

Summer 1999

What's Hot? What's Cool?

Bob Johnson

At the greenhouses at Santa Fe Nursery in Salinas, California, 4-in. infrared heating tubes are hung at the peak and run the length of the greenhouses. Behind the tubes, also running the length of the structures, are 12-in. sheets of reflector metal.

When the controls turn the system on, heat is directed from the tubes toward the greenhouse floor below. But rather than heat the greenhouse air, the heat is directed toward black-bodied objects below. This method of targeting the heat to the plants is the specialty of Growth Zone Systems of Mount Vernon, Washington.

"You use less fuel," said Growth Zone sales manager Jay Hibma. "And it decreases the incidence of disease because you're heating the plants."

Energy consciousness, encouraged by the high cost of power, continues to spur the development of more efficient and economical methods of controlling greenhouse climate. The high cost of energy has made the late 1990s the age of natural ventilation. And the latest approaches to heating are as high tech as infrared sensors, as traditional as wood chip boilers, or as low tech as simple attempts to fine-tune gas-powered boiler systems.

What's Hot?

While Growth Zone Systems has developed the high tech approach to targeting heat, Sunderman Manufacturing Co., Baltic, South Dakota, has developed a mechanical approach to putting the heat where the plants are.

"We use a series of poly convection tubes to force the air under the benches," said company president Paul Sunderman. "Instead of heating the greenhouse to 70°F and forcing the air down, we have the ability to put 100°F, or 120°F, air under the plant."

The result of concentrating the heat near the plants, rather than throughout the greenhouse, is a savings in energy. And it can also result in accelerated plant growth. "We've had people say they can save a couple weeks on growing time," Sunderman said.

Petaluma, California-based BioTherm has developed an energy saving system based on the simple fact that boilers operate most efficiently when they operate near rated capacity.

BioTherm began as a solar energy company. But when solar energy lost most of its government subsidies, the technology no longer penciled out. The firm then switched to modular greenhouse boilers, using a number of smaller boilers rather than a single larger unit. By controlling the number of units that are fired up, instead of running a large unit at a fraction of capacity, the system requires less energy when heating needs are less than full capacity.

"There are many times when a greenhouse is in a middle state of heating need and running a large unit at half speed is less efficient than running small units at full speed," said Jim Rearden, BioTherm president. "As opposed to a central heating system with a large boiler, we put in a number of smaller units. Heating in a large boiler is expensive; it is a more efficient use of fuel to heat the water with a number of smaller units."

The largest unit sold by BioTherm is a 50 hp, 1.8 million Btu unit that is 3 ft. long, 3 ft. wide, and stands 8 ft. tall. A conventional boiler, by comparison, might be 15 ft. long, 8 ft. wide, and 9 ft. tall. It could take as many as a dozen of the smaller boilers to meet the peak needs of a large greenhouse. "Compared to a traditional system, there can be a 30% reduction in energy and in energy costs," said Rearden.

Messersmith Manufacturing, Carney, Minnesota, still specializes in one of the oldest technologies—systems that allow boiler systems to heat water by burning wood chips and sawdust. The firm even has one California customer who is heating his greenhouses by burning walnut hulls.

The company originally began making units for the home but discovered in the 1980s that there is a market for larger units among greenhouse growers who are faced with huge energy needs. "We have growers who are saving thousands of dollars a year, even thousands of dollars a month," said Valerie Messersmith, company assistant to the president.

The availability of scrap wood is the key to these systems, and one grower in Racine, Wisconsin, hit the jackpot when wood chippers in the area learned that he could use their refuse. The wood chippers back their trucks up to his greenhouses and dump their waste, which is his fuel. His savings in energy costs have been so substantial that he has turned up the heat and gone from two crops a year to three.

What's Cool?

Energy cost is also the byword in cooling and ventilation, and the search for economy has made this an age of natural ventilation.

Related to natural cooling and ventilation has been a move toward using screens to retain heat or cold or to repel insects. With increased experience with screens has come increased innovation in finding ways to use them more efficiently.

"Installers are coming up with friction-free ways of moving the screens," said Les Evans, technical adviser for LS Americas of Charlotte, North Carolina. The advantage here is in both energy costs and in reduced wear and tear on motors.

Most environmental screening used by greenhouse installers nationwide comes from LS Americas. The firm manufactures the textiles used for heat retention and cooling. And in recent years, the firm has seen increased demand for insect screening.

The increased demand for environmental shades and curtains has meant increased attention to gaining an edge in the choice of material. A new standard in shading material could prove to be a more efficient aluminized shadecloth. "When you put a black shade over the greenhouse, the black cloth absorbs a lot of the heat," said Paul Jacobson, vice president of Edgerton, Wisconsin-based Green-Tek. "There is growing acceptance and interest in the alternative of aluminized shadecloth. It's a record year for us."

The aluminized alternative was first developed in Israel, where virtually all agriculture is under shade. The outside of the cloth is coated with a layer of aluminum that reflects the heat away from the greenhouse. The cost of the aluminized material can be as much as $.33 a foot, compared to $.07 or $.08 a foot for black cloth. But the added cost can be made up in energy cost and plant quality.

"We've had people report back to us as much as a 15% heat reduction," Jacobson said. "This gives you an advantage in plant quality, cooling costs, worker comfort, and, for garden centers, the longer you can keep a customer in your greenhouse, the better chance you have of snagging them."

There is an obvious explanation for the recent trend toward screens, shades, and natural ventilation that began two years ago, according to Francis Chester, vice president of Jacksonville, Florida-based Coolair: "There's no cost to it."

Coolair offers the same power ventilation systems as when Chester came to the firm fifteen years ago—negative pressure ventilation, exhaust fans, and evaporative cooling. "We're in the fan business, we promote power ventilation," Chester said. Coolair is among the firms waiting for the pendulum to swing back to power ventilation.

But Chester recalled a movement toward natural ventilation in the mid-1980s, and that trend lasted only a couple of years. "There were hot spells and people with natural ventilation were lost; they had no way of controlling it. Mother Nature doesn't always act the way you want her to," he said. "All we need is a really hot summer, and people will forget about natural ventilation."

Despite the trend toward structural ventilation and cooling, there are still innovations in electrical approaches. Aside from natural ventilation, the latest trend in greenhouse ventilation, according to Jay Stout, horticulture department sales manager of Acme Engineering and Manufacturing of Muskogee, Oklahoma, is horizontal airflow. HAF fans are now outselling Acme's Fan-Jet systems. Many growers believe it provides better air movement, according to Stout. But perhaps more important, it eliminates the nuisance of replacing the tubes when they wear out in about two years. "The tubes are not that expensive, but it's a labor thing," Stout said. "And a lot of growers would just rather be growers."

In 1996, Quietaire, Houston, Texas, introduced a smaller portable evapo fan. The 36-in. unit can be wheeled around the greenhouse on casters. "We're finding a lot of demand for the portable fan," said Quietaire president Don Dolson. "You can use them in garden centers, too, to make the customers more comfortable so maybe they'll stay around a little longer." Texas-based Port-A-Cool and Alabama's Hired Hand have also developed portable cooler units that they're now marketing.

Last year, Quietaire came out with a direct drive wall fan. This unit uses no belts and pulleys. The advantages of the direct drive fan are decreased maintenance needs and increased energy efficiency. Some growers, however, have objected that the direct drive fan is noisier than conventional fans.

What's Ahead?

With the continuing trend toward achieving economy by precisely targeting environmental controls, the most important item in the tool house of the future will be the computer. Although agriculture is among the slowest of industries in entering the high-tech age, computers are slowly showing themselves to be an indispensable item in the tool shed of the future. And no growers have been quicker to see the value of computer controls than greenhouse growers have.

All of the systems that control the temperature, ventilation, lighting, irrigation, or fertilization of the greenhouse can themselves be controlled by a computer. The shades and lights that control the length of the commercial greenhouse day, the heaters and air conditioners that control the temperature, and the misters that control the humidity can all be computer controlled. Hydroponic growers also control their irrigation fluid with sensors that monitor the nitrogen, phosphorous, and potassium content of the water and also the acidity and content, and all of it is controlled by the computer. "In horticulture, it is the job of the grower to create uniformity," said Alec McKenzie, owner of Argus Control Systems in White Rock, British Columbia. "If you lose control of the uniformity of the crop, you're out of luck."

The advantage of computer control is that it saves labor, is painstakingly precise, and maintains records of the use of every environmental system in the greenhouse, including records of the relationship between the greenhouse environment and yield.

The major expense and uncertainty in the most elaborate computer control systems have to do with the myriad mechanical devices, not with the computer that directs them. "The computer is the cheapest part, the cost of the lights is more than the cost of the computer to control them if you have a lot of different light requirements," said McKenzie. He estimated that typical computer control systems range from $10,000 to $25,000, but that economical systems are available for less than $10,000. And although even a modest computer system has the capacity for handling mind-numbing complexity, McKenzie—himself a former greenhouse grower—believes the soundest policy is to keep it as simple as possible and to accept added complexity and overhead only when there is a good reason for it.

Summer 1998

Greenhouse Heat, the Rocky Mountain Way

Paula A. Yantorno

In the floriculture industry, heating your crop is the No. 1 priority, especially during the snowy, winter months in Colorado. Center Greenhouse Inc.,

Denver, has managed to successfully keep the heat on over the years with heating systems, varying crop, available fuel, technological advances and, of course, cost.

When the business incorporated in 1950, Center Greenhouse was a carnation range with raised, redwood benches. The original boilers were coal-fired, Kewanee natural-draft boilers that were salvaged from an old cruise ship. In those days, heating was hard work. The fathers of current owners and cousins, Paul and Frank Yantorno, removed coal clinkers every night. Boilers provided steam-radiant heating with one 1¼-in. iron pipe run under each bench. The idea was to promote natural air movement and naturally dehumidify to keep botrytis levels as low as possible. The system allowed the Yantornos to grow quality carnations for more than twenty years.

Most large growing operations with gutter-connected greenhouses use a central boiler with steam or water to transfer heat. Heating companies such as BioTherm Hydronic Inc. and Delta-T Sales feel that using hot water to heat greenhouses and crops is a more progressive style of heating compared to conventional gas-fired unit heaters. With hot water heating, growers can create microclimates at different root zones with tubing on the ground, on benches, in baskets, around the perimeter, and in concrete slab heating in ebb-and-flood floors. However, unit heaters offer flexibility and low initial cost. Plus, if one heater goes down, you don't risk your entire crop. And you can easily add them to new or existing structures as your heating needs change.

Center's Heating History

In the early 1970s, Center's two original boilers were replaced with one Kewanee and one Cleaver Brooks natural gas and fuel oil–fired boiler because the utility company offered natural gas at a 50% discount in exchange for the right to interrupt service on high demand nights. Customers such as Center Greenhouse were then switched over to fuel oil. During the fuel embargo in the mid-1970s, Center removed the fuel oil burners and went to all natural gas. More than twenty years later, these fire-tube boilers (approximately 140 hp each) continue to produce heat with 15 psi of steam pressure.

When Paul and Frank began growing bedding plants in 1975, they removed soil from benches and laid the sideboards flat in the aisles, creating a giant redwood deck over the existing heat pipes. They quickly learned that steam pipes situated under the plants created a hot banding effect in the greenhouse. The result was a row of taller plants directly above the pipes and no plant uniformity through the greenhouse.

The following year, they changed their heating strategy. They removed the heat under the benches and installed Modine steam power-throw unit heaters with convection tubes. Three 1¼-in. steam lines were hung in each gutter to help melt snow. Eventually, the wood decking was removed, and the bedding plant crop was grown on a rock base on the ground. The only heat was from the power-throw units and convection tubes above.

Center's boilers deliver steam to Modine power-throw unit heaters that are made up of finned copper tubing with a fan that blows air over the finned tubes. As the steam goes through the copper tubing, it gives off heat and turns into liquid condensate. Gravity returns the condensate trapped in the power-throw unit to a holding tank where it's pumped back into the boiler and reused. The condensate retains heat, so it costs less to reheat and change back into steam than cold water. The fan blows the heated air into the greenhouse.

Center maintenance crews removed the convection tubes and installed horizontal airflow (HAF) fans throughout the entire greenhouse in 1990. The typical setup for Center's 50-by-200-ft. greenhouses is two 400,000-Btu Modine power throws in opposite corners. Three 20-in. HAF fans on each side of a house are spaced 50 ft. apart; fans on each side face opposite each other. Air movement is directed in a circular motion. This step dramatically evened out temperature variances and reduced fungicide usage because foliage is kept drier.

A definite need for under-bench heating arose again when Center began perennial propagation and seed propagation. Currently, Center's maintenance crews have been installing movable benches with 1¼-in. steam lines underneath. Installation includes one line every 6 ft., mounted at least 24 in. under the bench's surface. Center's growers have found that this distance is required to keep heat dispersed evenly and avoid any heat banding. There are four under-bench heat zones per 10,000-sq. ft. greenhouse to meet different crop requirements. The above-bench air temperature continues to be controlled by power-throw heaters. This setup, with cool air temperatures and warm soil temperatures, allows growers to maintain the perfect propagation environment.

Heating Options

In the 1970s when the Yantornos began growing bedding crops, they felt that Co-Ray-Vac infrared heating was the best seed propagation heating they could get. They found it to be very fuel efficient, but under greenhouse conditions where fog was necessary for maintaining humidity, the system didn't stand up well mechanically. The infrared heating was also installed in Center's retail store, which closed in July 1996. Presently, the Co-Ray-Vac heating is used on loading docks and in planting and production facilities, where it's the perfect heating application.

The simplest heating systems Center uses are located in the cold-frame greenhouses used for vernalization. One 350,000-Btu Modine gas-fired unit heater and one 12-in. HAF fan are hung in each 3,000-sq. ft. house. These gas-fired units aren't nearly as cost efficient as steam heaters, using more gas per square foot. They're old enough at this point that they will require increasing maintenance, so they'll be replaced with steam unit heaters in the near future.

For smaller operations that can't justify the cost of boiler heat, however, gas-fired power-throw unit heaters are the perfect heat source. This type of heating can be installed with little capital expenditure and produces immediate heat. Direct-fired units usually use air to move heat through ducts or convection tubes. Convection tubes are polyethylene film tubes with holes sized and spaced for the required heat distribution. They're placed overhead to heat floor crops or on the ground for bench systems.

A typical heating setup at Center Greenhouse, HAF fans and steam power-throw unit heaters.
Photo by Center Greenhouse Inc.

According to Ron Eberly, co-owner of American Clay Works in Denver and a distributor for Modine Manufacturing Company, growers in the West and mountain regions of the country are using a combination of strategies to achieve the best heating results. Many growers are removing glass roofs and re-covering with a single layer of polycarbonate plastic. Shadecloth is stretched underneath, and growing areas are heated with Modine power throws and convection tubes. HAF fans are used to redisperse hot air at crop height.

One improvement Ron sees is the use of stainless steel heat exchangers in place of aluminum exchangers that were often damaged by oxidation from a combination of moisture, combustion, and chemicals. Rob also says few high-efficiency power throws are sold in Colorado because most growers can't justify the 15 to 20% increase in cost for a savings of only 10% per Btu.

Computerized Controls

Temperature controls and alarms play an important part in greenhouse heating. When Center Greenhouse was a carnation range, thermostats in each house controlled temperatures. The chore of walking through the entire 80,000 sq. ft. of greenhouses and adjusting temperatures by hand took about thirty minutes every night to lower temperatures, then thirty minutes each morning to raise temperatures.

In the early 1980s, Center began working closely with Wadsworth Control Systems of Arvada, Colorado. They installed the first prototype of the Micro-Step Computer System, and Center's growers began using heat for dehumidification *and* temperature control. This also gave them the capacity to begin practicing negative DIF for height control. At the time, this was the ultimate control, and it worked perfectly for many years.

Computers can provide the optimum growing environment. Properly programmed sensing systems allow computers to anticipate light and weather changes and make the necessary adjustments in heating or cooling systems, saving energy and money. To have the programming capacity within Center's environmental controls, the system was changed in 1996 to Q-Com. Presently, the control system seems to be working well, with Center's staff continuing the learning phase.

The main low-temperature alarm system in the early years involved much time spent in the greenhouse and boiler room assessing the working status of the equipment. Paul and Frank's fathers have recounted many nights of sleeping next to the boiler in case of a failure. Eventually, they hooked low-pressure alarms to batteries with giant bells in their nearby homes—loud enough to wake the whole house!

The next step involved pagers that signaled Paul and Frank in the event of a heating failure. Today, radio signals are sent from the greenhouse computer controls to a security company that calls a list of cell phones linking Center's maintenance and grower personnel.

Power interruption can have serious consequences for greenhouse crops any time of the year, but nothing is more serious than a power outage midwinter, when greenhouse temperatures plummet to freezing levels in a matter of minutes. Standby generators are essential to maintaining a fully supported heating system. Center uses generators with automatic transfer switches. Power is interrupted for less than a minute during a utility failure.

It's necessary to have some type of backup in case of equipment failure, no matter what heating system you use. "It is better to have two smaller boilers instead of one big one or two smaller heaters in a greenhouse rather than one large," says Paul. "Our entire facility has always been set up with backup heat sources."

Selecting the Ideal

So what's the dream greenhouse heating system? Center's head grower, David Woodward, says, "Ideally, for the grower, if cost is not an object, bench everything and install under-bench heat, either water or steam, with changeable heat for the air above, regulated with separate controls."

This is because the root zone, rather than the foliage or soil media surface, typically requires the bulk of the heat. Root-zone temperatures ideally remain constant, optimizing root growth. "Under-bench heating, whether it's finned hot water or steam heat from boilers or a solar system, is superior for this phase of growing," says David. "Systems designed to heat a mass provide uniform heat, protecting the grower from the inconsistencies of the heat source."

Because air temperatures in the foliage zone generally need to be cooler, he suggests using power-throw unit heaters. Their flexibility in controlling air temperatures enables accurate DIF settings and facilitates other controls of diseases, foliage growth, and flower timing.

Summer 1997

Greenhouse Cooling Trends

Don Grey

Growers have different cooling and ventilation needs depending on crop, climate, time of year and budget. To help sort through these needs, we talked to growers and manufacturers to find out what's hot today and what's coming tomorrow.

Cooling and ventilation are broken into three major segments: structure, environment, and exclusion. Structural cooling includes a greenhouse's built-in ventilative capacity, such as retractable roofs, roll-up walls, roof vents, even the greenhouse skin itself. Environmental cooling includes anything that modifies greenhouse air, such as fog systems, exhaust wall fans, tube vent fans, horizontal airflow (HAF) fans, and fan-and-pad evaporative cooling. Exclusionary cooling involves heat blocking, including shadecloth, heat-reflective curtains, and shading compounds.

Structural Cooling

A first line of defense against excessive heat and moisture buildup is the greenhouse structure itself. Today's greenhouses have come a long way in design and environmental engineering.

Coverings

Greenhouse coverings continue to improve in durability, insulation, light transmission, and control over interior heating and cooling. Today's plastic film goes a long way toward reducing solar load, lowering inside temperatures and diffusing light. That's also the case with polycarbonate sheet technology, which now helps transmit more solar energy in winter and less during summer. One new sheet has a prismatic design that allows heat through in winter and reflects it in summer. It's said to work best on roofs or for east-, west- and south-facing walls, though it's less effective in high or low latitudes where the sun's rays are less direct.

Retractable-roof greenhouses

More and more growers worldwide are installing retractable-roof green-houses because of their flexibility. Growers who need basic winter protection from brief periods of cold but also want maximum ventilation during prolonged summer heat or humidity find these houses an excellent solution.

Likewise, those who need heated winter protection with good summer ventilation also find these houses attractive.

"They are the houses of the future," says Richard Wilson, Colorama, Azusa, California. "They have a lot of attributes to them." He currently has thirteen to fifteen acres under retractable roofs and likely will add more. Three styles are available: flat roof, peaked roof, and a new sawtooth design. Flat-roof houses are commonly used more as shade- and frost-protection structures, peaked roofs work well against heavy snow or rain and are often heated, and sawtooth structures permit open venting when other roof parts are closed.

It's this ability to vent and cool crops that sets these houses apart from fixed-roof, traditionally vented houses: Growers can fully expose crops to the outside environment, fully protect them, or leave them somewhere in between. Roofs can open to a greater degree, and depending on style, sidewalls can be fully or partially rolled up. Hook one up to an environmental control computer, and you have a system that can quickly respond to changing conditions. "It's nice to know you can completely open and close three acres in three minutes," says Rob Young, Young's Plant Farm, Auburn, Alabama. He has three acres of retractable-roof greenhouse that he uses for perennials and other crops.

With this degree of ventilation, you can cut disease problems because you can keep foliage drier. Daytime heat buildup can easily be controlled, especially during winter, and specific nighttime temperatures can be maintained. Growers who have retractable-roof houses also use traditional cooling equipment such as shadecloth, heat-retention curtains, and HAF fans. They allow even more control. For example, Mike Van Wingerden, Van Wingerden Greenhouses, Blaine, Washington, uses HAF fans to keep the air stirring, especially in colder greenhouses, to prevent humidity buildup. Sometimes CO_2 burners are necessary at night to keep foliage as dry as possible. Rob uses a heat curtain in his greenhouse.

Retractable-roof houses indeed have improved, manufacturers note, with tougher fabric, stronger supports, and better motors. Look for more improvements and new designs as manufacturers continue developments and vendors support them with new equipment.

Roll-up walls
Although retractable-roof greenhouses are gaining in popularity, many growers find traditional houses work just fine, with fewer up-front costs.

With roll-up sidewalls, these houses still can achieve a large measure of natural ventilation. Both gutter-connected and Quonset-style houses are available, covered entirely with poly or with a combination of poly and rigid sheeting.

The ability to roll up poly-covered walls entirely or partially by hand or with a controller to keep them out of the way is an advantage over drop walls. This degree of flexibility, at a relatively inexpensive price, allows you greater control over cooling and traffic flow throughout greenhouses.

Henry Huntington, Pleasant View Gardens, Loudon, New Hampshire, is sold on natural ventilation, though he wants better screening capabilities on vents. "My biggest priority is mixing screening with cooling," he says. "If manufacturers could come up with a way to have natural ventilation with adequate screening, that's what's needed." He says 60% of his operation is screened, though he's had to do a lot of modifications to make even that work. Still, he's already contemplating his next house, which he says will be polycarbonate with roof vents.

Vents

Single to double roof vents and wall vents provide varying degrees of performance, depending on the type of greenhouse and the ratio of vents to square footage. You'll have more control and better performance if vents are part of a control system because the system can better gauge factors such as temperature and humidity. Exhaust fans, shutters, vents, and cooling pad pumps can all be controlled by the system. You can program it to provide different stages of cooling (or heating). For example, Richard of Colorama has his double-Lexan plug house set up with several cooling stages. Double-butterfly ridge vents open wider and wider with each stage, allowing more natural ventilation. To reduce energy draw, he doesn't turn on fans unless absolutely necessary.

Environmental Cooling

You often need to modify your greenhouse environment to add or subtract humidity, temperature and air movement. Again, you have many options.

Fan and pad

Fan-and-pad evaporative cooling systems have been around for years and are popular favorites. They're simple to install and operate and require little maintenance, aside from occasional pad cleanings and replacements. They work in most conditions and many different greenhouse structures, assuming the length isn't too long. Many manufacturers sell fan-and-pad systems, and parts and pads are readily available.

Rob of Young's Plant Farm likes fan and pad cooling: "As far as greenhouse cooling goes, it's about as good as the industry will get." He says his ultimate greenhouse is glass with shading, with fan-and-pad cooling linked to environmental control computers.

Still, many growers find that fan-and-pad cooling isn't as effective in higher humidity. "You're not going to get as much cooling when the air is saturated," Richard of Colorama says. Likewise, Mike Poynter, Skagit Gardens, Mt. Vernon, Washington, finds that fan-and-pad cooling works best at his Northwest location when relative humidity is under 60 to 70%. Systems typically come in extruded aluminum and stainless steel, advantages for areas where high corrosion is a concern, though one new system coming to market is all plastic.

Exhaust fan speed and placement are critical in these systems. For optimum performance, enough air needs to be drawn through for full distribution. Experts say more than 100 to 225 ft. between pads and fans is pushing the limit of cooling pad effectiveness.

That's not the only drawback. Pads are most effective when they're clean. Manufacturers recommend regular cleaning to remove weed seeds, insect debris, dust, algae, and mildew, all of which can compromise pads and reduce their longevity. Some growers don't mess with pads other than when they install new ones, even though they aren't difficult to clean or to remove for winter storage.

Common complaints are pad life and expense. Manufacturers have improved pad composition over the years to offer longer life and prevent warping. On today's market you'll find cellulose paper coated with rot and algae inhibitors, bonded plastic fiber pads coated with absorbent plastic cellular foam, and pads made from aspen fibers. "I'd like to see the prices on pads come down," Rob says. "But I don't see how anything can outdo it."

One intriguing system manufacturers are talking about for the future is fan-and-pad fog. Instead of water running through pads, fog is sprayed through them, eliminating the need to recirculate water to and from a sump tank. And here's a new twist: evaporative portable coolers you can use most anywhere. Simply roll them into a greenhouse where spot cooling is needed or into a building for instant comfort; plug them in, and chill. Air discharge is up to 20°F cooler than incoming air.

High-pressure fog

This system can be used for a number of applications including evaporative cooling, humidifying, and applying foliar feeds, pesticides, and fungicides. A fog system stretches the limit further than fan-and-pad cooling because length or size of the greenhouse range or bay doesn't matter. Fog is delivered through a high-pressure feed line (typically copper, though some stainless steel pipes are available for areas with high-quality water) to a nozzle and orifice.

Another plus is cool air stability. Air from fan-and-pad cooling can heat as it travels from one end of the house to the other; fog doesn't do that.

Not all growers are sold on fog for cooling, however. "I've stopped using fog; it didn't work well for our location," Rob says. "We had 1½ acres of glass house under fog, and it didn't carry the mail for us."

Others tout fog's ability to cool for less money than other systems and keep water droplet size extremely small, which helps keep foliage dry. A fog system can differ its stages or zones of humidity output with easy control. Still, growers need to understand fog's limitations, especially in high-temperature, high-humidity conditions. Henry of Pleasant View Gardens is looking seriously at installing a fog system for poinsettia propagation, noting that fog has come a long way since his last system ten years ago.

A fog system can be expensive, particularly for smaller growers. But manufacturers are working on less-expensive systems to meet the needs of all growers. Nozzle longevity has improved over the years, though manufacturers know they still need to improve their nozzles' efficiency.

Air-over-water fog

This system isn't as common in greenhouses as in other industries such as textiles, but it does offer an alternative to a high-pressure system. It provides evaporative dry fog and humidification without wetting. Because it operates off of normal water pressure, you don't need a high-pressure hydraulic pump, one reason a high-pressure system is expensive.

Rather, an air compressor produces fine water droplets that are then released by compression into the atmosphere. You can regulate droplet size by adjusting the ratio of compressed air to water. For example, the system can go from fog spray to wetting spray by decreasing the air pressure. Though a high-pressure pump produces a minimum of about 1,000 psi, this system typically produces 30 to 40 psi of water and air, depending on droplet size. This also means you can use PVC pipe instead of more expensive high-pressure lines.

Although an air-over-water system can be less expensive up front, compressor operation can be costly in the long run.

Horizontal airflow (HAF)

Depending on your venting and cooling systems, moving air around in greenhouses offers several benefits. The longer the greenhouse is, the less wall fans can pull for end-to-end and side-to-side coverage. That's where HAF fans can help. Good air circulation can lead to healthier plants by cooling plants, lowering disease susceptibility, and promoting more uniform temperatures.

You can select from different HAF fans depending on your needs. At the top of the requirement list is efficiency: getting as much airflow as possible per watt of electricity used. Efficiency is important because you're drawing extra current for what can be sustained periods of use, a drawback for some. Fan capacity is important: how much air it can push for the size of house and type of crops grown. Also, consider location. Fans need to be set far enough from sidewalls and endwalls and spaced adequately, no more than 50 ft. apart, for best effect.

Positive pressure

Positive pressure in a greenhouse allows cool air to settle at crop level as warm air is forced to rise above the crop. Fans and pads are mounted at the same end, housed in a lean-to or cabinet outside of the house. The system pushes cool air from a blower through a thick cooling pad. Convection tubes are used to distribute cool air blown from the fan throughout the length of the house. Because the greenhouse has a positive pressure over outside air, insects won't be able to fly in when doors are opened—an added benefit.

This Florida greenhouse takes advantage of both environmental and exclusionary cooling, with a fan-and-pad system and overhead shade curtains. A unique feature of this facility: The cooling pads are mounted high on the sidewall and the fans are mounted in the roof. Rather than cooling the air at plant level, this design, combined with 14-ft.-high gutters, helps provide a more uniform greenhouse environment.

Exclusionary Cooling

Excluding excessive heat from plants can extend the performance of cooling systems or even sometimes reduce the need for them.

For shading, woven fabrics are less expensive than knitted ones and can be easier to install, but knitted fabrics tend to last longer. Each fabric type has advantages and disadvantages. Fabrics are available in different percentages of shading, from 30% to 90% or more.

Heat-reflective or thermal curtains have proved a benefit for many growers. Though more expensive than other fabrics, they reflect heat energy away from crops, meaning less heat buildup and fewer cooling demands. Mills are working to increase the longevity of fabrics, always a concern. Mills will continue to improve on and offer more metallic fabrics to do a better job of reflecting heat.

As retractable-roof greenhouses increase in popularity, look for improvements in their fabrics. One fabric manufacturer expects to see more emphasis on flame-retardant greenhouse fabrics. Some states are already looking hard at the potential fire danger of greenhouse fabrics. And we're already seeing a trend away from shading compounds to systems such as truss-to-truss shading, especially as technology progresses and prices decrease. After all, you want as much day-to-day control over the greenhouse environment as possible, and cooling is too critical to leave to chance.

Summer 1997

Cool Rules

Chris Beytes

The "greenhouse effect," the same phenomenon that has environmentalists up in arms over the threat of global warming, also causes the inside of your greenhouse to stay warmer than the outside ambient air. While this is a good problem in winter, it can be disastrous in the summer when the inside of your greenhouse can easy be 10 to 20°F hotter than the outside temperature. The solution? Force the warm air out and bring the cooler air in.

Doing this effectively requires proper engineering. The National Greenhouse Manufacturer's Association (NGMA) has developed standards for several aspects of greenhouse design. Here are some of their design recommendations for mechanical ventilation and cooling. Discuss these with your greenhouse builder the next time you plan a new construction project to ensure that you get the most effective ventilation possible.

Airflow rates. Airflow rates for cooling a greenhouse are determined by measuring cubic feet of flow per minute (cfm) for each sq. ft. of ground area. Eight cfm per sq. ft. is sufficient for a moderately shaded greenhouse with an interior light intensity of 5,000 f.c.; a 10,000-sq. ft. greenhouse would need fans capable of handling a total of 80,000 cfm.

Elevation. Interestingly, air's capacity to remove heat depends on its weight, not its volume. The thin (hence, light) air at high elevations isn't as effective at cooling, so you need to move more of it through your greenhouse. Greenhouses in mile-high Denver need more fan capacity than greenhouses closer to sea level. Engineers use an "elevation factor" based on barometric pressure to compensate for greenhouse elevation.

Fan tips. The NGMA suggests that you have from 100 to 225 ft. between your pads and your fans for maximum airflow and cooling efficiency. For longer greenhouses, consider installing pads at each end and fans in the middle, mounted either in the sidewall or the roof. In houses shorter than 100 ft., the air has difficulty reaching the velocity needed to keep the house from feeling clammy or stuffy. Engineers use a "velocity adjustment factor" that helps them increase the capacity of the fans and pads with these shorter houses. With any house, fans should be no more than 25 ft. apart along the exhaust wall of the greenhouse. This helps prevent dead air and hot spots between the fans.

When possible, install your fans on the downwind side of your greenhouse so that they aren't working against the prevailing wind. If you must put your fans on the windward side, your ventilation rating should be increased by 10%, and your fans should have motors rated at least ¾ horsepower.

When locating fans near an obstruction such as a fence or another building or greenhouse, leave at least 1½ times the fan diameter between the fan and the obstruction. In other words, leave at least 6 ft. between a 4-ft. diameter fan and an obstruction. Also, if fans of two houses face each other and are closer than 15 ft., they should be offset so as not to blow directly against each other.

Seal those leaks. A leaky greenhouse will allow warm outside air to bypass the pads, reducing cooling effectiveness. Be sure your greenhouse is relatively well sealed so that the fans and pads operate under a slight vacuum.

Pad pointers. Aspen (wood fiber) cooling pads should accommodate 150 cfm per sq. ft. of pad area. Corrugated cellulose pads (such as Kool-Cel pads) should be sized to handle 250 cfm (for 4-in.-thick pads) and 350 cfm (for 6-in.-thick pads). This can be reduced to 75% of the recommended area if the greenhouse design requires, but you should seal the house to keep air infiltration to a minimum.

Just as your fans should be on the downwind side of the greenhouse, pads should be on the side of the house facing the prevailing wind. However, you should arrange your greenhouses so that the fans of one house don't exhaust directly into the pads of the next house unless they're separated by at least 50 ft.

If your cooling air travels below your benches, it won't cool as effectively. Use baffles to force the air to above bench level.

Water works. Water flow to your pads should be at least ⅓ gal. per minute (GPM) per lineal foot for aspen pads, ½ GPM for 4-in.-thick corrugated pads, and ¾ GPM for 6-in.-thick pads. Design the system to provide slightly more than that, then use a valve to control the flow. Too much water will block airflow and reduce performance.

Your sump tank should have a capacity of ½ gal. per sq. ft. of aspen pads, ¾ gal. per sq. ft. for 4-in.-thick corrugated pads and 1 gal. per sq. ft. of 6-in.-thick pads. Provide a float valve to restore water lost by evaporation. Also, if your water has a heavy mineral concentration, provide a "bleed-off" valve to prevent buildup. A hose valve set to a slow drip will do the trick.

February 1998

Shroud Your HAF Fans for Best Results

Ted H. Short

Most growers have accepted the importance of horizontal airflow (HAF) fans for internal air circulation during the winter growing season. HAF fans are essential for uniform temperature, humidity, and carbon dioxide distribution. They can greatly minimize water condensation on plants, where many diseases like to develop.

However, one key HAF fan design factor that you should consider is fan shrouding. If you're only growing short plants such as bedding and plug plants, unshrouded fans can work quite well. But when the greenhouse gets filled with a lot of plant material, including hanging baskets, only shrouded fans will provide the desired horizontal airflow.

A shroud can be as simple as a sheet-metal ring or cylinder around the fan blades. The closer the shroud is to the blade tips, the more effective or efficient the fan is at moving air along the axis of the fan. Extremely high tolerances and high speeds result in jet engine designs.

The capacities of unshrouded fans are actually the same as shrouded. The undesirable characteristic of an unshrouded fan, however, is that it pushes most of the air directly off the blade tips, which can damage plants growing directly under (or above) each fan if the fan is located 2 to 3 ft. from the crop, as recommended.

Your HAF fan system should consist of fans moving air the length of each greenhouse. Fans are often spaced 50 to 80 ft. apart down one bay and aligned with similar fans pushing air the opposite direction down an adjacent bay. Fan diameter can range from 12 to 36 in., with the larger fans working best on deep canopy cut flower crops and trellised vegetables.

A shrouded HAF fan pushes air horizontally without an unshrouded fan's undesirable side effect of air blowing off the blade tips and down into the crop.

Fans, whether shrouded or unshrouded, should be designed to move about 2 cu. ft. of air per minute (cfm) per sq. ft. of floor area. For example, if a greenhouse is 40 by 200 ft., the total design airflow should be 16,000 cfm. Then comes the spacing and height of placement, and both are very critical.

Fans should be spaced down the center line of each greenhouse that is no more than 30 ft. wide and separated by no more than thirty times the diameter of the fan blade. For instance, if the fan is 2 ft. in diameter, the fan axles should be lined up and spaced no more than 60 ft. apart. The last fan (looking in the direction of airflow) should be no more than 60 ft. from the end wall.

The inlet side of the first fan (still looking in the direction of the airflow) should be about eight fan diameters from the end of the greenhouse wall. Again, if each fan is 2 ft. in diameter, the first fan should be no more than 16 ft. from the end wall.

Each shrouded fan should be 2 to 3 ft. above the top of the plants. (This is a problem for unshrouded fans, as they tend to damage the plants below.) If the velocity across the tops of the plants near the shrouded fan is too great, reduce the fan speed or angle the fan upward slightly. Technically, the air velocity across the plants should be no greater than 3.3 ft./sec. or 2.5 mph. With circulating fans, normal vent operation can be used. Less venting, however, will be required for winter humidity control. The fans won't greatly affect the amount of venting needed unless a fan-jet is installed to bring in outside air. For winter cooling, minimum venting doesn't seem to significantly affect the air movement by the fans.

We've come a long way with incorporating HAF fans into new and retrofitted greenhouse designs. Now let's see if we can do even better by selecting fans that move more air down the greenhouse and into the heavy plant canopies.

June 1999

It's Cold Out! So Why Ventilate?

A. J. Both

Why ventilate in the winter? Because greenhouse ventilation is necessary to provide humidity control and maintain adequate carbon dioxide levels. You may need to ventilate for temperature control, too; although, assuming the heating system doesn't overshoot the indoor target temperature, this is only needed when the sun's radiation overheats the greenhouse.

Under normal growing conditions, leaf stomates are opened during photosynthesis, allowing plants to take up carbon dioxide and, as a result, release water vapor. Therefore, the carbon dioxide concentration of the greenhouse air decreases while the humidity increases. Normally, the ambient carbon dioxide concentration ranges between 350 and 400 ppm (0.035 to 0.040%). Without the proper ventilation rate, a greenhouse crop can easily reduce the carbon dioxide concentration to 100 to 200 ppm or less, significantly slowing the rate of photosynthesis, and thus plant growth.

On the other hand, high humidity levels result in increased condensation on colder surfaces (e.g., greenhouse glazing material or plant leaves when their temperature is lower than the surrounding air temperature), reduced plant transpiration (which, in turn, reduces water and nutrient uptake), and increased risk of disease (e.g., mildew).

How Much Ventilation?

In colder climates, the general recommendation is to have winter ventilation capacity that's 10 to 15% of the maximum (summer) ventilation capacity. But what's the recommended maximum ventilation capacity? A frequently used—but not very appropriate—design criterion is "one air exchange per minute" (where the greenhouse volume is calculated without including the air volume above the gutters).

The more appropriate design criterion is 8 cu. ft. per minute (cfm) per sq. ft. of greenhouse area (10 cfm per sq. ft. for greenhouses without a thermal shade screen). This design criterion is more appropriate because the amount of solar radiation intercepted depends on greenhouse area and not volume. Note that this recommendation isn't affected by the height of the greenhouse. However, the recommendation of 8 cfm per sq. ft. should be increased when: (1) the greenhouse location has an elevation above 1,000 ft; (2) when the maximum interior light intensity measures over 5,000 f.c.; (3) when the desired temperature increase from inlet to fan is less than 7°F; and (4) when the inlet-to-fan distance is less than 100 ft.

Based on this information, the winter ventilation capacity for the average greenhouse should be around 1 cfm per sq. ft. of greenhouse area, or 1.3 cfm per sq. ft. for greenhouses with a thermal shade screen.

Mix It Up

In the winter, the incoming air is usually much colder than the greenhouse air. When this cold air is allowed to reach the crop, severe plant damage can occur. Usually a crop occupies the entire greenhouse floor area to maximize space use. Therefore, special measures are needed to prevent plant damage. When using a top-hinged ventilation window as air inlet (usually along an entire sidewall), care should be taken that the incoming air has sufficient velocity (at least 700 ft. per minute) so it mixes thoroughly with the warmer greenhouse air before it reaches the crop. If necessary, a baffle can be installed to direct incoming air up and away from plants.

A less common but very effective way to provide good control of inlet air velocity and ensure proper air mixing is to use a differential pressure sensor to control the opening width of a ventilation window.

Another ventilation method is a polyethylene tube installed several feet above the top of the crop canopy and along the length of the greenhouse. The tube is connected to the outside with a louvered inlet and tied shut at the other end. Once the ventilation fan turns on, incoming air inflates the tube and fresh air enters the greenhouse through holes along the entire wall of the tube. Designed for a sufficiently high airspeed (1,200 to 1,800 fpm), these poly tubes ensure proper mixing before fresh air reaches the crop.

A polyethylene tube along the top of the greenhouse can ensure proper mixing of cold air in the winter.

Take Control

You have to decide whether to ventilate for temperature, humidity, and/or carbon dioxide control. Plant requirements (including disease control) and energy costs will be the determining factors. For example, to dehumidify the greenhouse, the ventilation system can be turned on. This will drop the indoor temperature, requiring additional heating. The additional heating further reduces the humidity, but also increases energy use.

Whether you're using a ventilation window or a polyethylene tube, any effective, economical winter ventilation strategy is best implemented with the help of a computer control system that can adjust quickly and accurately to the ever-changing environmental conditions with minimal input required from a busy greenhouse grower.

December 2000

Outside the Box

Fred Kaiser

It's natural to think of your greenhouse environmental control system for controlling greenhouse climate and irrigation. But what about other uses? Growers tend to be incredibly resourceful, figuring out all kinds of interesting ways to use their tools. In some cases, the application can be so significant that it alone can justify the purchase of a system. Here are two.

Automatic Pest Control

If you've ever had to go around your greenhouse before making a pesticide application, turning off fans, closing vents, and opening curtains, then reopening vents and turning on fans for purging, you know what a bad job it is. A number of Q-COM customers have found ways to use their environmental control systems to do the job for them.

Kent Belau from Timbuk Farms, Granville, Ohio, was key in the development of a program for Q-COM's GEM software that lets you program up to four individual pesticide application steps: preparation, application, circulation, and purge. You enter the schedule for each of the events. You pick which day or days of the week, the start time and duration, and whether to make it a permanent or one-time event. Then you can program the equipment and temperature set point modifications for the following four stages:

Preparation. This is the period you'd use to prepare the greenhouse for pesticide application. You can preprogram any zone equipment you want to be overridden for this preparation cycle.

Application. This cycle is used to activate your sprayer to apply the pesticide. During this period, the spraying process is happening, whether from an automated fogger or other method. Usually the cooling system would be overridden so the pesticide isn't lost to the outside.

Circulation. The circulation period is used to distribute the pesticide. You can program the HAF fans to run during this period to circulate the pesticide for even distribution. You can also use this period to turn off all air-moving equipment to allow the pesticide to settle.

Purge. This period is used to purge the pesticide from the zone in preparation for the re-entry of people. During this time, the ventilation or cooling equipment is usually activated to allow remaining pesticide to escape outside.

During this portion of the program, there's a real danger of overcooling the house if the weather is cool. You can disable the purge if the zone temperature falls a certain number of degrees below your heating target. It will resume after the temperature recovers.

You can preprogram the computer to automatically control the greenhouse environment in your particular way for each of the steps that you use. You don't have to use all four stages. In fact, you can use it to only do purge, if you want.

Cutting Your Energy Bill

Utility companies frequently impose demand charges if your power consumption exceeds a predetermined threshold in any fifteen-minute interval throughout the day. In some parts of the country, this demand charge can be huge. Also, some utility companies offer rebates if you utilize energy-saving technology to keep your power below the demand thresholds. Incidentally, the demand thresholds aren't necessarily fixed. During peak usage hours, the threshold may be lower than, say, at night or on weekends and holidays.

Some of our customers have significantly reduced their demand charges using their environmental control computer, which is programmed by completing a form for the peak power demand permitted for that month. A wattmeter is installed, and the computer continuously monitors the power level.

If the power level comes close to the threshold, your computer can be set for one of two strategies. One is to power up the backup generator system. When the preset kilowatt demand level is exceeded, the generator will take over the electrical needs of the facility until the demand goes back to normal. Some growers, especially in northern climates, have found that one unseasonably warm spring or fall day can add a thousand dollars or more to their demand charges. (A typical demand charge is ten dollars per kilowatt, so adding 100 kW to your demand would do it.) So you may only need to run your generator for a few hours a month for significant savings.

Another is to do "load shedding," which is having the computer turn off some equipment. The program can prioritize what gets turned off first, second, etc. You might give up some cooling, but you can be certain that if you eliminate the demand charge, you'll save yourself a bundle.

November 2000

Feature Films

Ted Deidrick

Improvements in greenhouse films over recent years have followed two approaches. The first (predominant among domestic manufacturers) has been toward lowering costs while maintaining quality. With warranties increasing from three years to four, a grower's overall film costs drop. And by increasing mechanical strength, thinner films can be made as durable as thicker films, again cutting costs and reducing the volume of plastic to be disposed.

The second approach (more common with overseas manufacturers) has been to increase the value of films by including additives that benefit growers. Most of these affect absorption of specific wavelengths of light.

Because the basis of many specialty films is in selective transmission of different wavelengths of light, a brief review of light wavebands might be useful. On the left hand side of the scale is ultraviolet (UV) light, with very short wavelengths. This light has high energy and is responsible for suntans (and skin cancers). Next is the visible light, with wavelengths longer than UV. The visible light coincides pretty closely with the frequencies of light that the plant uses for photosynthesis (PAR, or photosynthetically active radiation). Just to the right of visible light is the near infrared radiation, which isn't used for photosynthesis, but impacts stem elongation and adds heat to the greenhouse. Finally, way off to the far right is longwave infrared radiation. This is radiation given off by warm objects (like the earth, greenhouse floors, etc.) as they cool.

IR (Thermic) Films

On clear nights, longwave infrared radiation given off by the earth escapes into space. On cloudy nights, some of this radiation is reflected back to earth. Films with IR additives act like the clouds, slowing escape of this radiation. Most analyses indicate that energy savings can recoup the additional cost of the film.

UV-Blocking Films

All multiyear films have UV stabilizers, which protect them from UV degradation. Still, some UV light goes through the film. In recent years, products with UV-blocking additives provide near-complete blockage of UV light.

Benefits are less fungal disease and insect pests. Research indicates that botrytis won't sporulate properly without UV light. Israeli researchers have seen a dramatic effect on insect populations because insects require UV light to see. In one tunnel trial, aphids in control tunnels were a hundredfold more frequent than in tunnels with UV-blocking films; thrips were sixfold more frequent, and whiteflies twofold more frequent. And insect-transmitted viruses were cut in half with UV-blocking films. While these and other tests look promising, the technology may only work in a totally enclosed tunnel. Any leakage of natural light into the house through a vent or door will negate the benefit of the film.

Further issues to be resolved include the impact on beneficials, on bee activity (for those with vegetables needing pollination), and flower color because flower color pigments can sometimes be induced or increased by UV light. Also, while most plants grow better with less UV, some argue that plants exposed to UV will be better prepared for planting outdoors.

Near-Infrared-Blocking Films

About 40 to 50% of the radiation that enters the greenhouse is in the near-infrared band. A greenhouse film that would block this light without impacting visible light would be a breakthrough, dramatically decreasing heat in the greenhouse and plant stretch, which is increased with high near-infrared levels. The problem has been finding a film additive that produces the desired results. There are a few commercial products that have begun to use this approach. The concern at this point is achieving stability of the pigment and the film.

Colored Films

A red film that would absorb radiation in the green frequency (not used by plants very efficiently) and re-emit the energy as red light was experimented with recently. Plants are green because they absorb (and use) most visible frequencies of light except green (which is reflected back to our eyes). Converting green light into red light increases the total light available to the plant. It also increases red light without altering infrared and thus should decrease plant stretch. Rose trials on the West Coast indicated significant increases in branching and rose yield, but the product is no longer available because the pigment changed color under prolonged UV exposure.

Copper-colored film functioned similar to thermal screens, providing shade during the day and retaining infrared radiation at night. This product also changed under UV exposure, so it is no longer available.

A blue film has also been marketed that is designed to provide fungus control, based on research that showed that blue light inhibited various fungi. This product hasn't gained popularity in the U.S. and it could be replaced with the UV-blocking films discussed above.

In addition to wavelength-specific films, watch for films with diffusive additives—reports indicate 7 to 10% increases in vegetable yields due to increased diffused light in tall-canopied crops.

May 2000

Shady Business

Chris Beytes

You can lower your greenhouse temperature by 8 to 10°F just by applying shade—a significant change when it's 90°F outside. But the big question is how to shade? Three basic methods are available: paint, shadecloth, and automatic curtain systems, each with benefits and drawbacks. Here are some thoughts on each:

Paint

One major advantage of paint (also called whitewash) is that it can help protect poly and fiberglass roofs, actually increasing their life by 50 to 100%, thanks to added ultraviolet protection. I've known Florida foliage growers who, by keeping their double poly painted year-round, can get more than six years from their three-year poly. Its white color will reflect most of the sun's heat away from the house, rather than absorbing it. Paint is also inexpensive—less than $.02 per sq. ft. (not counting labor) versus roughly $.10 to $.30 per sq. ft. or more for shadecloth.

Paint's drawbacks are numerous, however. It's labor intensive to apply—you mop or spray it on, which can be difficult on a large house. It's also tricky to apply paint uniformly for even shading. And you may have to apply several coats to get the desired degree of shade. Also, weather wears the paint away, gradually changing the level of shading. Most growers plan for this, applying it in the early summer, then allowing nature to slowly wash it off. You can even buy shade paint in different compounds that will last for a season or more and that are designed for poly or glass and other rigid coverings. How the paint wears off isn't an exact science, however. If you truly want full sun in the fall and winter, you've got to wash off the paint, which is more bothersome than applying it.

Shadecloth

For quick, accurate shading at a reasonable cost, try woven shadecloth. It comes in various densities, usually 30 to 90% shade, and in various sizes and types of weaves. I used it over the tops of the bays of my Florida greenhouse, putting it up in April or May and taking it off in October or November. We could put 30% shade over some bays, 50% over others, or even cover just half a bay, depending on the crop. We held it down using a special latch in our poly lock. One person could cover a 21-by-110 ft. bay in about thirty minutes. Taking if off is even quicker. Cost, as indicated above, varies widely depending on cloth density, construction, and quality.

Some growers hang standard black shadecloth inside their greenhouses. While this will shade crops, it won't keep heat from entering the houses—heat will build up above and around the cloth. It can also prevent airflow through roof vents. This method is best left for spot shade in emergencies.

A better solution is to actually suspend the shade above the house. David Wadsworth has done this over the sawtooth range at his Seffner, Florida, operation, Suncoast Greenhouses. This actually cools the air over and around the greenhouse and allows for better natural ventilation. A system like this can even be designed with several different percentages of shadecloth and an automatic drive system.

One problem with black shadecloth is that it absorbs any heat that hasn't passed through into the greenhouse and transfers it into the air around the house (if suspended over the house), into the roof itself (if draped over the roof), or into the greenhouse (if hung inside). I know my poly roofs didn't last as long as those of the growers who painted, but I made up for that in flexibility.

Automatic Curtains

That brings us to the most sophisticated way to shade: an internal shade curtain system. These are usually designed with aluminized shade fabric that actually reflects sunlight rather than absorbing it. This helps prevent heat buildup in the house. The curtain can be activated by a timer, a thermostat, or a light sensor.

Most new shade fabrics also do double duty as heat retention curtains, giving you energy savings in both summer and winter, albeit with some compromise compared with a dedicated heat retention fabric. For instance, Ludvig Svensson's ULS-18 cloth gives 85% shade and 70% heat retention. Cost for an automatic system runs roughly $.80 to $1.50 per sq. ft., depending on size. Larger jobs cost less per sq. ft. Payback can be based not only on crop quality, but also on greenhouse heating savings.

Automatic curtains have only two real drawbacks. First, most systems operate an entire house with one drive system: You shade everything or nothing. Second, suspending a curtain below your roof vents may block some airflow in a naturally ventilated house. Curtain manufacturers say this is negligible, but when you're trying to keep the house cool, every bit of airflow helps. If possible, suspend your system so it doesn't block roof vents.

May 1998

Chapter 5
Energy Efficiency

Heating Efficiency Basics

Chris Beytes

When shopping for a new heating system or upgrading your existing equipment for the upcoming season, it's helpful to have an understanding of the common terminology used to describe the three ways heating systems actually heat your greenhouse and the terms used to describe the three measurements of heating system efficiency. Heating methods and efficiency are closely linked, and the heat source you use should be properly matched to your heat distribution system.

The National Greenhouse Manufacturers Association (NGMA) recently published *Greenhouse heating efficiency design considerations* as part of its greenhouse standards. NGMA's design considerations give a good overview of heating methods and efficiency.

Heating Principles
All forms of heating fall into one of more of three basic principles, each of which is used in greenhouse heating.

Convection
Convection uses the forces of natural air circulation currents to transfer heat. Convection involves two basic principles: Cold air displaces warm air, and warm air rises in the presence of cold air.

With convection, heat is transferred by air currents, which transport energy throughout the structure. When these air currents pass by plant material, energy is transferred to the plant. Because of this, it's very important that some means of air circulation is used, such as horizontal airflow (HAF) fans, perforated polyethylene duct tubes, or ceiling fans, to assure the maximum amount of warm air is transferred to the plant environment and to evenly distribute heat throughout the structure.

Warmed air in the structure naturally rises and forms layers (called stratification), with the warmest layers generally at the highest points of the greenhouse. To maximize efficient use of the heat energy available, it's important to force the mixing and circulation of these warm air layers. Convection heat is also very valuable as a means of snow removal.

Conduction

Conduction uses direct application to transfer heat energy to the plant. Physically touching any warm object demonstrates the principle of conductive heating.

In greenhouses, this type of heating is most commonly distributed with hot water tubes, and occasionally with electric resistance strips, which are placed directly on the growing surface or in the growing media. The soil, containers, and growing surface in direct contact with the warm tubes or strips are heated and subsequently transfer that heat energy to adjacent material.

Radiation

Radiation uses electromagnetic infrared waves to transfer heat energy. As this is a little understood form of heating, its bears detailed explanation. If you ever have warmed yourself by a hot wood stove or warmed your hands at a campfire, you have experienced radiant heat. It's also demonstrated by standing in the sun on a winter's day or walking near a brick wall that's been exposed to the sun during the day. In these examples, although the air may not be warm, you're able to feel the heat energy radiating from these surfaces.

Efficiency

There are three common ways to describe heating efficiency:

Combustion efficiency

This is the most basic description of efficiency, and denotes the percentage of fuel burned and turned into heating energy.

Thermal efficiency

This is a measurement of the actual amount of available energy that transfers into the heating medium. It's derived by operating a piece of equipment at a steady rate and then measuring how much fuel is used versus how much usable heat comes out. It's most typically used in reference to boilers.

Distribution efficiency

This is the measure of how well your heating equipment actually delivers the BTUs to your plants and your structure. This expression addresses how energy is distributed and transferred to the objects requiring heat.

Distribution efficiency is greatly affected by the system you select and how you use your equipment. For example:

- Forced hot air systems' distribution efficiency is largely dependent on the means of air circulation in the greenhouse.
- Infrared systems, when properly installed, can transfer heating energy to crops very well without the necessity of air circulation.
- With hot water, distribution efficiency is tremendously affected if the supply and return lines are poorly insulated or uninsulated.
- Some hot water systems deliver heat much more efficiently than others do. Finned pipes heat air faster than bare pipes.
- With hot water, a high-efficiency distribution system coupled to a poor-efficiency boiler may be better than a high-efficiency boiler with poor-efficiency distribution.

Editor's note: To get a free copy of NGMA's greenhouse heating design considerations, contact NGMA, Tel: (800) 792-NGMA. You can also order the complete greenhouse standards book for $25.

July 1998

⌂

Which Fuel Should I Burn?

Jim Rearden

Energy is at the top of everyone's mind. The skyrocketing cost of natural gas has made headlines and brought the topic of efficiency and energy conservation to a high priority once again. This is especially true for heating fuel in greenhouse operations, as we rely heavily on adequate heading to produce timely crops profitably.

Looking back through my archive of old grower magazines, I noted there was a time in the early '80s when fuel economy was a highlighted topic of almost every issue. Back then, we actually had a true energy crisis due to short supply . . . not the "price crisis" that we're dealing with now as a result of deregulation of the utility companies. Many innovations in greenhouse operational efficiency, such as glazing technology, new heating concepts, thermal screens, and advanced control systems, came out of that crisis. Of course, some of the ideas, such as the grower who decided to raise rabbits under his benches to get a little extra "bottom heat," didn't make it. But for every "hare"-brained idea, there were others that stuck.

The reality is that, unless you're blessed to have your facility sitting adjacent to a bubbling geothermal hot spring, you need to create a strategy for navigating the current fuel market. Here are your options:

Natural Gas

Most growers have the luxury of having natural gas distribution lines connected to their facilities. Natural gas has been a blessing to our industry, as it has many attributes that make it far superior to the other options. Most growers use enough fuel to qualify to buy "direct purchase" gas from one of the large suppliers such as Enron Corporation; this means that you can buy at or near the "wellhead" cost and then pay a nominal transmission fee to your local utility, which owns and maintains the lines. Natural gas burns very clean, so maintenance on equipment is minimized. It's considered a "friendly fuel" by environmental groups and government regulators. Since natural gas delivery is on an as-needed basis, there are no storage issues, unlike other fuels that require tanks with their commensurate inspection and containment issues.

Oil

Heating oil is used by many growers as a primary fuel when they don't have natural gas available. This is very common in the Northeast, where the natural gas infrastructure doesn't exist. Oil comes with some baggage, however. Typically, oil-fired equipment costs more initially and requires more maintenance. Oil needs to be delivered in bulk. Also, storing oil on your site requires tanks that need to be inspected and maintained. And remediation of contaminated soil can be very expensive. Further, oil equipment is a struggle to get to burn cleanly and return the same kind of seasonal efficiencies that natural gas provides.

Recently, there's been a fair amount of interest in waste oil–fired equipment, but this probably isn't a viable option for larger operations. If you operate a cast iron or steel boiler, you'll need a burner that's specially designed to switch between natural gas and oil to use oil as your backup. And most gas-fired unit heaters can't use oil for a fuel source at all.

Liquid Propane Gas (LPG)

Propane was discovered in the early part of this century and has steadily grown in acceptance as a viable alternative for those who don't have natural gas. A by-product of fuel refining, LPG has many of the same characteristics of natural gas; with the proper equipment, it can be burned in the same heaters or boilers. It's very clean burning and friendly to the environment. Still, it needs to be stored on site. It's best to store a "transport load," which requires a 30,000-gal. tank—a "pig" in the industry vernacular. Having the ability to buy bulk will help you get the best deal per gallon. Also, LPG can be tricky to use properly. Many pieces of equipment are damaged each year by improperly vaporized fuel.

Electricity

It's only a viable heating fuel option for a few growers in North America. Typically, the delivered cost per heating unit is three to four times that of gas or oil. But if you're lucky enough to have very cheap electricity, you can heat with 100% efficiency, no emissions, and very low maintenance.

Wood and Coal

Several successful growers use wood chips to heat. However, the initial investment and extreme amount of storage space, labor, and maintenance make this an option for only the very few operations that can truly pencil it out. With wood and coal, one of the biggest problems is that the emissions from your smokestack can be especially noxious.

BTU Content of Various Fuels

Fuels	Unit of measure	Gross Btus per unit*	What we're used to paying
Natural gas	Therm	100,000	$.30 to $.60
LPG	Gallon	92,500	$.45 to $.75
#2 Fuel oil	Gallon	138,500	$.55 to $.80
Electricity	Kilowatt	3,412	$.06 to $.12
Wood	Cord	15-30 Million	N/A
Coal (anthracite)	Pound	13,000	N/A

*This number represents the gross amount of heat available per unit. The actual amount of energy you derive from each fuel unit is a function of the efficiency of the equipment you use to burn the fuel. The combustion and seasonal efficiencies of heating equipment vary widely. It's also important to factor any delivery charges, maintenance costs and labor costs associated with each fuel to determine its true economics.

Your Best Strategy

The most practical solution for most growers is to have natural gas with a backup supply of an alternative fuel. Whether the backup is LPG or oil is a big decision. If you're in an area with tightening air quality rules, LPG might be your only choice. There are now "aerification" units available that modify LPG to burn just like natural gas by adding air to change the specific gravity of the fuel. If oil is your primary fuel, LPG is a logical backup. Either way, you should shop aggressively for both. If you store large volumes on your site, you can swing a bigger hammer with potential suppliers.

If you were extremely savvy, you were able to lock in your natural gas prices for this winter on a contract purchase *before* the heating season. If so, you aren't suffering the fate of so many growers who are buying fuel on the "spot market" at five or ten times the usual price.

On the other hand, many growers decided not to lock in because the contract prices they were being offered over the summer were for as much as $.90 per therm (100,000 Btus), rather than $.20 to .30 per therm they expected. As one industry spokesman says, "They didn't realize they were entering a brave new world."

February 2001

Curtains: Your No. 1 Fuel Saver

John Walters

With the price of natural gas and other fuels going through the roof, your heat shouldn't be. There's no excuse for not installing thermal screens (also known as heat retention curtains or thermal blankets) in your greenhouses. Research institutions such as Rutgers, Cornell, and Penn State have documented energy savings potential of 60% in houses equipped with thermal screens. Other research has shown that screens are as cost effective as any energy conservation method. And cost analyses show that materials and installation expenses for a screen system can be recouped in one to three years.

But what do screens really do? Basically, they save on energy costs in two ways. First, screens cut down the amount of airspace in the greenhouse that needs to be heated. Second, thermal screens provide an insulation factor, keeping the cold out and the heat in.

Thermal screens improve both day and night environmental conditions, and they're now available in a number of different designs. To make a proper choice and achieve the desired results, it's crucial to realize that the screen is part of your total greenhouse system.

A Little Background

Ken Winspear, of the Silsoe Research Institute in the United Kingdom, is credited with developing the first internal greenhouse screen. Ken proved way back in 1948 that greenhouse curtains could be used to manipulate light and heat.

Imperial Chemicals, also from England, is credited with being one of the very first companies to make greenhouse curtains commercially available. At about the same time, a United States company called Simtrac began producing greenhouse curtains. Though now out of business, you can still find greenhouses with Simtrac curtain systems.

The Dutch, though often credited with inventing curtains, actually showed tremendous resistance to the use of internal curtains because they believed the loss of light and consequential loss of production wouldn't offset the energy savings. But this was when oil was cheap and energy savings weren't much of a concern.

By 1978, energy costs were soaring, and, given that growers spend somewhere between 70 and 80% of their energy dollars on heating their houses, the need for internal screens became obvious.

Screens vs. No Screens

If we look at temperatures and energy consumption in two identical greenhouses, one with a screen and one without a screen, we find two differences: First, the screen will allow for the heat to be switched on at a later time, as the temperature drops more slowly under the screen. Second, when the heat is switched on, less fuel is used for the set-point temperature. Using both effects, the total savings of this thermal screen can amount to at least 70%. As an added benefit, you can design a screened house with smaller heating units than required in an unscreened house.

Along with energy efficiency, research conducted by James Faust, Royal Heins, and Paul Kiefer found that thermal screens also increase plant temperature. According to their findings, plants remain warm due to their emission of long-wave radiation. Plants actually exchange energy with the thermal screen. They found that the colder the outside temperature, the more pronounced the benefit of the thermal screen with regards to plant temperature.

Screen Materials

Porous cloth materials are often used for shading and are made of white woven materials, but porous cloth is also a common material for internal curtains. The advantages of porous cloth are that it's easy to handle and it allows for water drainage. The major disadvantage of porous cloth is that it's not very efficient in retaining heat. The warm air flows easily through the cloth, giving it a heat transmission of 0.6 Btu/hr. This compares to having no curtain at all, which equals 0.8 Btu/hr heat transmission.

Nonporous materials such as polyethylene, when properly installed, offer a little over 0.4 Btu/hr of heat transmission. They're often used as blackout curtains for photoperiod control. But they do trap water and condensation, and they block out all light, which may not be desirable when trying to retain heat during daylight hours. They can also be heavy.

The third material for heat retention is aluminized fabric. The aluminized material is an integration of aluminum and thread. The aluminum reflects harsh sunlight while retaining heat radiation at night. It's lightweight for ease of handling and porous enough to not trap water. Aluminized screens offer roughly 0.3 Btu/hr of heat transmission.

Every greenhouse, whether production or retail (such as this new Nexus greenhouse at retailer Platt Hill in Illinois) will benefit from a thermal screen. Modern fabrics provide the benefits of heat retention and shading.

The majority of screens now available on the market has aluminum on the upper side, so the radiation of the sun is reflected upward out of the greenhouse and won't be converted into heat. This lets reflective aluminum screens reduce the temperature during the day. The material also has the advantage of being aesthetically pleasing. Another advantage of an aluminum upper side is its low emission value for long-wave heat radiation. This means that when you close the screen during the night, it'll reduce the heat loss, working like a Thermos to hold heat in.

Controlling Your Curtain

While curtains can be opened and closed manually, most growers choose to link them to their environmental control computer to automate them based on time of day, light, heat, humidity, or all of the above. But you can also use a simple time clock. Some growers have photo sensors that detect the light level and open or close the screen for shading. An advantage of a fully automatic system is that it can control the speed at which the screen opens to prevent it from opening too quickly and dumping cold air onto your plants.

When you should close or open the screen will depend on outside weather conditions. The screens can be opened slowly, or some growers wait until the sun warms the upper area of the greenhouse. In areas where snow is an issue, growers will leave the screens open to keep from isolating the top of the house from heat.

Keeping It Working

Maintenance of the screen fabric is minimal, as it's not exposed to the outside elements. Your biggest risks are gutter drips or water pipe leaks causing algae growth. Be careful trying to clean up such a problem, as most chemicals can be harmful to screen materials. Contact your curtain or greenhouse manufacturer for advice.

You do need to pay attention to the drive system that supports and moves the screen. Be sure that limits are set correctly to avoid stressing the screen or drive mechanism. You should check all moving parts for wear and lubricate them annually.

The biggest maintenance issue we see is worn monofilaments on sliding screen systems (where the screen slides on top of monofilament support wires, rather than being suspended below them). This is the biggest reason for screens failing before they should. If you see this happening, replace the worn wire immediately to prevent excessive wear to the screen. It's smart to install new support wires whenever you install new material.

The Payoff

During the past two decades, technology has revolutionized our industry. With energy costs so much at the forefront of the greenhouse business today, it's good to know there's a simple, proven technology that can quickly pay for itself just by the fuel it can save.

March 2001

Curtain Considerations

Chris Beytes

Have you given much thought lately to that big silver curtain that hangs overhead in your greenhouse? You know, the one your builder said everyone has so you might as well put it in while he was doing the construction?

If you're like many growers, that silver curtain—usually called an energy blanket, heat-retention curtain, or shade curtain, depending upon the fabric—isn't at the front of your mind. Controlled manually with a switch or connected through a sophisticated environmental control system, it quietly does its job, blocking sunlight in the summer or retaining heat in the winter.

Or does it? That's what we wanted to find out. Are there right and wrong ways to use an energy curtain? We asked John Bartok, extension professor emeritus, University of Connecticut, Storrs, for some general tips on getting the most from your energy curtain.

What's what?

First, how do you know if what you have is a true energy curtain—one that will keep heat out during the summer and hold heat in during the winter? Mainly by the weave, John says. High-tech curtain fabrics are generally made of an aluminized woven material. The more open the weave, the less shade the curtains give and the less heat they'll retain, but the more airflow they'll give. Paul Jacobsen, Green-Tek sales manager, says his company's Aluminet fabric is primarily designed to shade and to let heat and humidity escape. This is particularly good for warm climates. A curtain out of this fabric will retain some heat, but not as much as a dedicated energy curtain.

A fabric built by alternating open spaces and aluminized strips will increase the heat retention, depending on how tight the weave is. This type of material provides a good combination of shade, airflow, and heat retention in climates where cooling a greenhouse is a higher priority than heating.

LS Americas makes a fabric that alternates aluminum strips with clear plastic strips, offering a good combination of both shade and heat retention, albeit with less airflow through the fabric than an open weave material might give.

As an aside, how well air flows through the curtain is an important consideration for venting. With fans or fan-and-pad cooling, this isn't a factor, but with natural ventilation through roof vents, a tightly woven shade curtain may cause more heat buildup than it blocks out. That's why many houses are equipped with both automated shade curtains and heat retention curtains—probably the best solution if you can afford it.

A thermal blanket provides the greatest degree of heat retention, important in northern climates with a high Delta T (the difference between outside and inside temperatures). Thermal blankets are designed to provide some degree of insulation to retain the maximum amount of heat below the curtain.

Blackcloth curtains can also double as heat retention curtains. The challenge with these is that because they block out all light, you lose valuable growing time when you close them during daylight hours.

Up the Chimney

When should you operate your curtains? John says there are no hard and fast rules and that he doesn't know of any research on the best times to close or open curtains to maximize heat retention.

What's more important, he says, is to be sure your curtain is in good working condition and that it's tightly sealed all the way around the edges, with no holes or tears. John relates the story of one grower who installed a thermal blanket at a large greenhouse range. The only problem was that the curtain ended about a foot from the sidewalls all the way around. The grower's heating bills actually went up, John says, because of the chimney effect created by heated air rising through the gap. Once he sealed the gap, the curtain worked properly. So seal those gaps and holes!

Design Considerations

It's interesting to note how an energy curtain actually saves energy: by reducing the amount of greenhouse area exposed to the cold air. A greenhouse roof covers more square feet than the greenhouse itself because of its shape, whether bow, peaked, Venlo, or sawtooth. That's why it's best to hang the curtain horizontally under the gutters rather than hanging it up against the roof panels in a peaked house—you have fewer square feet of curtain exposed to the cold air.

Growers also ask about gutter height: Is a tall greenhouse more expensive to heat than a short greenhouse? Only by a few percent, John says, because going taller only adds a small amount of space that's exposed to the outside air (the added sidewall area). He says the increased temperature buffering of the large air mass gives your crops a much more consistent growing environment, which more than makes up for the slightly higher heating costs.

November 1998

Chapter 6
Irrigation

Modern Irrigation Management Systems

Don C. Wilkerson

Water and water management are essential parts of greenhouse crop production. However, our ability to efficiently deliver water when and where needed has always been a challenge. Granted, we've come a long way in the types of irrigation technology now available, but many growers haven't taken full advantage of these advancements. Today's modern application and control systems give growers an excellent means of precision irrigation that can improve growth, reduce crop time, cut labor costs, reduce insects and diseases, lower fertility costs, conserve water and protect the environment—and all at competitive costs. Here's a brief summary of those systems currently in use and a look at some of the new technologies currently being developed.

Watering Your Crops

Irrigation systems have a variety of properties that determine their suitability for use on various greenhouse crops. These properties not only affect plant growth but also nutrition, pest management, media choices, and other factors. It's important to ask the following questions when selecting a system:

Effectiveness. How well does the system deliver water to the target? Does the foliage get wet? Is it a high-volume or low-volume system? Is filtration required?

Efficiency. How much of the applied water actually reaches the target? Does the system require a large volume of water to thoroughly wet the growing media? Does the system produce lots of runoff?

Nutrition. Can you use the system to apply fertilizer?

Pest management. Does the system promote pest management problems? Is the foliage wet for extended periods? Does the root system sit in water during and following irrigation?

Environment. Does the system create a potential environmental hazard? Is there a large volume of contaminated water to dispose of? Does the system promote conservation of natural resources?

Cost. How expensive is it to install and maintain the system? What are the start-up costs versus long-term costs?

The following table reviews a number of irrigation systems using basic criteria to evaluate their use for greenhouse crops.

	Effectiveness	Efficiency	Nutrition	Pest management	Environment	Cost
Overhead (hand)	Acceptable/Poor	Medium/Low	Yes (limited)	Medium/Low	Medium/Low	Low
Overhead (impact)	Poor	Low	Yes (limited)	High	High	Low
Overhead (spray/mist)	Acceptable/Poor	Low	Yes (limited)	High	High	Low
Overhead (boom)	Acceptable	Medium	Yes (limited)	High	Medium	High
Drip (spit emitters)	Acceptable	Medium	Yes	Medium	Medium/Low	Medium
Drip (drip emitters)	Excellent	High	Yes	Low	Low	Medium
Subirrigation (mats)	Poor	Medium/Low	Yes (limited)	High/Medium	Low	Medium
Subirrigation (troughs)	Excellent	High	Yes	Low	Low	High
Subirrigation (trays)	Excellent	High	Yes	Low	Low	High
Subirrigation (floors)	Excellent	High	Yes	Low	Low	High

Overhead Systems

Hand irrigation is one of the most effective of the overhead systems. It's highly adaptable to a wide range of crops, limits runoff, and can be used to apply fertilizer. High labor is hand irrigation's biggest drawback. This is a major cost category that more advanced irrigation systems can reduce.

Impact sprinklers and spray/mist heads are inexpensive and cut labor, but their effectiveness is relatively poor. Although this system can be used for a variety of applications, wet and dry spots are a major problem, and system design is critical, in addition to the challenges created by excessive foliar wetting and large volumes of runoff.

Boom irrigation is a more effective means of overhead irrigation. Booms limit runoff and deliver water and chemicals directly to the selected target. However, the range of application may be limited (plug trays, packs, and smaller sized pots). Boom systems are usually fully automated and are frequently part of a total greenhouse system including benches and clear span house designs.

Drip Irrigation

Spit emitters in a drip irrigation system are generally limited to 1-gal. or larger pots. This is a relatively high-volume system, and emitters are rated by gallons per minute (GPM) at a given water pressure. If these system parameters are exceeded, the spitters may wet the foliage or miss the pot completely, creating an increased disease potential, improper watering, and water waste.

Drip emitters also have a limited range of application (4- to 10-in. pots). Drip emitters operate on a lower application volume than spitters, reducing the amount of water splashing on the foliage. These systems provide good water distribution within the container and are excellent ways of delivering soluble fertilizers. Both types of drip irrigation can be operated manually or automatically with timers or computer controls.

Subirrigation

Subirrigation mats have been used with various degrees of success but have a limited range of applications. These systems can limit runoff if water is recycled. Mats work especially well with small pots (4 in. or smaller).

Subirrigation using troughs, trays, or floors is adaptable to a wide range of containers and sizes. Because the water is recycled, most runoff problems are eliminated. Monitoring nutrients, pH, soluble salts, and contaminants in your subirrigation water requires good management skills. There are few pest problems associated with these systems, despite concern over the potential for root diseases.

Applying Fertilizer and Chemicals

Fertilizer injections (fertigation). Soluble fertilizer applied through an irrigation system is the most accurate means of delivering nutrients to your crops. Fertigation systems can be relatively simple (siphons, proportioners, ratio feeders, etc.) or more complex computerized units that adjust the amount of fertilizer injected based on inputs such as EC, pH, and flow. Most greenhouses use ratio feeders that inject premixed fertilizer on demand. The main difference between setups at various greenhouses is the volume of water that has to be provided. Several small injectors can be connected in series to increase capacity.

Acid injection. Many growers contend with extremely high pH/alkaline water that can interfere with the solubility of plant nutrients. An acid injection unit allows producers to inject concentrated acid (usually sulfuric acid) directly into the irrigation system. *This approach should not be confused with a system that merely allows acidification of the fertilizer stock tank.* A titration curve is required to determine how much acid is needed per gallon of irrigation water. Acid injection systems, like Progressive Pump's proportional injector, incorporate an in-line pH meter to adjust the amount of acid injected based on the pH of incoming water. This system provides the correct amount of acid to overcome high alkalinity and lower pH to a preset level for maximum nutrient solubility.

Computer monitoring and control. These systems provide growers with a variety of tools to improve management decisions. A computer-monitored system keeps track of important water quality factors such as pH, EC, flow, amount of fertilizer used, water temperature, dissolved oxygen, and much more. This information can be very useful in matching water quality to a specific crop, optimizing plant nutrition, and diagnosing plant problems. Computers help growers vary the amount and type of fertilizer used, select various sources of irrigation water, control flow from one section of the greenhouse to another, and much more. Computer-operated systems are becoming extremely valuable tools in developing comprehensive irrigation management systems.

Clean, Pure Water

Filtration. Good filtration is an essential part of any irrigation system. Turbidity, algae, and sediment not only clog equipment and emitters, they also promote the growth of harmful pathogens. The past ten years have seen good developments in filtration, including self-backwashing (self-cleaning) filters, improved sand filters, sediment membranes, spindown filters, and low-cost, replaceable cartridges. Chemical flocculents have also played an important role in this process. Netafim's spin-clean disk filter system is among the most popular on the market. This system provides filtration down to 130 microns and offers a self-backwash option based on pressure differential. Cost, capacity, and effectiveness vary depending on the system.

Reverse osmosis. Many growers treat water through a process known as reverse osmosis (RO) to remove potentially harmful salts. RO water is cheaper than distilled or deionized water, and the overall quality is the same. While it's possible to purchase an RO system, many units now in operation are under lease. This is often a better deal than owning a unit because service of the system's internal membranes is included.

Nana filtration (NF) is similar to RO but removes less salt from solution. NF water is also cheaper to produce, and there's less runoff to dispose of. There is growing interest in NF water for the production of nursery and floral crops, but little information is currently available on its use and maintenance.

Disinfection

Irrigation water may become contaminated with harmful pathogens. *Phytophtora* and *Pythium* are among the most common and devastating of those disease organisms that frequently attack greenhouse crops.

Chlorine. Disinfecting irrigation water is difficult at best. Chlorine is frequently used as an oxidizing agent to kill organisms in solution. Typically 3 to 5 ppm chlorine (with a contact time of three to five minutes) is sufficient to kill most harmful pathogens. However, due to the many safety and health restrictions placed on chlorine gas, most growers no longer rely on this technique.

Potassium hypochlorite. The latest approach involves the use of potassium hypochlorite as the source of chlorine. This system uses an electrolysis process to convert potassium chloride to potassium hypochlorite. The chlorine from potassium hypochlorite works similarly to traditional chlorination systems but without the health and safety problems associated with chlorine gas.

UV light. Ultraviolet light has also been used to treat irrigation water for harmful pathogens. However, adequate levels and exposure time to UV light are limiting factors.

Lasers. Plant pathologists are now studying the effects of lasers on pathogens in solution. This form of light energy can be effective, but it's difficult to recharge the system between laser shots to treat large volumes of rapidly moving water.

Ozone. Ozone is another oxidizing process that has been used on a limited basis for disinfecting irrigation water. Although ozone has demonstrated an ability to destroy a broad range of harmful pathogens, there are still many questions about the potential effect on plant nutrients as well as on the plant itself.

Eloptic energy (electrostatic precipitation, ESP). The jury is still out on the use of ESP for treating irrigation water. The claims seem to be almost too good to be true, but growers like Paul Wright of Rio Grande Nursery in Brownsville, Texas, swear by the positive effects it has had on crop quality.

"We've eliminated our salinity problems," says Paul, "and it's a lot cheaper than RO water." ESP uses a form of radionic energy that obeys some laws of electricity and some of optics. The system works by rearranging electrons in the water molecule, changing its ionic nature.

We still have a long way to go when it comes to managing irrigation systems, especially in the area of determining when to irrigate and how much water to add. Most of these decisions are based on intuitive observations rather than on something more concrete. Irrigation models using vapor pressure deficit or transportation come close to estimating plant needs. Also, tensiometers and gravimetric measurements can be used to monitor water status in the growing substrate. However, all of these systems require a substantial amount of tweaking to make them adaptable to a wide range of crops, container sizes, substrates, growing conditions, etc. Irrigation management is still a vast frontier of unknowns waiting for creative solutions, and researchers and manufacturers are working hard to find the answers.

Summer 1997

Easy Drip Irrigation

Chris Beytes

For a low-cost way to save money and resources while improving crop quality, nothing can beat drip irrigation. Sometimes called spaghetti tubes, drip irrigation systems deliver just the right amount of water to plants, cutting labor while conserving water and fertilizer. Best of all, drip systems are simple enough for any grower to install, whether in a greenhouse or outside.

But simplicity is probably drip irrigation's downfall. To deliver accurate and consistent irrigation to each pot on the system, drip irrigation needs to be properly designed. Too many growers simply put in a ¾-in. main line, then branch off from that to supply black poly pipe that feeds each bench or row. This will get the job done, but not with any degree of consistency.

Rather than get into the fluid dynamics required to design a drip system from scratch, I thought I'd share the setup of the system from my old greenhouse, which was designed by a University of Florida agricultural engineer and was based on manifolds. Nine years of consistent pot plant production proved the system's accuracy. Plus, having installed it myself in several slightly modified configurations, I know it can be easily adapted to a variety of situations. Here are the details:

First, city water was supplied through a 1½-in. PVC line. At the head-house, this line first connected to a filter (20 mesh), then to a fertilizer injector. Next in line was a pressure-reducer valve, which dropped the city pressure of 50 to 60 psi down to a more drip tube–friendly 15 psi.

The 1½-in. line then headed into the greenhouse at the main aisle to supply eighteen 5-by-50-ft. benches, nine on the left side of the house, nine on the right. This is where the manifolds come in.

Just after entering the greenhouse, the main line branched into the first manifolds: two parallel 1½-in. lines that ran about halfway down the center aisle (underground, of course). When the lines were opposite the fifth benches, each turned 90 degrees and then branched into the second mani-folds: two 1¼-in. lines, one heading farther into the greenhouse to between benches seven and eight, and one heading back toward the door, stopping between benches two and three. Both lines turned 90 degrees and again branched into manifolds, this time reduced to 1 in., heading along the base of the benches. From this 1-in. line, ¾-in. lines branched upward to feed the nine benches on each side of the house. Each bench had its own valve and a ¾-in. black poly tube that ran its length and was equipped with drip tubes and Stuppy emitters. Drip-tube length was kept to 2 to 3 ft.

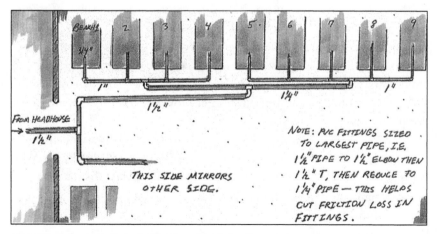

Diagram of a simple but effective drip irrigation system.
Illustration by Chris Beytes.

This system fed half of my greenhouse; the other three bays had their own main supply, injector, and pressure reducer. I could water nine benches at a time, three or four if I was fertilizing. I also used this design to feed misters in my stock house, and it worked great, although I couldn't irrigate as many plants at once, as the misters flowed more water than the drippers did.

The Scientific Side

I talked with Johan Oostenbrink, product manager with Netafim, Fresno, California, to learn a little of the science behind the design. He says the manifolds minimize friction losses (and hence flow losses) in the pipes. Because the manifolds give longer runs of larger pipes, the system can carry more water. They also help equalize the pressure and flow going to each bench. A properly designed system, he says, should have water flow within 5% plus or minus from one end of the bench to the other.

If you're in doubt about whether this system will work in your particular application, check with your irrigation supplier. They can tell you if you need to adjust any of your pipe dimensions.

April 1998

Just-in-Time Watering

Peter Ling and Robert W. McMahon

Watering plants is easy—just pick up your garden hose and spray. Watering plants *correctly* is a much more challenging issue. Plants need water to transport nutrients and to cool themselves. Overwatering wastes water and causes higher humidity in the growing area. This can lead to disease problems and even costs you more to heat your greenhouse, as a good part of heating energy is used to dry your floor instead of providing a warmer environment for plant growth.

Proper watering provides sufficient water for plant growth while helping you control the relative humidity to promote plant health. It also cuts down your heating bill, reduces runoff, and saves water. Call it just-in-time and just-the-right-amount watering. Here's why you want to do it and some tools that might help.

Water as Growth Regulator

Water is an excellent nonchemical growth regulator, especially for bedding plants. While plants need water to grow by increasing cell count and size, high turgor pressure in cells promotes stretching that results in larger leaves and taller plants.

To limit plant height through irrigation, you water lightly but frequently, but only after some water-stress symptom such as wilting is evident—"just-in-time" watering. The water used by plants under this production scheme mainly helps the plants to cool themselves, not to grow.

The amount of time you can go between waterings without permanently damaging your plants is affected by climate conditions. You need to water more frequently under hot and dry conditions when plants get warmer; you can water less frequently under cloudy and humid conditions when plants are cooler. But how good are you at judging what just-in-time and just-the-right-amount mean for your crops?

Experienced growers say they can judge a growth medium's wetness by either looking at or feeling the soil mix or by picking up the plants. However, their estimates could prove to be way off. During a growers' meeting, we asked participants to estimate the soil moisture level of some plants, and then we checked them with a soil moisture sensor. The closest estimates were only 50% off the meter readings, while others missed by as much as 250%.

Eliminate the Guesswork

Accurately estimating the environmental conditions and the available water in the soil are important for just-in-time and just-the-right-amount watering. Sensors that monitor environmental conditions and soil moisture measurements are invaluable for maximizing the potential of water as a growth regulator while preventing crop damage from excessive water stress. Good sensors will tell you how much water is in the growth medium and how hot and dry the greenhouse is, letting you make an intelligent decision on when and how much to water. You can buy portable sensors with displays, and sensors with electrical outputs that can be easily connected to computers.

One simple moisture sensor is a tensiometer, which consists of a porous cup attached to a vacuum gauge. You insert the cup into the soil mix and fill it with water. As the soil mix dries, water leaves the cup and the resulting tension (vacuum) is recorded on a gauge. We've seen growers get good results using tensiometer output to trigger solenoid valves, which turn on their irrigation system at a preset soil moisture level.

As with any tools in the greenhouse, using tensiometers correctly separates the best growers from good growers. Here are a few tensiometer tips:

- Fill the cup with water and check for leaks. Without water, the tensiometer won't work, and a leaking system will give an erroneous reading.
- Place the sensor tip where it counts—at the root zone.
- Have good contact between the porous cup and the soil, and insert the cup in a single stroke to reduce airspace between the soil and cup.
- Calibrate your tensiometer for different soils; the relationship between the tensiometer reading and water content varies among soil mix types. Careful calibration will let you determine the correct water content level from tensiometer readings for different growth mixtures. Some companies sell "low-tension" tensiometers specifically designed for soilless media and sandy soils. This is what you want for greenhouse use.

Tensiometers are inexpensive (about fifty-five dollars), yet they give useful soil moisture information for good watering control practices. More sophisticated tools, such as time domain reflectometry (TDR) sensors, light accumulators, weighted leaf sensors, and canopy temperature sensors, can be integrated into computer-controlled watering systems for precise watering control.

While sensors can never replace a good grower's feel for a crop's growth and vigor, they can help with production decisions by providing accurate information about the growing environment.

April 1999

Save Water, Save Money, Save Time

Don C. Wilkerson

When you're thinking irrigation, it's important to consider factors such as regional and environmental differences, the thousands of different crops produced, water and water-quality issues, nutritional requirements, cost, and personal preferences before making a decision. To help you choose the system that's right for your needs, here's a combination of personal observations and some informal research I've conducted in trying to make heads or tails out of the irrigation haze.

The Old Standbys

The most basic forms of irrigation, hand and overhead (sprinkler type), are still the most widely used systems worldwide. Although we would like to think our industry is rapidly moving toward more high-tech methods of delivering water to crops, we still rely heavily on these two relics of the past. It's hard to argue with success, and both hand and overhead irrigation systems are easy to install, relatively inexpensive (if you don't count labor or crop damage/loss), and, except for an occasional kink in the hose, simple to operate.

Needless to say, when compared to other systems, hand and overhead irrigation aren't the most labor efficient or cost efficient. Nor do they have the least environmental impact. However, both are here to stay.

One of the most recognizable trends in drip irrigation is in hanging basket production. Anyone who has ever pulled finished baskets with spaghetti tubes and drip emitters knows that much of the irrigation system frequently disappears in the process. In addition, the rate of application and the distribution of irrigation water can be less than uniform.

The newer, automated basket lines (the ECHO System, by Cherry Creek Systems) move baskets on a large conveyor to a watering station. Here, a solenoid-operated irrigation head applies water. Fully programmable, the volume of water applied to each basket can be adjusted based on crop, size of basket, stage of growth, type of growing media, environmental conditions, etc. This system can also be used in combination with fertilizer and acid injectors, chemigation, and other system components. It can be retrofitted into existing greenhouses and can accommodate two to three layers of baskets.

Another relatively new development in the area of hanging basket production is the use of in-line drip emitters. In-line systems are very similar to conventional drip systems; however, they don't use spaghetti tubing between the emitter and the polyethylene header. Instead, the emitter is inserted directly into the header line, and baskets are hung beneath. Once again, the rate of application and uniformity of irrigation are critical, and each type of emitter has unique characteristics. Most in-line emitters can be closed when a basket is removed.

Clogging can be a problem anytime a low-volume system with a relatively small orifice is used to irrigate greenhouse crops. Filtration is important and may be required depending on the source of water. However, I've probably seen more problems from PVC shavings (a self-inflicted wound) than I have from poor water quality. In some areas, algae growth inside PVC pipes can also create clogging problems. This may require something as simple as painting exposed pipes or as sophisticated as different water-treatment procedures.

Subirrigation

Ebb-and-flow benches are an important means of delivering irrigation water to crops. However, the newness of this technology seems to have worn off somewhat since its initial introduction. It's hard to fully understand why this has occurred, but factors such as cost, increased water management concerns (nutrition, EC, pH, diseases), difficulty in retrofitting older greenhouses, and decreased concern over irrigation runoff have all served as influences.

The use of flood floors, on the other hand, is on the rise in many U.S. regions. Growers are still faced with cost and water management issues, but the advantages seem to outweigh the disadvantages. The ability to use this system with a variety of container sizes and spacing combinations, coupled with more efficient water use, make flood floor systems extremely attractive.

Boom Watering

The use of overhead boom irrigation is also growing rapidly. Several different systems are on the market, but the basic operation is the same. A fine spray of water is precisely applied over the tops of flats, trays, and pots. In many systems, the boom travels from one end of the greenhouse to the other on a truss-mounted track. Other systems use a free-traveling boom with a separate drive system. Most booms have fully adjustable spray bars and nozzle settings to water in pressures from a fine mist to a heavy watering. Many systems are also programmable, and watering intervals, volume, and start-stop times can be preset.

Increased precision and reduced labor costs are among the most important advantages of overhead booms. These systems are right on the money when it comes to supplying a consistent amount of water to the crop. Although some systems require a separate boom setup for each house, newer systems make it easy to move one boom mechanism from one house to another.

In some situations, however, the use of boom irrigation is difficult. Booms are wide and require a clear-span greenhouse for optimum efficiency. Because water is applied overhead, they can increase the potential for foliar diseases. Also, they aren't always suitable for use on all crops. Initial costs can be substantial, and occasional maintenance is necessary.

Water Treatment Systems

Filtration is a very important part of an irrigation system. Turbidity, algae, and sediment not only clog irrigation equipment and emitters, they also provide an essential component for the growth of harmful pathogens. Filtration can be expensive, and other, more passive methods of reducing sediment (grassways, weirs, and volume control) can be employed.

There have been numerous advancements in this area in the past five to ten years. These include self-backwashing filters, improved sand filters, sediment membranes, spindown filters, and low-cost, replaceable cartridges. Chemical flocculents have also played an important role.

Acid Injection

Many growers have to contend with extremely high pH/alkaline water. These conditions can directly interfere with the solubility of plant nutrients in the stock tank, irrigation lines, and media. An acid-injection unit allows producers to inject concentrated acid (usually sulfuric) directly into the irrigation system. This approach shouldn't be confused with a system that merely allows acidification of the fertilizer stock tank. A titration curve is required to determine how much acid is needed per gallon of water. Acid-injection systems incorporate an in-line pH meter to adjust the amount of acid injected based on the pH of incoming water. It provides the correct amount of acid to overcome high alkalinity and to lower pH to a preset level for maximum nutrient solubility.

There are many trendy things going on in irrigation technology, and it's a challenge to stay on top of the most recent developments. But the bottom line is . . . the bottom line. No matter how many bells and whistles a new piece of technology might offer, they're meaningless if it isn't economically feasible. Before investing in any system, carefully study up-front investment and operating costs and overall flexibility/adaptability to a variety of production systems.

The Great Flood

Chris Beytes

Growers have really latched onto the idea of ebb-and-flood irrigation. It's a great labor saver—no emitters to stick in pots—and it's environmentally sound, letting you capture and reuse excess irrigation water.

There are three main ways to provide flood irrigation: troughs, trays, and floors. Each offers benefits and drawbacks, but having three choices means there's something for every grower and every situation.

Troughs

Flexibility and adaptability are what make troughs so desirable for growers who want to retrofit ebb-and-flood irrigation onto an existing bench system. Made of galvanized steel, aluminum, or plastic, troughs run either across or down the benches. They come in 5 to 7½ in. widths to accommodate pots in sizes from 2 in. up to 8 in.

They're tilted slightly (4 to 5 in. per 100 ft.) so water fed in at one end runs down the trough and out the other end into a return gutter or floor drain. The water runs slowly enough that plants sit in a shallow pool of water.

Because troughs don't have to be fastened to the base, you can adjust the spacing between them or add or remove troughs for various plant sizes or crops. They even work on rolling benches if you use flexible tubes to feed water to them and set up some sort of floor gutter or drain to catch runoff.

Zwart Systems, Grimsby, Ontario, Canada, can roll-form seamless troughs to any length. Cost depends on width, with a 7⅜-in. trough priced at $0.68 per linear ft.

If you put six troughs on an existing 5-by-100-ft. bench, your cost per sq. ft. would be about $0.80. A new metal base would run about $1.75 per sq. ft., bringing a new system up to $2.55 per sq. ft., without plumbing.

Trays

The next step up from troughs is trays—standard benches, either stationary or rolling, that you can flood with water. Unlike troughs, a valve at one end lets the trays fill with water for a predetermined time, then lets the water drain out. These offer more crop uniformity and overall space efficiency than trough systems but are more expensive, starting at about $4.00 per sq. ft. for a 6-ft.-wide tray, according to Midwest Growmaster, St. Charles, Illinois.

Trays are perfect for retail use. You can buy freestanding trays in nearly any size. You can fill them with a garden hose or a temporary connection and drain them into a floor drain. Because they're freestanding, you can move them around to rearrange your garden center while gaining the benefits of quick, neat, uniform irrigation.

The best way to combine efficient irrigation with internal transport is to use Dutch trays equipped with a floodable bottom. They give you the ultimate in crop spacing flexibility and mobility, at a price: about $5.00 per sq. ft. for the trays and rollerbond (the rails the trays ride on), without any plumbing.

Along with flexible plant spacing and labor savings, trays offer the added advantage of better space use—a properly designed tray system can give you 80 to 90% space use, compared with 60 to 70% for stationary benches and 70 to 85% for rolling benches.

But the main reason to invest in trays is for mobility—you can roll your crops into and out of the greenhouse very efficiently. This system is for serious growers who want to make a major, long-term investment.

Floors

Flood floors give the best of (almost) all worlds: maximum space use and labor- and water-saving irrigation. The drawback? Plant mobility—human labor is still the best way to put plants down and pick them up.

The cost for floors is probably the most variable of the three systems because you can do a little or a lot of the work yourself. Also, 70 to 80% of the cost is in the concrete work, which can vary considerably. Plan on $4.50 to $6.00 per sq. ft. for a complete system, which also includes in-floor heat.

Remember, if you install Dutch trays at $4.00 to $5.00, you still need a concrete floor, a heating system, and the irrigation plumbing. Prices for the other ebb-and-flood systems also don't include any plumbing or heat.

March 1998

Eliminate Runoff with Flood Floors

William J. Roberts

Dutch greenhouse operators are leaders at reducing greenhouse runoff. Several years ago they agreed by handshake with the Dutch government that there would be no runoff from greenhouses by the turn of the century. This gentleman's agreement actually became a law with the date moved forward to 1997. All greenhouses had to meet this requirement, which may explain why 15% of Dutch greenhouses are now empty: Operators couldn't comply.

In the United Kingdom, new groundwater regulations went into effect April 1. Although somewhat different in thrust than the Dutch law, they have the same intended effect: reducing groundwater contamination.

Dutch and U.K. growers are using two systems to meet these environmental requirements: ebb-and-flood bench systems, and ebb-and-flood floor systems. North American growers have also embraced this technology. Both systems require the same basic components, including water and nutrient holding tanks, pumps, irrigation controls, watertight tables or floors, and under-bench or in-floor heating systems. Here's a look at the fastest growing system, flood floors.

Flood Floors

In an ebb-and-flood floor system, the entire floor or sections of the floor become large "benches" containing the irrigation water. This system has become popular in the Netherlands, with more than 1,200 acres reportedly constructed in the last ten years. The system actually combines three management systems into one: watering, heating, and internal transport. It turns out that each of the three components of the system is very efficient, and most growers are happy with the results of the ebb-and-flood floor system. Electric forklifts are used to convey the product to the headhouse area, and space use is nearly 90%. Another benefit is lower energy costs; nighttime set point temperatures can be 5°F lower without any negative effects on the crop because the microclimate at the canopy level on the floor is at the desired temperature for optimum growth.

Special Equipment

Flood systems require several holding and mixing tanks, depending on the desired number of fertilizer solutions. Filtration is mandatory to limit large particles of media, leaves, and other debris from plugging the system. Normally, the entire flow is run through simple self-cleaning gravity filters on the way back to the holding tank. Computers maintain proper EC and pH in the various storage tanks.

The greenhouse is usually divided into zones of 1,000 to 3,000 sq. ft., depending on the greenhouse design. Each floor section can be flooded and drained independently through an underground system. A section of 3,000 sq. ft., flooded to 1½ in. in fifteen minutes, requires 3,500 gal. of water and a delivery and return system capability of handling 233 gal. per minute. Good engineering design with appropriate pipe sizes, particularly on the gravity return system, are a vital part of the overall design.

Growing on the Floor

In-floor heat, combined with excellent drainage, help ensure that the floors are dry most of the time. This prevents excessive water evaporation and also prevents the spread of disease.

Disease spread is still one of the major concerns with ebb-and-flood floor systems. Fungi, bacteria, and spores can be transported by the watering system, so sanitation is imperative. There are three sterilization

A heated flood floor is three management systems in one: heating, irrigation, and material handling.

methods used to overcome these potential problems: pasteurization, ozone treatment, and ultraviolet light—all of which are expensive to purchase and maintain. Some research work on very fine sand filters has been done in the Netherlands and seems promising.

You need to consider the type of media used for growing the plants. A mix with at least 10% air is required when soil is in the saturated condition, and the container must maintain good contact with the floor.

Managing fertility is also a challenge with subirrigation systems. Nutrient solutions should be maintained at low concentrations because the frequency and style of watering could cause a buildup of salts.

The duration of each watering should be long enough to allow the potting medium to approach field capacity. This varies for the size of the container. For flats and plugs, this may be only three to four minutes. For 3- to 6-in. pots, this may be ten minutes. Larger containers or tubs may require twenty minutes.

May 1999

Flood Floor FAQs

Ratus Fischer

Thinking about adding a particular piece of technology to your business but have lots of unanswered questions? So do many other growers. That's why we're starting a new series called FAQs (frequently asked questions). The first installment (and the source of the idea) is from flood floor expert Ratus Fischer, who says that growers have so many questions about flood floor technology that he wrote them all down to help his staff. Here they are, to help you decide if flood floors are appropriate for your business.

Q: How do you prevent the spread of disease through the water?

A: By preventing pathogens like *Phytophthora* and *Pythium* from getting into the water in the first place. With short watering times of less than ten minutes, the water on the floor begins draining away while the last bit of water is still entering the container. This one-way movement practically prevents pathogens from leaving the container. Spores in the water are likely to settle in the water storage tanks, where we try to let them rest undisturbed until clean-out time.

Floor heat will provide optimal temperatures to keep the roots happy and make them less susceptible to pathogens. Subirrigation keeps the foliage dry, which keeps foliar diseases at bay. Growers with flood floors commonly report their disease problems have decreased rather than increased.

Q: Can we use fungicide drenches on flood floors?

A: As yet, no fungicides have been labeled for application through subirrigation water. They can be applied from above as usual.

Q: Isn't salt accumulation a problem with subirrigation?

A: With any subirrigation, some salt accumulation occurs in the top layer of the soil. Yet very few crops seem to respond negatively, not even Easter lilies with their crown roots. Of course, low-salt fertilizers should be used.

Q: Do we have to change our fertilizer concentrations?

A: Yes. Start out with 50 to 75% of the concentration recommended for overhead watering. Since the water is recirculated, all fertilizer will end up in the plants and not in your well.

Q: Are special containers needed to grow on the floor?

A: No. Most pots and bedding trays on the market will work. On rare occasions, trays with unusually small drain openings have been seen floating.

Q: Which crops will grow best on flood floors? Can we grow bedding plants?

A: Flood floors will work great with all but very few potted crops, from miniatures to baskets. Most growers use the floors for bedding as well. There are some limitations, though. With flood floors, each watering is a full watering, and the small cell packs tend to stay saturated longer than larger containers. Bedding crops that need withholding of water should be watered overhead during those phases of growth. Since the watering with flood floors is very even, crops can be dried out more between waterings before the first plants get damaged.

Q: Can different crops and container sizes be grown on the same floor section?

A: Yes, as long as the crops have similar watering needs. The size of the container doesn't matter much, since any size container with an appropriate soil mix will soak up water to its capacity within the normal flooding time.

Q: How deep should the water be on the floors?

A: As soon as the water makes contact with the soil, the capillary action begins. For all but very large containers, 1 in. of water is sufficient. The systems are normally designed for water depths of up to 2½ in.

Q: How do I provide different fertilizer solutions to the floors?

A: Most flood floor systems have two or three tanks with different fertilizer solutions or plain water. Each floor section can be watered with the appropriate fertilizer mix or concentration.

Q: What kind of fertilizer-mixing system do I need for flood floors?

A: Most likely, a simpler one than your equipment supplier thinks. If you're willing to switch some suction tubes, a basic proportioner will do. Fully automated systems require a bit more hardware. Since the water that comes back from the floor is practically unchanged from what goes to the floor, we need only supply a preset mix to each flood floor tank.

Q: Can we retrofit existing greenhouses with flood floors?

A: Yes. The systems can be adapted to just about any greenhouse layout, as long as each flood section in itself can be kept or made level. The watering sections usually correspond with the bays or houses—typically 1,000 to 6,000 sq. ft. in size. The same is true for floors in newly constructed houses.

Q: For which sizes of greenhouses are flood floors suitable?

A: There's no limit to how large. One flood floor tank system can supply six acres or more of growing area. The only limit is how long a watering time for the whole system is acceptable. There's also no real limit to how small.

Floor heat maintains the ideal root temperatures, prevents excess humidity in the crop zone, and dries the floors quickly, preventing the growth of algae. *Photo courtesy of GreenLink.*

Even a few hundred square feet can be feasible, if the added complexity of full automation isn't required.

Q: Is floor heat necessary for flood floors?

A: Yes, unless the greenhouse is located in a subtropical climate. Floor heat maintains the ideal root temperatures, prevents excess humidity in the crop zone, and dries the floors quickly, preventing the growth of algae. And you still need overhead heat. If the floors were to provide all the heat in the greenhouse, they would be too hot for the plants.

Q: Can flood floors be used outside or in retractable-roof greenhouses?

A: Yes. Rainwater will drain through the same system as the floodwater, but is directed to the outside instead of into the flood system tanks.

Q: How much pitch does a flood floor need?

A: The less pitch there is, the less water is needed to cover the whole floor, but the risk of puddles increases accordingly. A good concrete crew can pour a largely puddle-free floor with a ½ in. of fall over six to ten feet.

Q: How can you keep the flood floor from cracking?

A: Pouring good concrete floors is as much an art as a science. Small cracks are usually only cosmetic and don't cause leakage. If large cracks occur, some of the following advice may have been ignored: Keep the moisture in the concrete while curing, cover the floor with plastic (or water) for seven to fourteen days, and create sufficient control joints.

Q: How can we avoid puddles, and when are they a problem?

A: Use a good vibrating screed adjusted to a perfect V or W shape, fight with your concrete crew to maintain a stiff concrete mix with a slump of no more than four, and place the concrete carefully, without unmixing it by excessive raking and pushing around.

A puddle on the floor is only a problem if it doesn't dry out within a couple of hours after watering. Algae will grow, and plants sitting in the puddles can get watered beyond their comfort. A rule of thumb: Throw a dime into any standing water—if the water covers it, it's a puddle.

Q: Do you need a special contractor to pour a flood floor?

A: Yes and no. Most quality-minded contractors can pour a good flood floor. Since pouring precisely pitched floors is quite different from pouring flat floors, it helps considerably if the contractor is willing to listen to others who have done it before. If you want to eliminate the "guinea pig" factor completely, try to work with someone who has previously done flood floors.

Q: Should I get professional help when designing a flood floor system?

A: If you wish the system to perform as desired, that's an excellent idea. Once the concrete is poured, changes tend to be on the expensive side.

Q: What's the average cost of a flood floor system?

A: A complete system will cost in the range of $4.50 to $5.50 per sq. ft. Costs will be lower if much of the work can be done with in-house labor. These figures include everything from design to operating system: piping, all components, concrete, floor heat (without boiler), and labor. The concrete work accounts for around 60 to 70% of the cost.

With a flood floor system, you not only pay for a watering system, but you also have a concrete floor for maximum flexibility and sanitation and floor heat for optimum control of growth. Savings in labor, improved plant quality, and low maintenance costs over many years of use offset the relatively high initial investment.

Q: Is there equipment available to move pots and trays?

A: Not as much as we'd like to see. Conveyor belts are quite common. Visser's forklift-based Space-o-Mat works well for larger batches of same-size pots. The latest development for larger operations is growing flats and pots on floodable pallets, which are moved by a gantry system.

March 2000

How Small Can You Go?

Ratus Fischer

In the relatively short history of flood floor irrigation, mostly larger greenhouse operations have installed these systems. The reason small growers haven't yet made use of this technology isn't necessarily the high initial costs, but more likely lack of information and experience. With little support available from the irrigation industry, it takes a good measure of pioneering spirit—and considerable financial resources—to take the leap into flood floors.

But this has changed now. Small- and medium-sized growers are discovering that they can use flood floors to gain the same benefits larger growers see: labor savings, uniform watering, dry foliage for reduced disease problems, flexible use of the growing space, low maintenance, and full water recirculation.

The Technical Side

There's no limit to how small and simple flood floors can be—a tree nursery in Oregon lines a 100-sq. ft. section of greenhouse floor with plastic and fills it with a garden hose. However, different sized flood floor systems call for different designs. Simply scaling down a large system will make it expensive and is often impractical. But there are some features common to flood floors of any size:

- The plants sit on concrete floors, which are pitched just enough to ensure puddle-free drainage.
- Curbs or rubber barriers separate the floor area into manageable watering zones, which generally correspond to the bays of the greenhouse.
- Each watering zone is filled 1 to 2 in. deep with water and then drained. The plants sit in the water for less than ten minutes. This is time enough for the capillary action to provide a thorough watering but not long enough to allow pathogens to migrate from pots into the surrounding water.
- In-floor heat is crucial for the optimum microclimate and provides valuable control of the root temperatures. Larger floor heating systems typically tie in with the overhead heat. Small systems can be as simple as a household water heater and a circulation pump connected to in-floor tubing.

Other features vary with the size and application of a system. A system of 100,000 sq. ft. or more typically has from ten to a hundred watering zones of 2,000 to 6,000 sq. ft. each; short watering times of an hour or less per acre; two or three solution storage tanks that allow the grower to choose between fertilizer mixes or plain water; low maintenance water filtration; and fully automated operation, often integrated with an environmental computer.

As the systems get smaller, the picture changes. The number and size of watering zones decreases. More and smaller zones add flexibility but cost marginally more to install than fewer large ones. And there's less need to push for high speed—even a "slower" system will water everything in less than an hour. However, we still want to be sure the water doesn't sit for more than ten minutes on any watering zone.

As for fertilization, experience shows that a choice of one or two fertilizer solutions covers the needs of most small growers. With an appropriate design, it's easy to add more tanks later, if needed. The higher costs for in-ground tanks are usually justified in larger systems; smaller systems typically have aboveground tanks for ease of installation. The size of the tanks is largely determined by the size of the watering zones, not by the number of zones in a system.

Even the smallest systems normally run unattended on a programmable irrigation controller. However, automated switching between fertilizer solutions and the associated tank refilling add costs that generally aren't justifiable with small systems. In most cases, a simple proportioner can handle all fertilizer mixing needs.

In a nutshell, with proper design, a small grower can realize nearly all the benefits that the big growers get from their flood floors: quality watering, recirculation, and basic automation.

It's the Economy

No matter the size of a flood floor system, the initial investment is considerable. Realistically, you're looking at $4.50 to $6.00 per sq. ft. But don't stop reading yet! These numbers include all materials and all (often hidden) labor costs. And the investment buys you more than just a laborsaving irrigation system. You get concrete floors for flexibility and sanitation, in-floor heat for better growth and disease control, and technology that will keep you ahead of any coming environmental runoff regulations.

Flood floors are also a long-term investment, with ten to twenty years of low-maintenance operation. But for many smaller growers, such up-front investment is out of reach, even if it pays back handsomely. That's where another aspect of flood floors comes in: Practically all the technology involved is simple. If you've got some basic handyman skills, you and your crew can do almost all the work yourself. And not all work needs to be done at once. It's common to put the piping into the ground, pour the floors in stages, and add tanks, pumps, and controls as your wallet allows. Well-drained concrete floors are assets even before the flood system is operational.

Speaking of concrete, 60 to 70% of the cost of flood floors lies in the concrete work. Sophisticated concrete pouring and finishing equipment can be helpful, but isn't essential for good floors; experienced and careful people are. Laser leveling is indispensable.

Also, while there are a few special components required for flood floors, such as self-cleaning high-volume filters, large water valves, and rubber water barriers, most other materials can be bought locally.

When Not to Invest

Now that you know how easy flood floors can be, there are some situations where they're not a good investment, regardless of size. These include:

- Inexpensive greenhouse space that's used only seasonally for bedding plants. While many bedding crops do well on subirrigation, it's really the potted crops where the payoff for flood floors comes in.
- Older, existing greenhouses where the floor system is likely to outlast the structure.
- When growing crops requiring lots of handwork and manual labor. In these situations, ebb-and-flood bench systems may be more appropriate. However, given flood floor benefits and the reasonable cost, more and more growers are finding ways to adapt their crop production techniques to floors instead of benches.

Flood floors are essentially simple. But well-functioning simplicity is the result of competent design and lots of experience. Before you commit to a flood floor, connect with growers who've built and operate systems—they're more than willing to talk about them. And talk to professionals about how they can tailor a system to your specific need. This way, you'll prevent unnecessary expenses. As the interest in small flood floor system expands and grows, there will be design and component packages available on the market that will simplify construction and lower costs.

Summer 2000

Water Works

Bill Sheldon

Greenleaf Nursery, one of the country's largest growers, pumps 2 million gallons of water daily from eastern Oklahoma's Tenkiller Reservoir. Yet by day's end, the 570-acre facility will have pumped nearly double that amount—3.5 million gallons—through the nursery, thanks to $2.5 million recycling system.

The recycling project at Greenleaf's Oklahoma facility, located thirty-five miles east of Muskogee, near the Arkansas border, consists of some ninety miles of pipe, 10,500 sprinkler heads, and eight gravity-fed holding basins with a combined capacity of 17 million gallons.

They started the recycling project in 1989, with the first five years consumed in buying needed land from the Corps of Engineers. Rather than pull water continuously from the reservoir and let it run back into the ground naturally—taking nutrients and other runoff contaminants with it—Greenleaf pumps reservoir water up 150 ft. into a gravity-fed ditch system that supplies the eight holding ponds, which supply various areas of the nursery. All the water applied through the overhead system that doesn't get used by the plants is recaptured by an underground drainage system. "Some water could get pumped in our internal system three or four times in a day," says Dave Morrison, vice president of operations. Dave adds that the new system has cut Greenleaf's use of lake water in half.

Greenleaf has had plant production at this location since 1960—there are also sites in El Campo, Texas (about seventy-five miles southwest of Houston), seventy miles east of Raleigh, North Carolina, and another in eastern Oklahoma (near Ft. Gibson). Greenleaf products are shipped directly to three thousand retail mass merchandisers in forty states, Canada and Mexico. Combined production is more than 18 million liners; 400,000 bare root trees; 900,000 seedlings; and 12 million finished plants. Propagation primarily is in woody ornamentals, but they have a good representation of ornamental flowers.

Dave says the project is entirely voluntary and there still are no laws that require such recycling. "We felt someday we'd be forced into doing this, so we wanted to get ahead of that and do it our way. We used our own crew for a lot of construction, saving a lot of money."

Distribution channels (right) carry runoff water into holding ponds for recycling. The tank on the left is just a temporary holding area for water destined for one of the eight main ponds.
Photo by Bill Sheldon.

Mark Andrews, superintendent of research and development, offers another advantage to recycling besides water savings. "Oklahoma State University has monitored storm water discharge [from the nursery], expecting to find nutrients going into the lake. Actually, nutrients weren't flushing out of the storage basins—which surprised us."

Water quality is always an issue when you're recycling. Greenleaf does daily monitoring of water, while state and federal inspectors do periodic testing of the reservoir. Diseases aren't a problem in the system. "It's amazing . . . when water is held in basins, pathogens are decreased," says OSU professor Sharon von Broembsen, an extension plant pathologist who has monitored the system. "Nutrients are increased, and pollution of local water supplies is being eliminated. We've often tested water coming out of their system, and it's at levels of drinkability. What Greenleaf is doing works."

Although Greenleaf's project is on a very large scale, those involved feel the recycling program can be advantageous for medium-sized and small operations, too. "If you're closer to a city, your nursery might have more visibility and get more attention from clean water folks, so you ought to look into it," Mark says.

Sharon suggests that a system even as small as a concrete septic tank is feasible. She thinks retail nurseries and garden centers also ought to look into the program, adding that there are significant enough cost savings in water and fertilizer for smaller operations to invest in an appropriate system.

"Even a small volume of irrigation runoff with concentrated nutrients can end up in local streams," Sharon warns. "In urban locations, owners may find themselves responsible for storm water quality that discharges across their property. Channels can be designed to divert this water around the nursery to avoid mixing with irrigation runoff containing fertilizers, herbicides, and pesticides."

Sharon does note some possible disadvantages that smaller operators might consider, including installation costs, possible build-up of salts in the water, herbicide and pesticide contamination, and the potential distribution of weed seeds. However, "the primary disadvantage of a capture-and-recycle system is the possibility that waterborne pathogens will be recycled back onto crops, resulting in increased disease problems," she points out. But her research has shown that this hasn't been the case at Greenleaf. "These systems make good sense from a practical perspective. Water costs are reduced, a constant water supply is assured, storm water is controlled more effectively, and overall management flexibility is enhanced."

Another contributor to the science of the system is Jim Leach, who has been the technical lead in monitoring the system for the Oklahoma Conservation Commission. He says the recycling "creates awareness and is a good education program, especially for employees."

While the science is important, Mark has to consider the end result—the impact on Greenleaf's customers. "[Recycled water] is actually beneficial with woodies—they grow better with less fertilizer. The roses get much better bud color. We maintain a predictable product. But I'm not sure the buyer has necessarily noticed a change in the product."

January 2000

Chapter 7

Carts

Who's Got the Carts?

Chris Beytes

We recently received an intriguing letter from a Georgia bedding plant grower who was inquiring about the whereabouts of his shipping carts. It seems that, like most growers, by the end of the bedding plant season, he has fewer carts than he started with.

Not that he expected us to know where his carts were. His was more of a philosophical question: How can something the size of a cart vanish like a sock from a dryer?

His letter described the typical situation: He delivers carts to a store. Later, a competitor's driver, in a hurry to get home, invariably picks up some of his carts. When the driver gets back home, the greenhouse owner may decide to simply ship the wrong carts out with the next order heading in the general direction of where they came from, assuming they'll eventually get back to their rightful owner.

"Now it's January, and we're still short more than 20% of our carts," he laments. "Somebody has them, but rather than calling the rightful owner and straightening it out, nothing gets done. Is it not time that our industry deals with this problem and puts some ethics and honesty into the cart equation?"

Coping with Cart Loss

Ethics and *honesty* are pretty strong words. Do we have a cart theft problem? Or is it carelessness on the part of drivers and store managers and ambivalence on the part of business owners? We thought we'd ask around a bit to get some more opinions.

First, when it comes to vanishing carts, he's right on target. We've certainly heard the complaint before. It's common practice for growers to order a fresh batch of carts each winter to replace the ones that mysteriously vanished last season. Our grower says he lost 20% of his carts, which is high according to our informal polls—3 to 8% is more common. But if you have

3,000 carts, that's 90 to 240 carts, and at $300 to $500 per cart, you're losing up to $120,000. Most growers simply write this off as a cost of doing business with the chains. (Or do you have nerve enough to send The Home Depot a bill?)

What about unscrupulous growers actually stealing carts? Admittedly, we heard secondhand tales of growers who have found a competitor using their carts for in-house transportation. Most growers, however, have hundreds or even thousands of carts; a few stolen ones won't help their business. So, that can't explain the thousands of carts lost each year.

Careless drivers do sometimes bring back the wrong carts, in which case growers told us they'll try to call the rightful owner—who may also have gotten the wrong carts—to arrange a swap. Growers say they do what they can to prevent the problem, but a lot of carts look very similar, and drivers will argue that their schedules are too tight for careful cart identification.

Stores also add to the problem, with naive employees using grower carts as though they were store property. And we've heard of drivers from another greenhouse "temporarily" using someone else's carts to unload his product.

Solutions

Here are a few things that growers are trying to do about cart losses.

Paint

You can paint your carts, either with a few splashes of color or by spraying the whole thing. Cannon Equipment says some growers request custom-painted carts, which adds twenty dollars to the price per cart. However, we were told of a Northwest grower who paints his carts Day-Glo orange and still loses them.

Unique sizes

Some growers have gone to a unique size to prevent driver confusion. This seems to be one of the simplest solutions, provided you need new carts and can come up with a size that fits your truck and your flats while still being one of a kind.

Engraved names

Cart manufacturers now routinely stamp business names, addresses, and phone numbers on carts. Some growers put an 800 number on their carts to make it easy for someone to notify them of a lost cart. But it still requires a harried truck driver to look at each nameplate.

Bar codes

Most growers track where each cart goes. If one's gone at the end of the season, they know where it was last sent. Some track by numbering their carts and recording where they're shipped; others use bar codes and hand scanners. One East Coast grower has bar codes on the bottom of each cart and scanners embedded in the floor at the entrance to each loading bay. Every cart is automatically scanned when it goes in or out of a truck, updating the computer.

Cart bounties

Pay your drivers a dollar bounty for every cart they bring back. That works for one large grower we talked with. Another said he plans to implement a bounty program this year. That keeps drivers on the lookout year-round.

However, make sure you tell them it's a dollar for *your* carts only. Otherwise, we'll know where to look for all of the missing carts next season.

March 1999

Cart Attack!

Chris Beytes

Powell Plant Farm lost just 80 of their 9,200-plus carts last season. How'd they keep track of them so well? By simply "managing their system."

Rough estimates suggest that there are more than a million carts being used to move plants from greenhouses to retailers in North America. But if casual surveys indicate that growers "lose" anywhere from 3 to 15% of their carts each season, some 30,000 to 150,000 carts—worth $300 to $800 each—are lying around unclaimed in the backrooms of retailers or in cart yards at the wrong greenhouses. And that's just one season's worth.

What can be done? Growers have tried bar codes, embossed nameplates, and custom paint colors, only to still come up missing hundreds of carts at the end of the season. Now there's even talk of cart "networks" or "pools," global positioning system chips embedded in carts, national cart-tracking Web sites—and even asking retailers to pay for missing carts.

At least one grower says such drastic steps aren't necessary. Powell Plant Farm, Troup, Texas, uses 9,200 carts to deliver 160 acres' worth of production across much of the U.S. Yet their typical annual cart loss over the last three years has been just 1.0 to 1.5%. How do they do it? By managing the system, says Powell's chief information officer, Les Johnson. "But you've got to have the right method of tracking a rack," Les adds, as we talk in his office about Powell's system. "You can't just throw them out there without your name on them or without a label and expect them to come back."

Here, then, is the Powell system and how they manage it:

Prevention

Les defines "loss" in two ways: physical loss and logical loss. Physical loss happens when the cart is truly gone from the system. Maybe someone else picked it up or stole it. Or else it was damaged in some way that makes it unusable. Logical loss is when your cart is still out there in the system, but you don't know where. It might be in the backroom of a retailer or at the wrong retailer. Or its bar code was scanned incorrectly or not at all, so the cart isn't where your computer says it should be.

Powell's starts with a very standard cart. Their 9,200 carts are standard Cannon units with no special paint or modifications. They have "Powell Plant Farm" embossed into the metal. There's also a plastic bar code sticker that gives each cart its own unique identification number. The number is also printed under the bar code so the cart can be tracked by scanner or human eye.

In addition, there's a Plexiglas panel where each order's routing ticket goes. The routing ticket tells what trailer the cart gets loaded into, how many carts are in the order, and what store the order will go to. The routing ticket also has its own bar code, indicating the order it goes with.

When the carts are loaded into trailers, the cart bar code and the routing ticket bar code are both scanned using a PDT 3100 Symbol Technology handheld scanner. This will update a computer file with the

Their name embossed in metal, a bar code with a human-readable number, and a place to firmly attach a routing sheet—that's all Powell Plant Farm needs to manage their fleet of 9,200 carts.

information about where each cart is going. Once scanned, Powell's knows which carts are at which customers, the delivery date, and the order number the cart was carrying.

Before drivers leave with an order, they're given a cart pickup list. This tells them what carts should be ready for pickup along the routes they're about to drive. The list can be generated by state, city, zip code, and individual store location. It's also based on a forty-eight-hour turnaround: Les gives customers two days to receive the order and empty the cart. Once a cart has been out that long, it automatically goes onto the available-for-pickup list. One truck can hold twenty-seven to thirty-two assembled carts; Powell's drivers will try to pick up as many as fifty-four disassembled carts.

What about half-empty carts? Powell's drivers are responsible for consolidating carts so they can retrieve as many as possible. Powell's in-store merchandisers help with this process.

Right now carts are scanned when they leave the loading dock; they aren't scanned back in when they're brought back to the greenhouse. Les says that recording returning carts is currently a manual process, but they may change to a scanning process.

Quick Turns

With just 9,200 carts to serve 160 acres of production, Powell's depends on turning carts quickly. One way to do that is with central pickup points. During the peak of spring, they maintain a cart yard in Dallas and in Houston (and expect to have one in Atlanta). One driver does nothing but drive the routes, picking up empty carts and taking them to the pickup yard, where employees disassemble them. Les says this allows his other drivers to drop full carts at the stores then pick up a full load of empties for the return trip, saving time and letting Powell's turn each of their 125 trailers in one and a half to two days. The big challenge is tracking each cart from the customer to the pickup point and then back to the greenhouse. To this end, the pickup point is treated just like another customer.

There are times when Powell's won't leave carts at a store, such as during slow sales times, past a certain delivery mileage, if they know they won't be doing a second delivery run in a certain area or to certain customers, or if they know they won't be back to a customer in seven days. The routing tickets specify if carts shouldn't be left. It may take time for the driver to unload the carts, but it speeds turns and cuts down on potential losses.

What about those carts that do happen to get "logically" lost? Les says they do several things. First, merchandisers and drivers are expected to keep an eye out for carts at all times. Having merchandisers in stores prevents carts from finding their way onto other trucks or into the backroom of the store. They help locate carts that didn't get scanned or weren't scanned properly. Powell's also asks customers to call if a cart is at a store for more than a few days.

Along with finding their own carts, drivers are trained to not bring home somebody else's carts. In fact, bringing home the wrong carts is grounds for disciplinary action, Les says, like getting a speeding ticket.

Managing the System

Overall, the cart-tracking system at Powell Plant Farm is fairly simple and uses technology available to any grower. You don't even have to have a bar code and scanner, just a number. So why do so many other growers, using the same system, seem to have much higher losses?

Les says that maybe growers working in high-density markets, such as the Northeast, have a tougher time. He adds that some growers may have created problems for themselves by starting out too casually with their cart program, shipping them to retailers more on good faith than with a formal tracking plan in place. As the number of carts increased, the system eventually got out of hand, and retailers have become conditioned to take carts for granted. To Les, the solution doesn't lie with more technology or with shifting the burden to the stores or even a third party. Growers can manage their own carts.

"I don't care if you do it with an Excel spreadsheet or with pencil and paper," he says. "You've got to have a way to track when that rack left this facility, and it has to be a designated, very distinguishable asset—that means numbered—and that asset has got to be tracked to some place. And when it gets there, you better know that it's there, and you'd better have a way to track it to get it back."

January 2001

Growers against Rack Theft

Troy Bouk

At GrowerExpo 2001, held in Chicago in January, I had the opportunity to represent Fernlea Flowers as one of five participants on a panel of experts from varying segments of our industry who discussed the topic, "Carts: Gotta Have 'Em—Now How Do You Keep 'Em?"

One idea that attracted attention was the hiring of detectives to build cases against known rack thieves, who would then be prosecuted.

The idea originated at our Apopka, Florida, location this past year. A trucking company was offloading plant material on Wellmaster racks identical to those we use, with one exception: all the bases were painted black (ours are lime green). However, on closer inspection, we realized the racks were, in fact, ours. Underneath the black paint was our lime green paint, plus two holes under the tongue of each base matched perfectly with holes that we drill to install our bar codes. The bar codes, however, had all been removed.

We'd received several reports of a central Florida plant carrier doing this, but now we had considerable proof. We called the local police to make a report, yet despite all the evidence, they said they wouldn't take any action. They said they'd have to catch the culprits actually taking the rack from one of the stores we ship to in their district. Plus, they added, they don't have the resources to undertake such a campaign.

Next, I contacted the Federal Bureau of Investigation, since transporting stolen property across state lines is a federal offense. The FBI agent I spoke with said that, although a crime was being committed, he couldn't commit any resources to catch the thieves. He did, however, make the following recommendations:

- Send registered letters to as many growers in our industry as possible telling them that use of our racks by any entity other than Fernlea is strictly prohibited and that if caught, the offending entity would be subject to prosecution.
- Hire good investigators (such as ex-FBI agents) to stake out and thoroughly document the thefts.
- Use the evidence to prosecute to the fullest extent of the law.
- Take out full-page ads with industry magazines such as *GrowerTalks* to notify the industry—including major retailers—about who was convicted for rack theft.

The agent believed that, by doing this, the risk of prosecution would be such an overwhelming deterrent that rack theft would be dramatically reduced.

But detectives aren't cheap, especially when you consider that it may take days to stake out stores, follow trucks, and prepare evidence. However, when you compare the cost of prosecution against the cost of tracking racks and replacing lost racks, it seems quite reasonable. (We don't consider a rack to be missing unless two attempts have been made to retrieve it from the store and the rack has been missing for more than three months.)

Jack Van de Wetering, Ivy Acres, Long Island, New York, suggests that a group of the largest growers join together to fund a program to fight rack theft. It would be called Growers Against Rack Theft, or "GART." This would substantially increase the funds available to fight rack theft and ultimately reduce everyone's rack collection costs. So far, Fernlea, Ivy Acres, New York's Kurt Weiss Growers, and Maryland's Bell Nursery have committed to funding this effort.

I've proposed that the contributors to GART each identify problem regions. We'd hire detectives to operate in the most frustrating areas first. We'd educate them on identifying each member's racks and authorized versus unauthorized trucks. The program would be administered by Pam Jones of Fernlea Flowers, who'd hire the detectives and act as liaison between detectives and GART members. Costs would be divided among all members of GART based on the number of racks each member owns as a percentage of the total racks owned by all members.

This program isn't intended to prosecute growers who occasionally retrieve other growers' racks. Rather, GART is being established to stop the deliberate use of our racks by others.

How will we differentiate between accidental retrieval and theft? Quite simply—Fernlea never uses another grower's racks to ship our product. We make all attempts to return the rack to its owner. We expect other growers to extend us the same courtesy.

For information on joining GART, please call Pam Jones, Tel: (850) 442-6188, ext. 266.

March 2001

Chapter 8
Maintenance and Damage

Crank Case

Jennifer Duffield White

When you've got a stuck tractor behind the greenhouse and a busted flat filler in the production barn, preventative maintenance is the last thing on your mind. But making time for it may save your sanity and keep the list of technical emergencies from growing.

Whether your business is half an acre or more than fifty, in one way or another your greenhouse is automated. You may not have the latest transplanter or environmental-control computer, but keeping the simple gearboxes and driveshafts on your vents and curtain systems trouble-free is essential for every grower. Preventative maintenance from the start saves time, resources, and a lot of worry.

With sixty acres of production facilities, Mark Sheldon, maintenance manager for Green Circle Growers, Oberlin, Ohio, and his staff of twelve have enough to keep them busy. In fact, we were lucky to catch Mark in early February when they were in the middle of production, with plenty of equipment to repair.

Eliminating problems from day one isn't just a philosophy at Green Circle: It's a necessity. With acre after acre of mechanized equipment and a slew of technical difficulties each day, Mark has found that simple periodic checks make gearboxes the least of his worries. Of course, Mark has seen faulty gearboxes in his day, but says the best way to come out ahead is with prevention. "There's a wide range of gearboxes out there," he says, adding the recommendation to "buy decent quality so you don't have to maintain it as often."

An important but overlooked aspect of gearbox life is installation. Mark suggests taking extra time to make sure the box is level and the breather is straight up and down. If the boxes are installed properly with care, Mark sees fit to check them once a year. "Generally speaking, if you keep track of the oil level and check for leaks, then you shouldn't have too many problems," he says.

Ridder USA and Wadsworth Control Systems, both of which manufacturer gearbox systems for greenhouses, agree that proper installation should eliminate difficulties. But if you do run into problems, especially leakage, don't let things go. While a box might still run for several more months without failure, it will save money and time in the long run to take care of any problems, even minor ones, immediately. "Getting by" isn't good enough.

Most gearboxes take oil or grease. Some, such as those from Wadsworth Control Systems, use synthetic grease that doesn't require replacement. The gearboxes at Green Circle Growers take 90-weight oil, but when Mark does need to add lubrication, he says, "We usually go with a good-quality red grease."

Mark tends to see more of his maintenance problems with fan belts and louvered vents. As far as driveshafts are concerned, proper installation is key once again, along with good welding. He does see more wear on the rack-and-pinion systems because they use aluminum racks, which wear down more easily. "You can't run metal against metal," he adds, saying that regular lubrication is imperative on these installations.

George Dean, owner of Wadsworth Control Systems, recommends that rack and elbow pinion arms be lubricated with Teflon grease at least twice a year. Along the same lines, he tells customers to test their torque and limit switches twice a year to ensure proper operation.

March 2000

Fire and Sparks

Chris Beytes

Probably half the greenhouses in America have a welding outfit on the premises for making light repairs and fabrications. If you don't have one but think you could use one, here are some welding tips from David Sprinkel of the Hobart Institute of Welding Technology in Troy, Ohio.

Welders

Gas welders

The most traditional style of welding is with an oxyacetylene torch, but that's being phased out by arc welders, David says, because the torches are slow and tricky to learn. Gas welding outfits are most often used for brazing and cutting.

Arc welders

These are sometimes called "buzz boxes" or "stick machines" for the welding rod or "stick" used with them. They plug into a 220-volt electrical service and are available in AC or AC/DC models. A small machine will weld steel from 16 gauge up to about ¼ in. thick and costs as little as just a few hundred dollars. Larger machines will handle thicker metal and work more quickly.

According to David, the most versatile machines are AC *and* DC. These let you choose AC or DC welding rods, depending on the job you're doing, such as deep, heavy welding or shallow, smooth finish welding. You can't weld aluminum with a small buzz box; that takes a big industrial arc welder.

You may also have heard of TIG welding. TIG stands for *tungsten inert gas* and is a type of arc welding that uses special rods and a tungsten electrode shielded by inert gas. David says it's most often used for high-quality work and on specialty metals.

Wire-feed welders

Wire-feed machines eliminate the need to hold and feed the rod by hand. Instead, an electrode wire is fed through a gun automatically. David says they're great machines for beginners and are also good for thin material that's easily burned through. Wire-feed welders are fast and, with the proper setup, can weld aluminum. As with arc welders, the larger the machine, the heavier the material they'll weld. You can buy small, 110-volt wire-feed welders for under four hundred dollars.

Wire-feed welders are also called MIG welders, which stands for *metal inert gas.* The gas is used to shield the molten metal from the atmosphere and comes from one of two sources: the wire, which generates its own gas as it burns (self-shielded wire), or from a gas bottle on the machine—the gas is fed through the nozzle of the gun to shield the weld puddle.

What's Best?

David says there's a lot of overlap between stick and wire welders, and each has its strong points. Stick machines are quick and easy, and you can equip them with long cables for accessing hard-to-reach areas. Wire welders are easy to learn to use and are fast, but you have to work within about ten feet of the wire-feeding unit. Gasoline-powered welder/generator combinations that let you weld or generate electricity for power tools can be a good buy. They're available as stick or wire machines.

What You Shouldn't Weld

According to David, while there's no governing body watching over your minor repair work, there are at least two areas off limits to amateurs: structures and pressure vessels.

Structural welding, such as building a packing barn, is governed by the American Welding Society Structural Code; you must be certified and follow set procedures.

Pressure vessel welding—such as your boiler system—is governed by the American Society of Mechanical Engineer Pressure Vessel Codes. Again, only certified welders can work on these systems.

Rather than just reading the manual and burning up some metal, take a welding course at your local vocational school or adult education center to learn the basics. If you want more advanced training, a specialty school, such as the Hobart Institute of Welding Technology, can equip you for the big jobs.

April 2000

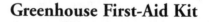

Greenhouse First-Aid Kit

Sara Rowekamp

When you entered the horticulture industry and decided to become a grower, did you have any idea you'd also become an electrician, plumber, and maintenance manager in addition to a plant grower?

By now, of course, you know you'll wear each of these hats at one time or another throughout your work week, and it seems that your need to switch hats occurs at the most inopportune times. Whether it's over the weekend when it's hard to get parts, or in the heat of the day when all the plants need watering, or perhaps late at night when all the hardware stores are closed—that's when trouble usually arises.

For that reason, it's good practice to have spare parts and tools on hand to make quick repairs. Sometimes a problem is easy to fix on the spot, while at other times you'll only be able to make a short-term fix, saving the true repair for later. In either case, a greenhouse "first-aid kit" will alleviate some of your troubles. Here's what we recommend you have on hand:

Greenhouse Structure
- One roll wide poly tape. You never know when a tear will occur, such as when a trapped bird will attempt to break through the roof rather than going out the entrance door. Patching a tear early will keep you from losing the whole roof later.
- One spare roll double polyethylene. Be sure to work your spare roll of film into your reroofing rotation so it hasn't dry-rotted when you need it.
- Glass panes. For when that rock slips out of the hand of an innocent child.
- Polycarbonate/acrylic panels. This stuff is pretty tough, but it will break because hail is an amazing thing. Or that innocent child may have a great pitching arm.
- Spare inflation fan. If the current blower goes out, the wind picks up, and you don't have a backup blower, you may need that roll of poly sooner than you thought.
- Several lengths of poly lock or wiggle wire. Once again, wind and unsecured plastic aren't a good combination.

Basic Tools and Spares
The tools in your first-aid kit should not be the same tools you use everyday for maintenance—this ensures that the tools you need are there when you need them. In this kit, include:
- Screwdrivers (including Phillips and slotted, a nutdriver set, and a TORX driver set)
- Pliers with wire cutter
- Basic wrench set
- Utility knife
- Hammer
- Flashlight
- Tape measure
- Self-tapping (TEK) screws
- Nuts, bolts, screws, and nails
- Grease and penetrating oil
- Duct tape
- Electrical tape

Other tools you find yourself using often
- Ladder, because you never know how high your equipment is until you need to repair it.
- Electric drill, with attachment for driving self-tapping screws.

Environmental controls, motors, and electrical
- Fuses for environmental controls. Keep on hand at least one of each amp fuse your equipment needs. Don't cheat and use the incorrect fuse.
- Multimeter to test electrical wires for current.
- Spare vent motor or an alternate method of opening vents. A few spare racks for these vents would be helpful, as well.
- One or two spare fan motors, and several belts for the fans. When you're rooting poinsettia cuttings in the heat of summer, you can't risk any lack of air movement and cooling.

Plumbing
- One length of each size PVC you have around your greenhouse.
- An assortment of PVC fittings: couplings, 90s, Ts, caps, and plugs.
- PVC cement and cleaner.
- Solenoid valves.

Heaters
- Lighter or matches to relight the pilot.
- Torpedo heater in the event the heater just won't work. If you don't want to invest in a backup torpedo heater, contact your local tool rental service to request an after-hours phone number to call for someone to meet you at night in the event the need for a heater arises.

Shade and evaporative cooling pads
- Roll of monofilament wire to replace broken or worn wires in your shade system.
- Spare pump for evaporative cooling system.

You may never be prepared for every emergency, but with these items on hand, a breakdown will be an obstacle rather than a catastrophe.

June 2000

Rust Never Sleeps

Chris Beytes

A grower friend of ours called recently to inform us that he'd just spent a ton of money replacing the bottom few feet of all of his greenhouse columns, as rust had practically eaten them off at ground level. "If this is a common problem, half the greenhouses in the country could be ready to blow over in the first high wind, and growers don't even know it," he warns.

While this surely isn't the case, we thought we should take a look at the special challenge of burying steel in wet, salty dirt and concrete and having it last as long as possible. After all, the columns are responsible for holding up your entire greenhouse structure.

According to Linda Barnett, vice president of sales for Stuppy Greenhouse Manufacturing, Kansas City, Missouri, the basic nature of the greenhouse environment, with its moisture and chemicals, is tough on steel, especially when it comes in contact with the ground. "You can't pile dirt around a column and keep it wet all the time and expect it to last," she says, adding that growers are often in a hurry to get a new house up and don't take the time for simple measures that can prevent rust.

The Problem

The mechanical tubing used in greenhouses is manufactured from long, narrow coils of flat carbon steel that are fed through rollers to form a tube. The seam is automatically welded, and the tube passes through a zinc-galvanizing bath for rust protection. The tube's interior is protected with a zinc-rich paint, and the exterior is coated with polymer coating for added protection. Then the tubing is cut to length. If your greenhouse builder is using quality tubing, such as Allied Tube, Conduit's Gatorshield, or Century Tube Corporation's Mechani-Max tubing, you can be sure that you're getting the best available.

That doesn't mean, however, that it won't rust, especially in the tough environment of a commercial greenhouse. The problem isn't just moisture, says Century's Tim Ogg. Low soil pH and high salinity play a major role, so the region of the country you're building in may impact the life of your steel. Coastal areas with shallow, salty water tables are especially vulnerable, as are areas with extremely acidic soils.

The chemicals your columns are exposed to also contribute to rust. For example, steel used in cattle buildings has a very short life because of the constant exposure to urine. We certainly don't have that problem, but fertilizers and pesticides can be just as caustic, especially if you use spray methods that allow chemicals to saturate the soil directly around columns.

Internal moisture is yet another battle. Condensation can puddle inside the column, or rain leaks at the gutter can allow water to get in. Drilling a weep hole in the column at ground level to allow moisture to escape is a good solution, but this breaks the galvanized coating, allowing rust to gain an easy foothold. So be sure to seal the edges of any holes with a zinc-rich primer.

The Solution

Just how do you protect your greenhouse columns? Allied's "Tech Bulletin #51-95" offers builders several suggestions for extending column life. First, if you're setting columns in concrete, make sure you use a Portland cement–based product. Its high alkalinity helps protect steel from rust. Gypsum-based concrete is usually lower in pH and is also slightly water soluble and can soften when exposed to moisture, allowing rust-inducing water and oxygen to penetrate. Concrete should extend above the soil line and should be slightly pitched on top for drainage.

If you're setting columns without concrete, they should be protected with roofing tar, shrink-wrap PVC tube, or a heavy, waterproof paint. Make sure any coating extends above the soil line. And as with weep holes, make sure you seal the edges of any saw cuts or holes with a zinc-rich primer.

Allied has recently introduced a new product, ArmorCoat, that they say improves the corrosion resistance of their standard steel tubing by four to five times. ArmorCoat is a thermoplastic coating that can be applied to a specific location on the tube, such as at the bottom 3 or 4 ft. of greenhouse columns. It offers an added measure of protection against ground-level rust without the hassle of applying tar or other coatings.

Greenhouse manufacturers are well aware of the risk of column rust and should offer specific solutions to customers who want added protection for their greenhouse columns. However, they can't force preventative measures on you if you're not willing to pay for them.

Remember, protecting your greenhouse columns isn't something you can do after the concrete is poured. Spending some extra time and money up front can mean years of extra life from your greenhouse.

June 1998

Keep Maintenance Top-of-Mind

P. Allen Hammer

Using the "fix as needed" approach for your greenhouse heating and cooling equipment is the worst management system you could choose. However, I think it's an often-used approach. I see at least one greenhouse heater pollution problem each year. I've also seen cooling fans blowing into the greenhouse because the wiring was backwards and fans running at half speed because of loose belts.

I'm convinced that heating and cooling equipment is often the least maintained of greenhouse equipment. However, let's start the discussion of heating and cooling equipment at the selection stage, because that's also very important.

Buy Right, Install Right

Heaters and fans installed in the greenhouse should be designed for greenhouse use. The greenhouse is a harsh environment that requires special considerations for heating and cooling equipment. This can be particularly true for greenhouses that are not used for periods of the year when the equipment can be exposed to extremes in environment. The equipment manufacturer should adhere to the National Greenhouse Manufacturers Association (NGMA) design standards for the greenhouse. Purchasing your equipment from these manufacturers ensures that you're getting greenhouse-rated equipment.

Greenhouse heaters and fans should be installed according to manufacturers' specifications. Different types of heaters—natural gravity vented, power vented, and those with separated combustion areas, for instance—use very different approaches to ventilation, each requiring specific installation details.

Except for electric unit heaters, all greenhouse heaters require venting. A proper vent cap must always be installed on the vent pipe to protect the heater and to avoid backdrafts. Provide a fresh air intake of 1 sq. in. of free area for each 1,000 Btus burned. The height and length of your vent pipe and chimney stack must meet specific design criteria to function properly—it's not as simple as buying a heater, hanging it in the greenhouse, and attaching a vent pipe and chimney stack.

Another very important consideration in selecting heaters and fans is determining size (heating or airflow capacity) and the number of units you need. There are several excellent references that can help you determine greenhouse heating and cooling requirements. Manufacturers will also help with these calculations.

In addition, I think it's important to follow several very important rules in selecting heaters and fans: First, always equip a greenhouse with at least two heaters and two fans. Multiple units provide the opportunity for staging and give you some backup in case of equipment failure. I also suggest using two-speed fans, as this gives you even more cooling flexibility.

Along with fans, evaporative cooling pads are strongly recommended for summer cooling, even in the Midwest. Even on humid summer days, evaporative cooling pads will provide a much-improved growing environment over fans alone. Properly designed, constructed, and maintained greenhouse evaporative cooling systems are amazingly efficient and inexpensive to operate for the benefits they give.

Seasonal Systems

Winter and summer ventilation are equally important; however, the mechanics of accomplishing them are very different and often misunderstood.

Summer ventilation using fans is usually designed to provide one air exchange per minute in the plant growing area to reduce greenhouse air temperature and provide fresh air. Hot air in the upper roof area usually isn't disturbed, and horizontal airflow (HAF) fans are generally turned off.

Winter ventilation is used to reduce greenhouse temperature, provide fresh air, and reduce greenhouse humidity. But to keep from overchilling your plants, winter ventilation is usually done with very little air exchange. To prevent plant damage, the cold winter air should be mixed with the warm greenhouse air before reaching the plants. Fan-Jet systems or a tube system mounted in the roof area of the greenhouse provides the needed mixing of the ventilation air. Remember that an exhaust fan must be operated in conjunction with the Fan-Jet system to provide fresh air intake as air is exhausted.

Except in the warmest climates, greenhouses must be designed and constructed with a winter ventilation system. HAF fans may provide the needed mixing of internal greenhouse air, but they won't properly mix the cold ventilation air into the warm greenhouse air.

Maintenance Check

I wish I could provide one uniform checklist for greenhouse heating and cooling system maintenance. However, the wide diversity of greenhouse systems requires individual maintenance lists to ensure optimum performance of individual equipment. When you purchase heating or cooling equipment, you should ask for specific maintenance checklists for that equipment. And once you have these lists, make sure you actually perform the maintenance.

The chart "General Maintenance Guidelines" on the following page provides some basic rules of thumb for maintaining greenhouse heating and cooling equipment. And here are a few additional helpful heating and cooling hints we've learned from experience:

- Give it a number. It's useful to number or somehow identify each heater, fan, pump, and valve in your greenhouse. This system lets you easily record maintenance and repairs and makes it less likely that you'll miss the maintenance on a piece of equipment. It also provides a record of repairs to help identify problems with specific equipment.
- One-man job. Assign heating and cooling equipment maintenance to one individual. Develop a maintenance schedule and require a written record of performed maintenance and repairs. Any database software works great for such record keeping.
- Heat, don't cool. Ventilation exhaust fans should not operate at the same time that unit heaters are operating.
- Dry daily. Evaporative cooling pads should be allowed to dry out sometime during a twenty-four-hour period to reduce algae growth.
- Go digital. Computer control of heating and cooling equipment provides more uniform environmental control and supplies a record of equipment function. It also provides an opportunity to reduce unnecessary cycling, optimizing your equipment function.
- Go up. Because of their larger internal volume, tall greenhouse structures provide better environmental control conditions for plants than short structures, particularly with cooling and humidity control.

Don't Ignore It

Heating and cooling problems generally don't kill plants. Instead, they most often cause very subtle growth problems that are difficult to diagnose, causing growers big headaches. Such problems also cost lost greenhouse profits through reduced plant growth and plant quality.

General Maintenance Guidelines

Monthly During Equipment Use

- Check heater and fan belts for correct tension and signs of wear. Keep a supply of belts and pulleys on hand.
- Oil nonsealed bearings on motors and fan shafts.
- Check heater pilot or electronic ignition for proper function.
- View flame for proper color and size.
- Make sure chimney vent is working properly and vent pipe doesn't show excessive soot accumulation, which would indicate a combustion problem.
- Check heater fresh air inlet and make sure it's functioning.
- Oil fan louvers.
- Clean strainer on evaporative cooling pad systems. Provide algae control in the water for the pads.
- Check water pH and soluble salts levels in cooling pad water. Correct the pH to the 6.0 to 9.0 range and reduce salt buildup by allowing a small amount of water to bleed off. Make sure water flow is adequate to keep the pad system saturated.

At Least Yearly, or More Often, as Required

- Check heat exchanger for cracks. This check would make most sense in the fall.
- Replace heater fuel filters.
- Check all fuel valves and pumps for proper function.
- Check fuel nozzles, electrode adjustments, electrical controls, limit switches, and fuel pressures.
- Check chimneys and vent caps for debris (bird nests are a favorite), cracks, and rust holes.
- Replace polyethylene ventilation tubes.
- Conduct a combustion test. This generally measures CO_2 output and other products of combustion.
- Check fan motors and fan blades for proper function and wear.
- Calibrate thermostats.

Growers must realize that heating and cooling system maintenance is every bit as important as controlling insects and irrigating the plants. You can't afford to ignore it.

Summer 1999

From the Top Down—Re-covering Poly Greenhouses

Don Grey

Many growers choose polyethylene greenhouse film to cover everything from hoop houses for overwintering to heated and cooled freestanding and gutter-connect houses. A properly covered house will protect plants through all kinds of conditions. But sooner or later they need to be recovered— or reskinned—with new film. Growers and suppliers share their tips and techniques for this routine but critical task. After all, there's more than one way to skin a greenhouse.

Poly Coverings

Today's poly films are better than ever, but they don't last as long as glass or rigid sheeting. So poly needs to be changed on a regular schedule depending on its thickness and rating and where and how it's being used. Poly typically comes in one- to three-year ratings (ratings reflect durability against weather and ultraviolet ray degradation). It comes in white, clear, and colored, in single sheets or in two sheets melded into a tube, and in different thicknesses.

Manufacturers fold the poly in several styles—center, gussetted, or double-gussetted, for example—so make sure you buy it folded to your specifications. How it's folded determines how you put it on your house.

A single layer of one-year poly may be suitable for mild climates, whereas a three-year film installed in a double layer typically works well for greenhouses in more demanding weather conditions. The air inflation between the two layers provides excellent insulation, strength, and durability.

"Plastic requires more maintenance than glass, but it still results in a tremendous heat savings compared to glass," says Jim Gapinski of Heartland Growers in Westfield, Indiana. Heartland grows potted and bedding plants in nearly three hundred greenhouse bays. "Make sure you buy your poly from a reputable dealer," Jim recommends. "Have your best people put it on. It's there for three years, so make sure it's done right because you want that poly to last."

Inspection First

To help your new poly last, first look for problems with the old roof. Before you reskin your houses, inspect the existing poly for wear points, especially premature wearing. This could indicate problems with loose or defective poly locks, which can cause poly to rub against roof supports and shorten its life. Look for areas that are torn or punctured and repaired with poly repair tape. Also look for sharp metal shards, nails, or wood slivers and file or sand them smooth. Remove old lath boards and nails.

Off with the Old

After inspecting the existing poly cover, it's off with the old and on with the new. It's tempting just to unfasten the old poly and let it drop to the ground, but careful removal can help keep the film clean for recycling.

Tanasacres Nursery Inc., Hillsboro, Oregon, a potted and bedding plant grower, folds the plastic in half or thirds, starting from the endwalls. For longer houses (most are 28 by 100 feet), workers cut the poly into two or three sections for easier folding. At least 75 to 80% of its houses are covered in one-year poly, so they're usually uncovered in June, when bedding plants don't need supplemental heat, and reskinned in September in time for poinsettia production. The film is recycled, so cleanliness and neatness are important.

Important for removing poly are calm, dry days. You don't want poly flapping or blowing around as it's coming off. Likewise, it's very difficult to pull wet poly, so wait until rain and dew are gone.

Here's an interesting twist: While most growers remove old poly first and then reskin with new, one Northwest grower simply lays new poly atop the old and then pulls the old layer down through the greenhouse. Because the old poly film is still durable and stretched taut, workers can walk right over it, if necessary, and pull the new poly into proper position. The old layer is then unclipped from the poly locks, folded, and fed through the bows into the empty house.

On with the New

The first rule in covering greenhouses is the most obvious and practical: calm, still days are essential. Even the slightest breeze can cause problems. You don't want the film flapping around or blowing away. Ron Schmidt, a production manager at Woodburn Nursery and Azaleas Inc., Woodburn, Oregon, relies on a commercial agricultural weather forecast to pinpoint still days. "Even with a mild breeze, you can't do much," he says. "The biggest obstacle is the wind." When conditions are favorable, work crews reskin as many houses as possible.

Getting the poly up on top or over the house is probably the next biggest challenge. For freestanding houses, it's common to pull the poly from one side of the house to the other, but this isn't recommended; it's best to keep the poly off the ground to keep it clean and avoid snagging or tearing the film. Instead, hoist the poly to roof level, set it on the ridge, and unfold the sides. Tanasacres Nursery, for example, has a device it uses for its freestanding houses to lift the poly to roof level. It has metal poles on each side that fasten to a tractor's scoop to hold a poly roll. Once hoisted, the poly is unrolled over the top, down the sides and endwalls. A crew of four will cover as many houses as possible, loosely fasten the plastic, and then go back to finish clipping the houses more securely. Endwalls are done first, followed by the sidewalls. The crew can cover a house in about twenty minutes.

Gutter-connect houses are more challenging. At Heartland Growers, Jim uses a forklift and a pallet to lift a poly roll to roof height. A crew of six (two to unroll the poly and four to pull it down the gutters and clip it in place) can cover a bay in about twenty minutes. Heartland uses a three-year poly tube and typically reskins its houses in October.

Ron says Woodburn Nursery built a jig that holds a poly roll (locked so it doesn't slip), which fastens to a 4-by-8-ft. safety cage. A forklift hoists the cage, jig, and poly

You can use brute force, forklifts, front-end loaders, or homemade stands to get the poly onto the roof. With this design, workers don't have to lift heavy poly up to roof level.

to just above roof level. A worker inside the cage feeds the poly off the roll. Four workers on each side of the house's gutters unroll the film and set it in place. The bottom layer is clipped at the corners and center; the top layer is installed next. Then everything is fastened securely. "The bottom layer is pulled tight, and the top is left a little looser," Ron says. "When it's inflated, we want a 6-in. balloon effect."

With a crew of ten, it takes about twenty minutes to skin a house. The nursery typically reskins at least eighty houses each September, usually on a three-year cycle.

Latching It Down

It's critical to pull the poly to its desired tension and hold it in place. Poly should be pulled just tight enough to eliminate wrinkles and keep water from forming puddles, but not so tight that it stretches. If the poly is stretched too tight during warm weather, it can't contract during cold and may tear.

Once the new poly is in place, it has to stay there. That's where a good lock is important. On steel greenhouses, most growers use commercial poly locks to secure the film. You'll find at least two basic locks: clips or springs, and wire inserts. They cost about the same, are quite secure, and can accommodate several poly layers.

Clip-type locks are made from aluminum and are fairly durable, so they can be used year after year. Some locks use a plastic insert to hold the poly. The clip or spring has a base and top section. It comes in styles for flat and arched roofs. Simply insert the poly film into the base and attach the top. Today's locks won't cut the poly, and they hold it intact, even in strong winds. "For larger gutter-connect greenhouses, I'd use a clip," says Gary Baze of Conley's Manufacturing and Sales, Pomona, California. "I have more confidence in it. I know from experience that when a good quality clip goes into a good quality base, it's there to stay."

Wire locks also perform well. An extruded aluminum frame houses one or two wires that are used to secure the film inside the extrusions. Two wires allow you to anchor a double-poly roof one sheet at a time, a handy benefit. They also work great on flat, straight roofs, but don't appear to be as effective on sloped or arched roofs, one supplier notes.

Locks do have a limited life, so inspect them carefully when the house is reskinned. Sometimes a clip just needs a new rubber gasket.

Keep in mind that locks can and do malfunction. One grower sends workers out to walk the gutters in windy weather and inspect the locks just to make sure they will hold. "You'll know in winter if the clips pop out of the house and it deflates," he says.

Some growers use wood lath strips on their greenhouses or hoop houses to secure poly. Lath doesn't work as well as poly locks. Although cheaper up front, in the end the strips are more time consuming to attach. If you do use lath, make sure you fold the poly to the outside to prevent water penetration, which over the course of a season can rot the lath. Also, use form or two-headed nails, which are easier to remove.

Inflation

Double-poly houses need proper inflation to achieve full insulation and strength. Six to 8 in. of airspace between layers is a suggested optimum. Two to 3 in. may not be enough in many areas, but 2 ft. is excessive. Uniformity between layers from one end of the house to the next is important.

Guard against overinflation. Again, poly stretched too taut during summer can't contract in winter and is more likely to form condensation during winter. Use a manometer, an inexpensive tool that measures air pressure, to gauge the amount of air pressure between the two poly layers. Insert the manometer's rubber tip between the two layers so that it's pressurized and look for a reading between 0.2 and 0.4 in. on the scale. Check with poly manufacturers for their specifications.

Use blowers to keep the insulating air level between the poly layers inflated and constant. Blowers (often called squirrel cage fans) are small and relatively inexpensive. It's best to use air pumped in from the outside, so a blower with an intake and exhaust manifold is necessary. That's because air drawn from inside the greenhouse is moist, heated, and often contains chemicals, which can cause condensation, channel heat from the inside, and degrade the poly. Use fans big enough to inflate the amount of covered square feet; a variable-speed motor or an adjustable baffle over the intake will let you vary the blower's output.

Before installing new poly, check the blower motors to verify that they work and are adjusted properly. To be safe, check them monthly. Because they are on continuous duty, you may want to replace motors when you change the poly. Then, after you install the poly, make sure the blower fan is hooked up. Cut a hole in the bottom poly layer and attach it to the fan's brackets. You'll want a tight seal around the fan's base to prevent pressurized air from escaping.

Maximizing Poly Life
Some growers have been known to paint or coat the greenhouse's tubing to prevent poly abrasion, says Conley's Gary Baze. Although he doesn't know growers who paint the tops of arches, it's true that poly degrades much quicker where it touches the metal, particularly in areas with high sunlight levels, he says.

Instead of painting the tubes, Woodburn Nursery installs a house's structural purlins on top of the tubes rather than underneath. The poly sits atop the purlins instead of directly on the tubing and lessens abrasion. It's this attention to detail that leaves nothing to chance for such a routine but critical task as covering and protecting your crops.

March 1998

Snow Business

Chris Beytes

How can you prepare your greenhouses for snow? Ideally, your greenhouse designer has already handled the important part: engineering your structure to meet the specific snow load requirements for your locale. But that doesn't mean your structures are immune from disaster. Here are some tips from Steve Woods, a risk control engineer with Florists' Mutual Insurance, that may keep you from losing a structure this winter.

Snow Loads

Greenhouse engineers design snow loads into structures using a national snow map, which outlines the ground snow load for regions across the country. (Snow is measured in pounds, not inches, for engineering purposes.) For instance, central Texas gets 5 lbs., northern Kansas gets 20 lbs., and North Dakota gets anywhere from 35 to 50 lbs. on average.

The map also shows areas where snow conditions vary widely enough that you need to check local building codes. For instance, Kodiak, Alaska, has a 40-lb. rating, while Fairbanks is at 100 lbs.

That's why it's so critical that you buy a greenhouse that's engineered to stand up in your part of the country, Steve says. Shallow-pitched roofs that work fine in the South won't shed snow adequately in New York. And a gutter-connected house designed for California probably won't stand up to heavy, wet snow collecting in Minnesota.

Anchorage, Alaska, grower Lee Risse is glad his greenhouse was properly engineered.
Photo by Stuppy Greenhouse Mfg.

Heat 'Em or Lose 'Em

Assuming your existing structures are properly engineered, what should you do to prevent problems in the case of a blizzard?

Lack of heat is the No. 1 cause of greenhouse collapse, Steve says. Florists' Mutual won't even pay a claim on an unheated house, he says—policies specify that structures must be heated to a minimum temperature, usually 50°F. (Cheaters beware: Experts can tell if you turned on your heaters *after* the roof caved in.)

Floor heat, which is great for plants, won't melt snow from your roof. It's critical to have good heating up high in your houses, especially along the gutters. And don't wait to bring the temperature up—it's easier to keep a house warm than to get it warm.

Also, a closed energy curtain may prevent the snow from melting. Be sure to open your curtain *before* snow starts to accumulate.

Heating works because greenhouse roofs have very little insulation value, with one exception: double poly. If snow is starting to accumulate on your double poly roof, shut off the inflation blower. That will let the roof deflate, removing the insulation value and allowing the outer layer to heat up enough to melt the snow. Be careful, however, that you don't wait so late that the weight of the snow causes your roof to "bathtub" inward.

When Disaster Looms

What if you've done everything right, but accumulating snow is threatening your structure? Steve says after moving plants to a safer location (if possible), it's time to consider sacrificing your covering.

Contact your insurance agent before you take that step—most likely, they'd rather pay for a new roof than an entire structure. However, "if it's a matter of saving your structure or getting to the phone, go ahead and cut that poly," he says. Be careful when knocking out glass panes, and don't risk a worker's compensation situation.

What about Retractables?

Like rigid-roof greenhouses, retractable roof greenhouses, if properly engineered, will stand up to snow. Cravo Equipment, Brantford, Ontario, Canada, has engineered structures to handle up to 30-lb. snow loads.

Graham McDonald, Cravo's marketing manager, says all of the above rules apply: You must heat your greenhouse, you must open the energy curtain if snow is accumulating, and you must start heating early to keep the snow from getting ahead of you. Retractable roofs *shouldn't be operated* when there's snow on them! But as with rigid roofs, if the structure is threatened, better to lose the roof than the whole building.

Editor's note: Load standards are available from the National Greenhouse Manufacturers Association, Tel: (800) 792-6462.

December 1998

Gone with the Wind

Bob Johnson

It's a decision no grower ever wants to face: Hurricane-force winds are approaching and forecasts say they'll reach your greenhouse within the hour. And the question is: Should you cut off your poly roof and sacrifice your crop, or leave the roof on and risk the entire structure?

It's a decision best made at the last minute, or at least at the last hour. And the answer often has as much to do with a grower's past experience as with the prospects for imminent catastrophe.

"People make the call an hour or so before the hurricane hits because [hurricanes] can change directions in a hurry," says Craig Humphrey, vice president of engineering at Colorado-based greenhouse builder Nexus Corporation. "If they've had a bad experience with hurricanes, they might tend to cut the roof. If they've had thirty years of experience with inferior structures, they might also cut the roof."

Greenhouse structures are rated according to their ability to withstand strong winds. At Nexus, there's about a 20 to 25% cost difference between the lowest rated structure, able to withstand winds up to 70 mph, and the highest rated structure, able to withstand winds up to 120 mph.

"If their structure is designed properly, they shouldn't have to cut the poly off," Craig says.

Of course, there's a major strength difference between single layer poly and double poly. "A single-layer plastic is going to go a lot quicker," says Gene Giacomelli, professor of bioresource engineering at New Jersey's Rutgers University. The double poly can remain strong as long as the electricity stays on and air is being pumped between the layers. "We have examples of double-layer poly staying on in Taiwan in typhoons, and that's a strong storm."

But Gene confesses that to cut or not to cut is a tough call. "There's not much you can go on. When you cut the roof, you're sacrificing your plastic and your crop just to save the metal structure, and that's an act of desperation. At that point, Mother Nature is in charge."

Hurricane Andrew, in 1992, remains the benchmark by which other disasters are measured. "Andrew was the biggest by far, the most damaging to the industry by far," says Pete Fornoff, vice president of Florists' Mutual Insurance, the largest greenhouse insurer in the U.S. "We approached $20 million in losses. But there were growers who were uninsured or were insured by someone else—the gross losses were much more."

If you do decide to cut loose the plastic when a major storm is approaching, you may face a second disaster when you try to explain your decision to the insurance company. "I can't tell them not to do it, but they're going to have problems with insurance," Pete says. "The plastic won't be covered, and [whether] the crop [is covered by insurance] will be debatable." According to Pete, nearly all insurance policies have a clause excluding compensation for intentional damage. That clause would appear to clearly exempt the insurer from paying for a roof that was deliberately cut.

Insurance headaches can even follow a storm when the wind, not the grower, has torn the plastic roof from the house. Apopka, Florida-based V. J. Growers Supply experienced heavy demand for both poly and shade cloth after Hurricane Andrew and when Hurricane Irene hit last fall.

"Some of them are still replacing the plastic because they have to get it cleared with the insurance," V. J.'s sales representative Linda Jonas told us three weeks after Irene. Those delays were happening even though the plastic was largely damaged by the storm, rather than as a result of deliberate decisions to save the house by cutting the plastic.

So the question remains: Should you cut your roof? It all comes down to which loss might be greatest: The roof, the structure, or the crop. Only you can answer that question.

January 2000

Twice Shy

Chris Beytes

It was November 11, a cool fall evening in Virginia, and Jeri LeMay was making her regular, end-of-the-day walk through Battlefield Farms. Most everyone else had already headed home. Jeri could see that the poinsettia crop was coloring up nicely, just about ready to ship. The production barn was brimming with cartons and sleeves. Rolls of new poly for the roofs were stacked high. Pots and trays were stockpiled for spring. Everything was in order.

Her walk was suddenly interrupted by smoke and flames coming from a corridor. Obviously too big a fire for her to handle, Jeri quickly called 911 to summon the volunteer fire department from Rapidan, fifteen miles away.

But within minutes, the fire, later determined to have started in the cart charging station, had spread into the main barn, where the massive stockpiles of combustibles fueled it into an out-of-control inferno. The blaze jumped the walls of the barn and roared into the greenhouses, leaping from bay to bay on the closed shade curtain. Within five minutes, it had burned through ten acres of greenhouse. Pipes melted, glass shattered, poly vaporized, pots, trays, and even plants burned.

The assessment of the damage began before the smoke had cleared, as maintenance manager Alan Helwig began plotting ways to get power and heat to the four undamaged acres to save the remaining crop. But how would he call for supplies? The phone service was fried. The boilers, the main electrical service, trailers, forklifts—everything was in the production barn.

Head grower Marc Verdel had just stocked the seed cooler for his plug crop. It was in the barn, along with the remains of the soil line, seeders, and transplanter.

Years of growing records were in the office, which was . . . in the barn, along with every record the company had ever kept—personnel files, customer lists, orders, and accounts payable and receivable. And they discovered too late that the backup computer files they'd been making wouldn't work.

All of which leads to the moral of the story.

"We were planning all along to pull the offices and boiler room and everything separate," owner Jerry van Hoeven told us as we met briefly in his pool house turned temporary office. "We had them all in one barn. If that had been separate, at least we wouldn't have lost everything at once."

How many greenhouse operations have everything—power, heat, production equipment, and office—all located in one central barn, as Battlefield did? Most that we visit. How many growers have taken the precautions that

Battlefield is only now taking after the fact—building a separate, free-standing office, installing firebreaks in the new warehouse, storing chemicals and fertilizers in isolated rooms, and investing in flameproof shade fabric sections to help prevent fire spread in the greenhouses? Few, very few.

Much can be written about Battlefield's amazing recovery and about the help they received from employees, family, friends, the community and the industry. It's an inspiration. But Jerry makes a more important observation about the disaster and the improvements it forced him to make: "After the fire we could afford it. Why couldn't we afford it before the fire?"

May 2000

Index

Page numbers for photographs are **bold**, and page numbers for tables are *italic*.